The Greatest Racehorse?

The Greatest Racehorse?

Man o' War and the Judgment of History

Mark Shrager

ECLIPSE
PRESS

Essex, Connecticut

ECLIPSE PRESS

An imprint of The Globe Pequot Publishing Group, Inc.
64 South Main Street
Essex, CT 06426
www.GlobePequot.com

Distributed by NATIONAL BOOK NETWORK

British Library Cataloguing in Publication Information available

Library of Congress Cataloging-in-Publication Data available
ISBN 978-1-4930-8888-1 (paper : alk. paper)
ISBN 978-1-4930-8889-8 (electronic)

♾™ The paper used in this publication meets the minimum requirements of American National Standard for Information Sciences—Permanence of Paper for Printed Library Materials, ANSI/ NISO Z39.48-1992.

Contents

INTRODUCTION

Ranking America's Best Racehorses

MAN O' WAR!

The exclamation point following the name of this singular Thoroughbred is not merely the author's; it is the world's. It is virtually 100 percent certain that if you are a follower of the Sport of Kings, you have known of Man o' War's name, his exploits, his legend, from approximately the moment you became a racing aficionado. Even if you are not a fan, if you know the name of only one Thoroughbred racehorse, that horse will almost certainly be the chestnut 1917 foal of the stallion Fair Play and the mare Mahubah: Man o' War!

And if you choose to engage with the sport and learn anything of its history, you will quickly recognize that among fans of Thoroughbred racing, the name Man o' War demands an exclamation point.

There are, if the reader would like to see them, some seconds of grainy, hundred-year-old film showing Man o' War winning his final race, a match race against Sir Barton at Canada's Kenilworth Park. Man o' War runs with his head high, not normally considered an ideal characteristic for a racehorse, but to say that it works for him is the height of understatement. In the film clip, Man o' War is well ahead and speeding farther away from his beaten rival. There is nothing Sir Barton can do about it; he is confronted by a far more talented runner.

As the two horses turn into the stretch and the camera operators crank the film through their primitive photographic machinery, Man o' War is extending his lead entirely on his own, his jockey making no effort to push his mount to run faster. Following the race, jockey

Clarence Kummer would report, "I did not urge Man o' War. I just let him finish under restraint and had a hard time to hold his head." Kummer was a powerful rider who would one day be honored with a plaque in Thoroughbred racing's Hall of Fame. It required all of his strength and riding guile to prevent Man o' War from running too fast for the colt's own good.

You cannot hear it on the film (in 1920, the year of this long-awaited match race, the talkies were still in the future), but somehow you can imagine this amazing horse, having dominated, desecrated, diminished, all but destroyed another luckless rival, snorting with a mixture of satisfaction and superiority—but also with frustration, for Man o' War, surely the fastest, most powerful racehorse not merely of his generation but many generations, was almost never allowed to experience the full speed and power of his own uniquely efficient persona.

This was both an inevitability and a necessity. Allowing Man o' War to run without restraint would needlessly risk injury. Both Man o' War's owner, Samuel Doyle Riddle, and his trainer, Louis Feustel, knew there was no need for the prodigious colt to run at maximum speed, for even a geared-down Man o' War would almost certainly win anyway. He lost only one race in his sterling career, and this under the flukiest of circumstances.

There was also a longer-term strategy requiring consideration. Larger margins of victory and faster times would result in more weight being placed in the hidden compartments of Man o' War's saddle in future races, with an increased likelihood of injury and defeat. It was therefore very much in Man o' War's long-term interests to win comfortably but not overwhelmingly.

And so his jockeys were usually instructed to put forth only the effort necessary to ensure another victory, for "too much weight," as the racing axiom goes, "will stop a freight train." The racing secretary, whose job it is to bring fields of Thoroughbreds to the wire as closely as possible by assigning more weight to the better horses, was Man o' War's enemy; the most effective counter-weapon was a jockey pulling back double, if necessary, on the colt's reins.

Thus Man o' War was seldom permitted to experience his own unbridled power. Had he been able to read his press clippings and formulate his feelings in words, the colt likely would have expressed exasperation at article after article proclaiming that he had earned his most recent victory with ease—but "under restraint." No American horse had ever run faster at a mile, at a mile-and-an-eighth, at a mile-and-five-eighths. Nevertheless, the turfwriters insisted, had Man o' War been allowed to run at full speed from start to finish, he would have run even faster.

Today, Man o' War has become something far more than merely the most revered, most beloved racehorse in the history of what was once, long ago, America's favorite sporting pastime. He has been assumed, almost by acclamation, to be the fastest, strongest, most perfect specimen of the Thoroughbred ever produced in America.

He has been the subject of more books than any other racehorse, more articles, more online acclaim. When the editors of the *Blood-Horse*, the prestigious chronicler of American Thoroughbred racing since 1916, published *Thoroughbred Champions: Top 100 Racehorses of the 20th Century*, their all-inclusive survey of the most outstanding Thoroughbreds for one hundred years, their cover boy and #1 selection was not Secretariat, with his Triple Crown sweep; nor Citation, racing's first million-dollar earner; nor Kelso, with his five Horse of the Year titles; nor Dr. Fager, with his record for the mile that has stood for more than a half-century. It was Man o' War, about whom they proclaimed:

> *Most champions, even great ones, define themselves on the racecourse. We admire and understand their shiny strengths, but in so doing we also come to understand, or suspect, their limits. Those who saw Man o' War apparently found no hint of limit. At all distances, he was overpowering.*

And yet it seems, if not impossible, at least highly unlikely that racing could have continued for what is now more than a century since Man o' War humiliated his final rival, without producing at least one competitor better than the most acclaimed runner of 1919 and 1920. The breeding of fast equines is a scientific pursuit, and the very nature of science is to discover better solutions, create better products, invent better processes.

Since Man o' War's day, scientists have discovered powerful antibiotics, split the atom, conquered the scourges of smallpox and polio, sent modern-day explorers to the moon, connected the world via the internet, and uncovered many of the secrets of the human genome. We clone plants and animals, we send electronic telescopes into space to discover and explore heavenly bodies never seen by the human eye. We transplant organs to extend and enhance the lives of individuals whose cases would once have been considered hopeless.

Theoretically, at least, our onrushing science and technology should also have impacted all aspects of what we still sometimes call the Sport of Kings. In many ways, it has. Track management techniques have been improved, leading to faster race times and safer surfaces; training regimens of the past have been all but reinvented, leading to new ideas about how runners should be conditioned and prepared for competition; equine nutrition has been studied and more nutritious feeds created; crippling injuries that might once have ended equine careers and brought top racers' lives to a tragic close are treated with improved surgical techniques. In equine breeding, as well, science has been a boon; this is no longer a sport in which those seeking to create faster racehorses must rely on so unscientific an approach as "breed the best to the best and hope for the best."

So why should Man o' War's amazing physical attributes, his speed, his raw power, never once have been exceeded by the product of an equine breeding industry that seeks, with supreme passion, scientific fervor, and ever-growing financial incentive, to create stakes winners, Triple Crown immortals, champions, Hall of Famers?

In few other sporting endeavors would it be suggested that an athlete who excelled during the Woodrow Wilson administration, at the time of Prohibition, at the conclusion of the First World War, remains the standard for unexcelled excellence in their sport's history. Even baseball's Babe Ruth, whose records had once seemed unassailable, was finally overcome by the likes of Henry Aaron, Mark McGuire, and Barry Bonds.

And so it seems appropriate to ask: Could any racehorse who has tread the turf in the years since Man o'War's long-ago days possibly have represented an improvement over this legendary beast?

Since the horses who might challenge him cannot be available to demonstrate their relative excellence by running rigorously controlled match races, the best we can hope to do is compare statistics and memories and anecdotes. Which leads to the next question: In the absence of a scientifically valid answer, how does one go about deciding whether any of the approximately 2.3 million Thoroughbreds that have been registered to race in America can legitimately challenge Man o'War as a claimant to the title America's Greatest Racehorse?

It would seem a pretty straightforward undertaking, wouldn't it? Racing has always celebrated runners with speed, stamina, and that indefinable but self-evident quality it describes as "class," and we can go beyond those words to define the qualities that have traditionally been expected of the truly gifted Thoroughbred. Among the most important of these are:

DOMINANCE. Dominance over other good horses is certainly a fundamental element of Thoroughbred excellence. A vast difference exists between being a champion racehorse and merely being a contender, and an essential component of that difference is that the best of the breed should be consistently able to outrun—to dominate—those who are merely very good.

GAMENESS. We respect Thoroughbreds such as Man o'War, who won major races by immense margins. But we also hold a soft spot for horses like Affirmed, who so often prevailed in head-bobbing, heart-tingling finishes, persevering even against the likes of so powerful an opponent as Alydar. We revere Thoroughbreds with this rare quality, the sort who look the opposition in the eye and refuse to allow them past.

BEATING GOOD HORSES. For generations, we've employed a demeaning term to describe runners who prevailed over opposition that seemed only so-so: "He didn't beat anybody." It was a critique that might have been leveled against the likes of Native Dancer and Tom Fool, and arguably might have been applied even to Man o'War himself. To demonstrate excellence on the racetrack, it is necessary not merely to win but to win over top competition.

WINNING MAJOR RACES. All of these attributes, of course, are expected to occur in important races with top-dollar purses and long histories of bestowing renown upon horses we recognize as top-quality. A long winning streak in ordinary races, even a string of wins in less important stakes, may define a "nice" colt or filly but will not elevate a good racehorse into the realm of immortality. Only important races can truly bestow importance.

PRECOCITY AND STAYING POWER. We reserve our loftiest praise for Thoroughbreds who defeat their peers in traditional 2-year-old races, then compete with distinction in classic contests at age three. We are even more impressed by runners who then continue to prevail at ages four and beyond, in classic races such as the Suburban Handicap, the Santa Anita Handicap, and on Breeders' Cup Weekend.

VERSATILITY. In earlier days, the sport might have defined "versatility" to mean the ability to win at one, two, three, or four miles, and in multiple heat races on the same day. But Thoroughbred racing has evolved from those days, and Ten Broeck, who once held six separate American records at distances ranging from one to four miles, no longer exemplifies versatility in racing's modern era. Today, success in sprints and routes, on dirt and on turf, over fast tracks and in the slop describes versatility in the Thoroughbred.

OVERCOMING ADVERSITY. We also respect racehorses who overcome adversity to earn racetrack glory. Runners who win despite having to conquer the pain of a serious injury or illness certainly deserve our respect, and as we total up the debits and credits of candidates for the title "Greatest Racehorse," this is yet another factor that should not be overlooked.

LONGEVITY. Historically, racing fans have been drawn to Thoroughbreds who raced season after season, shouldering high weights and taking on all comers. Often, these have been geldings, horses that could not be retired at an early age to rich stud careers, and so were kept on the track, overcoming the best of successive generations of horses. Runners of this sort often surge up leading earners lists, sometimes seizing the top spot as they continue their careers.

Extreme longevity, however, works against the chances that a horse will be seen as an all-time champion. Every athlete, however gifted, eventually discovers that age can never be outrun. Injuries mount up, losses accumulate with the sheer numbers of races, and, for the best of these multi-generational stars, strings of victories lead inevitably to racing secretaries piling on ever higher weights in the effort to create better wagering races.

RECORD TIMES. Yet another factor that designates an exceptional horse is their ability to run distances faster than any horse has ever covered them. Stakes records are important indicators of ability, track records even more so, American and world records best of all. Surely, any horse that can run a commonly contested distance faster than any other horse in history stakes its claim to being a runner of significance.

AWARDS. We believe in the ability of those who follow the races most closely to discern which are the best Thoroughbreds of their time, as reflected in the season's year-end awards. We accept that divisional championships, Eclipse Awards, Horse of the Year trophies, and, most importantly, Hall of Fame inductions reflect the most honest appraisals of the most committed followers of the sport, and accept their validity as indicators of exceptional equine quality.

We can also discuss a number of other qualities that have been traditional measures of equine excellence but for various reasons have declined from earlier days:

MONEY EARNINGS. Obviously, winning substantial amounts of money deserves a measure of acclaim. In modern-day racing, however, we recognize that the sport's inflated purse structure ensures that the most successful racehorses will record vastly higher earnings than earlier champions could possibly have collected. Indeed, inflation has rendered almost meaningless the amounts earned by even the most accomplished runners from earlier eras of the sport's history. To give just one example, Arrogate is the current leading money winner with earnings of $17,422,600; Man o' War won $249,465. No one who knows anything about racing—or about economics—will ponder these figures and conclude that Arrogate must have been nearly seventy times as good as his rival from pre-inflation 1919 and 1920.

CARRYING HIGH WEIGHTS AND GIVING WEIGHT TO OPPONENTS. There was a time, not so long ago, when the best horse in a major race would routinely be assigned 130 pounds or more and be asked to defeat other runners carrying substantially less weight. It was a prerequisite of excellence: If you could carry high weights and concede weight to good rivals, you must, by definition, be an exceptional horse.

Sometimes this was taken to extremes. On July 4, 1921, Hall of Famer Exterminator was assigned 140 pounds in Latonia's mile-and-a-half Independence Handicap (he finished sixth); on a warm August Saratoga day in 1936, the prodigious weight-carrier Discovery, who had won the previous year's Merchants & Citizens Handicap under a mere 139 pounds, was assigned a 143-pound impost (bet down to odds-on despite this burden, Discovery finished sixth to the mare Esposa under a feathery 100 pounds).

Nor were these isolated instances. The Hall of Fame mare Pan Zareta was assigned 140 pounds or more in seven of her 151 starts, and one day at Juarez won under 146 pounds, defeating a colt carrying an even 100. The mighty Roseben raced 111 times over the course of his seven seasons of competition, carrying 140 pounds or more on twenty-nine occasions and winning fifteen. His highest weight assignment, on two occasions, was 150 pounds, and he ran second under this onerous load both times. His plaque in the Hall of Fame is much deserved.

The practice of assigning extreme high weights has largely been abandoned by racing secretaries, who no longer allocate 130-pound weight imposts to 2-year-olds and rarely pile so great a burden even on older, more mature horses. In an era when equine deaths on the track become headline news and truly outstanding Thoroughbreds with the ability to attract record crowds to racetracks can also earn record stud fees, dangerous weight assignments are no longer the norm. While we recognize the excellence of horses from yesteryear who carried unconscionable weight imposts to victory, this is best viewed as a historical anomaly, rather than as an example to be followed. And one can only add, "Thank goodness."

CROP SIZE. The numbers of foals registered with The Jockey Club as potential racehorses have varied tremendously over time. The official records—which in the earliest years of racing reflect only estimated numbers of foals—count a total of just 3,950 registered foals during the ninety-year period from 1803 to 1892—about forty-four possible racehorses per year, on average, based on records accumulated after The Jockey Club's inauguration. For many years thereafter, registrations remained few, given economic issues and the small purses typical of the times.

During the 1910s, which included Man o' War's birth year of 1917, the numbers continued to be low—Man o' War's crop, in fact, was the second smallest of the twentieth century, with only about 1,680 foals registered—but with increasing prosperity and rising purses, foal crops gradually expanded, until by the mid-1980s more than 50,000 foals a year were being produced, a thirtyfold increase annually over Man o' War's day. It is perhaps no accident that the 1986 crop, the largest in history at 51,296 foals, brought us the outstanding Easy Goer and Sunday Silence, as well as Hall of Famers Open Mind and Safely Kept. We will explore the importance of crop size as a reason to believe that Man o' War's excellence might have been equaled or even exceeded through the sheer numbers of history's larger crops of horses.

UNDEFEATED RECORDS. Over the course of racing history, a handful of runners—usually with very short careers—have achieved undefeated records. A runner such as Colin or Personal Ensign or Flightline, with a glorious "0" in their loss column, will always capture our attention. Even a brief and tragic career, such as that of the 2-year-old filly Landaluce, who won five smashing victories in five 1982 starts prior to her untimely death, can quicken our heartbeats with an excellence that seems nothing less than the runner's birthright.

But since even the best of horses usually lose at least once, we must ask: Is an undefeated record a requisite for excellence, or is it merely a reflection of great good fortune—or sometimes of lesser competition? We concede Man o' War a place among the very best, despite his one shocking defeat. Can we demand that other runners have won every time before they can be compared to the top Thoroughbreds of the past?

WHAT MIGHT HAVE BEEN. Also deserving of a place in our discussion are runners who, for reasons beyond their control, lost the opportunity to maximize their records due to disabling injury or tragic premature death, or because they were retired from racing at an early age. Neither injury nor early retirement is the fault of the horse, of course, but it is one more consideration as we attempt to determine who might have been history's greatest racehorse.

And so we have our task. We might think of Man o' War as the "reigning heavyweight champion of the world of racing," his record nearly perfect, his fast times and crushing victories demonstrating his unquestioned ability. He will serve as our equine John L. Sullivan, taking on every contestant in the house in comparisons with other runners who have raced with distinction in one or more categories. We will compare:

- Man o' War with Secretariat in asserting dominance over good horses.
- Man o' War with Affirmed in demonstrating gameness.
- Man o' War with Count Fleet in defeating good horses.
- Man o' War with Forego in winning major races.
- Man o' War with Seattle Slew in demonstrating precocity and staying power.
- Man o' War with Dr. Fager in demonstrating versatility.
- Man o' War with Citation in overcoming adversity.
- Man o' War with John Henry in achieving longevity.
- Man o' War with Swaps in setting records.
- Man o' War with Kelso in earning awards.

In considering lesser qualities, we will also compare:

- Man o' War with Spectacular Bid as a money earner.
- Man o' War with Exterminator in carrying and giving weight.

- Man o' War with Easy Goer and Sunday Silence in representing their foal crops.
- Man o' War with Flightline in earning outstanding records.
- Man o' War with Ruffian in achieving excellence despite limited opportunity.

Before beginning these horse-vs.-horse comparisons, however, it is important to add one concept to our overview of racehorse greatness—the recognition that the horse is not responsible for anything that affects its racing record. The horse does not determine its workout schedule or its schedule of races; it does not decide whether it should race at age four or retire as a 3-year-old. The horse does not treat its own injuries, does not deliberately break slowly in a crucial race, and never determines the tragic circumstances that produce an equine death on the racetrack. The horse's record is, in a major way, the result of human machinations; the horse is never even asked its opinion on the matter. Our philosophy, as we consider the horse-vs.-horse comparisons in the forthcoming chapters, can be summarized in one sentence: "The horse gets full credit for its accomplishments, but nothing is the horse's fault."

And with that understanding firmly in mind, let's seek to answer the question: Who was America's greatest racehorse?

PART I
EXCELLENCE

Man o' War at age two. (Keeneland Library Cook Collection)

CHAPTER 1

Man o' War

MORE THAN A CENTURY FOLLOWING HIS FINAL VICTORY, MAN O' WAR remains, for many, the enduring example of greatness in the Thoroughbred racehorse. The immortal champion won twenty of his twenty-one starts, often by overwhelming margins and in record-shattering times. Though his last triumphant foray around a track occurred in 1920, and even after his records have long since been eclipsed by such modern titans of the turf as Kelso and Dr. Fager, Swaps and Secretariat, he remains, for many, the gold standard for the sport.

The accolades for the colt nicknamed "Big Red" for his powerful, muscular frame and his bright chestnut coat have continued long after his premature retirement from the races at age three, and, indeed, long after his death, at thirty years of age, in 1947. Following his departure from the racetrack, the charismatic Man o' War was visited by thousands of fans annually at owner Samuel Doyle Riddle's Faraway Farm in Kentucky.

In retirement, Man o' War was assigned a groom, Will Harbut, to explain the stallion's career to the thousands of visitors who came to Faraway Farm, and over the years Harbut's presentations became more elaborate. The great turfwriter Joe Palmer described a day when he brought a visiting British royal, Lord Halifax, on a tour of Kentucky horse farms, and concluded the day with a visit to Man o' War. Harbut spent twenty minutes expounding the glories of Man o' War, his sons and grandsons, and Palmer later described the groom's denouement as "almost art":

He broke all the records and he broke down all the horses, so there wasn't nothing for him to do but retire. He's got everything a horse ought to have, and he's got it where a horse ought to have it. He's just de mostest horse. Stand still, Red.

"That's worth coming halfway around the world to hear," remarked Lord Halifax.

Most Thoroughbreds are assigned January 1 as their official birth date, but not Man o' War, whose March 29 birthday was celebrated with cakes, telegrams from admirers, and, occasionally, a nationally broadcast birthday party. His public funeral, marked by what the *Los Angeles Times* described as "elaborate rites," was broadcast to much of the nation via radio.

The famous stallion's passing was national news, mourned in headlines throughout the North American continent. "Man o' War, Nonpareil of the Turf," proclaimed the *St. Louis Post-Dispatch*; "Man o' War, Greatest of Thoroughbreds," trumpeted the *Louisville Courier-Journal*. The *Knoxville News-Sentinel* described him as the "Champion of Champions"; the *Calgary Albertan* declared him the "tops in history." The *Lexington Herald*, which lauded Man o' War as the "World's Most Famous Race Horse and Sire," counted over 2,000 "solemn but dry-eyed" mourners attending the departed stallion's last rites.

And over the years since his passing, the unbridled adulation for the Thoroughbred with the all-but-unblemished record has continued unabated. Walter Farley's semi-fictional children's book, *Man o' War*, published in 1962, introduced young readers to the sport's acknowledged superhorse and remains a beloved part of many racing fans' childhoods. Joe Palmer described Man o' War in terms approaching poetry—or was it divinity?—"as near to a living flame as horses ever get, and horses get closer to this than anything else." And, Palmer added,

Even when he was standing motionless in his stall, with his ears pricked forward and his eyes focused on something slightly above the horizon which mere people never see, energy still poured from him. He could get in no position which suggested actual repose, and his very stillness was that of the coiled spring, of the crouched tiger.

Almost from the beginning, the imposing "Big Red" seemed larger than life. Purchased by Riddle on August 17, 1918, for $5,000 from a sale of the yearlings of leading breeder and owner August Belmont II, Man o' War was not even the highest-priced yearling in the sale. That honor went to a colt called Fair Gain that sold for $14,000; the second-highest sale price was $13,600 for a colt that would be called Rouleau, who would face Man o' War twice during their 2-year-old campaigns and never get close. Riddle apparently believed that, even if Man o' War proved too slow to win flat races, he might grow into a useful jumper. Fortunately, this was a route Riddle found it unnecessary to pursue.

Man o' War wasted little time demonstrating which of the Belmont yearlings had the greatest value. Entered at Belmont Park on June 6, 1919, in a field of seven non-winners, the son of Fair Play, following two minutes at the post as the official starter patiently attempted to wrangle the nervous youngsters into some semblance of order, broke alertly from an outside post. He raced along for a while, observing events alongside the early leader, then burst away, winning the five-furlong contest on Belmont Park's straight course under jockey Johnny Loftus, who would escort Man o' War throughout his 2-year-old campaign. Two runners, 7-to-1 Retrieve and 20-to-1 Neddam, whose names would be long forgotten had they not briefly trod the same turf as Man o' War, pursued the 3-to-5 favorite in second and third place, at an appropriately respectful distance.

Man o' War would never be anything but odds-on when he went to the post, his odds ranging from 9-to-10 in one race during his 2-year-old season to 1-to-100 several times as a 3-year-old. On one occasion, it was reported that a wealthy sportsman had wagered $100,000 on Man o' War at 1-to-20 odds, and when challenged to explain so risky a bet, he asked, "How else am I going to earn $5,000 in two minutes?"

Returned to Belmont Park for the Keene Memorial Stakes just two days after his maiden victory, Man o' War faced five rivals on a track surface labeled "slow." Man o' War didn't care about track surface; his desire was only to run. He broke well under a 115-pound impost, dueled briefly with his opponents, then left them behind, winning over the five-and-a-half-furlong straight course by three lengths at odds of 7-to-10. On Watch, who would win twenty-three races over the course of his career but would lose all four times he faced Man o' War, was second, with Anniversary third and Hoodwink, who the following year would be the foil in one of Man o' War's most celebrated races, trailing home last. The *Louisville Courier-Journal*, already recognizing the 2-year-old as something possibly very special, described him as "a whirlwind."

With a stakes victory now on his resume, Man o' War was assigned a 120-pound burden twelve days later in the five-and-a-half-furlong Youthful Stakes, an impost that in light of the colt's subsequent weight-carrying prodigies seems a pittance. This time, Man o' War was away in front and never looked back, overpowering his three rivals by two-and-a-half eased-up lengths while conceding twelve pounds to On Watch and fourteen to the overmatched Lady Brummel and St. Allen.

Man o' War returned to the barn after the race with no apparent problems, so two days later he was back in competition, assigned to heft 130 pounds in Aqueduct's five-furlong Hudson Stakes. The public backed him overwhelmingly in spite of the high impost, even after the spirited colt improvised a full somersault prior to the race, tossing Loftus like a rag doll. Could Man o' War possibly win again, despite these concerning circumstances?

Man o' War did not disappoint. After breaking through the barrier before the start, he ran as though 130 pounds was a mere triviality, scoring in wire-to-wire fashion, with runner-up Violet Tip making no impact despite a twenty-one-pound edge in the weights. *The Daily Racing Form*'s chart caller was clearly impressed, commenting that "MAN O' WAR set a great pace from soon after the start, drew away easily after rounding the last turn and was easing up in the final sixteenth."

Aqueduct's six-furlong Tremont Stakes, its name appropriately honoring a brilliantly fast 2-year-old of the past, and Saratoga's United States Hotel Stakes were next added to the big colt's victory skein, each in front-running style, each under 130 pounds. In the latter, featuring a large $10,000 purse, a field of ten went to the starting line, including Upset, who would shortly play a pivotal role in Man o' War's juvenile season, and multiple stakes winner Bonnie Mary, second high weight at 127 pounds and recent winner of the Fashion and the Great American Stakes. It was a fine field of 2-year-olds, and Man o' War dusted it off easily, opening a large lead and sauntering to the finish unchallenged. As he awaited his next race, Saratoga's six-furlong Sanford Memorial Stakes, it was already appearing possible that this extraordinary colt might prove to be literally unbeatable.

Or so it seemed.

But lose he did, unbelievably, before some 20,000 astounded witnesses, and even more amazingly, he lost not to Golden Broom, a $15,600 yearling whose selling price more than tripled the amount paid for Man o' War, but to Upset, who had been left behind with the rest of the opposition just eleven days earlier in Saratoga's United States Hotel Stakes.

It required a sequence of disastrous events to bring Upset home ahead of Man o' War, and after the race many, whether witnessing the scene firsthand, learning of the outcome in one of New York's hyperactive poolrooms, or reading their morning newspapers the following day, believed that the fix must surely have been in.

This belief, never proven, may also have had its impact in the administrative upper echelons of the sport. Months later, The Jockey Club, racing's supreme licensing authority for jockeys and trainers, would refuse to issue a license to either Upset's winning jockey, Willie Knapp, or to Man o' War's rider, Johnny Loftus. The Jockey Club never issued an explanation, but as the sport's monolithic judge, jury, and executioner it was not required to explain nor to provide an avenue for appeal. Willie Knapp and Johnny Loftus would never again earn their living as jockeys.

The events leading to Man o' War's only career loss may have begun the evening before, when Mars Cassidy, who served as official starter for more than 50,000 races over the course of his forty-year turf career, celebrated his birthday with a large coterie of friends and acquaintances. The celebration may have involved more alcoholic beverages than was prudent, for the next day Cassidy called in sick. In his absence, the task of starting the day's races at Saratoga was assigned to C. H. Pettingill, who for years had earned his living sending fields of Thoroughbreds on their way. After many years serving as a placing judge, however, he was badly lacking in recent experience.

As the prolific racing writer W. C. Vreeland would opine the following day to his Brooklyn Daily Eagle readers, "Why he was selected [as official starter] is one of the mysteries of the turf. Anyone else would have been better."

Starting a field in those days meant lining a group of runners up behind a string or a webbing that would spring upward at the push of the starter's button, but this was merely the mechanical aspect of the job. Just as important was the task of dealing with nervous horses and devious jockeys seeking to gain an advantage by outbreaking the opposition. It was a difficult, nerve-wracking job, one that required both a sensitivity to the needs of the horses and an iron will for dealing with the tiny but competitive men on their backs.

Pettingill was haunted by the memory of one race. The 1893 American Derby had offered an enormous $49,500 winner's purse (the Kentucky Derby's purse that year was just $4,020), and as a result had seen false start after false start, as the jockeys sought every advantage for their restive mounts. As tension grew by the moment, an increasingly frustrated Pettingill waved his red flag repeatedly to recall the field for another try.

The harassed official starter infamously kept the field at the start line for an hour and a half, the crowd roaring its displeasure, before finally sending them on their way—by which time the race favorite, a nervous colt named St. Leonards, had descended into exhaustion. As the Chicago-based newspaper *Inter-Ocean* described the fiasco the following day:

> *When they arrived at the post the trouble began . . . why a starter like Pettingill should take almost two hours to get them off is a mystery. . . . There is no doubt that the best horse, St. Leonards, was beaten by this tiring process. . . . In the hour and thirty odd minutes at the post there were twenty-five breaks, in which one or more horses ran from an eighth to a sixteenth of a mile. Twenty-five eighths of a mile both ways would be six miles. In fifteen of these breaks, St. Leonards was among the first three, and usually the first. It is safe to say, therefore, that St. Leonards ran three miles before the race.*

On Sanford Memorial Stakes Day, Pettingill, perhaps recalling this traumatic long-ago embarrassment, kept the field at the string for just three minutes, but then sent them off to a ragged start, with Golden Broom and Upset away well, and Man o' War and Donnacona breaking flat-footed. This time, Pettingill did not wave his recall flag.

Some would claim that Man o' War was backing up when Pettingill released the field, perhaps even turned the wrong way, but the official *Daily Racing Form* chart claims only that "MAN O' WAR began slowly."

Loftus attempted to undo the evolving disaster by saving ground, but succeeded only in exacerbating the situation. He scraped the paint racing around the turn, then reached the top of the stretch with Golden Broom and Upset well within reach but forming a box that prevented the straining Man o' War from flying past. Jockey Willie Knapp aboard Upset stated later that he could hear Loftus shouting—all but begging—to let him through, but Knapp held his ground, blocking Man o' War's path. This was, after all, not the most gentlemanly of sports, and Knapp was not Man o' War's press agent. He and Upset had a race to win.

By the time Loftus was able to take Man o' War up, go around the fading Golden Broom, and, for the first time ever, apply the whip on Man o' War it was too late, and the supercolt followed a half-length behind Upset. "If I had taken him to the outside an instant sooner," said Loftus in the next day's *New York Herald*, "he would have won, for he is the gamest and most courageous horse I ever rode. He would have caught Upset in a few more jumps." But of course, horse races are never scheduled for six furlongs plus a few more jumps. It didn't help that Man o' War was carrying 130 pounds, Upset just 115.

Vreeland, who had savaged Pettingill in his *Daily Eagle* coverage, was no kinder to Loftus. "That [Man o' War] failed," Vreeland wrote, "was due entirely to his rider, Johnny Loftus. If Loftus had been a stable lad instead of the premier jockey of America, he could not have ridden a poorer race. Loftus made three mistakes, all costly. Man o' War overcame two and would have made amends for the third if the error had not been committed so close to the winning post."

The press would emphatically inform its readers that none of this was a reflection on the colt. "Man o' War, Although Beaten in Sanford Memorial, Outclasses Field of Juveniles," thundered the *New York Herald*, and its veteran turfwriter, Henry V. King, informed his readers that

"[Man o' War] was fifty pounds better than any horse in the race." This sentiment was echoed by Vreeland, who stated emphatically that Man o' War remained "the champion . . . [m]ake no mistake about that . . . [h]e never was so great as he was in defeat." These were far from the only affirmations of Man o' War's self-evident superiority.

Even the racetrack itself came in for criticism—indeed, criticism that is still proffered today in Saratoga's none-too-complimentary nickname. The 1919 Sanford Memorial is one of a handful of races (another is Secretariat's loss to Onion in the 1973 Whitney Stakes) that have led to Saratoga's receiving the portentous moniker "The Graveyard of Champions."

Loftus was reportedly heartbroken by the loss; Riddle and the rest of the Man o' War contingent were gracious in defeat, and ten days later, in the $10,000 Grand Union Hotel Stakes, it was time for Man o' War and his maligned jockey to make amends. Penalized ten pounds for his shocking victory, Upset carried 125 to Man o' War's 130, with eight other owners and trainers hoping for their own headlines but realistically racing for third money. August 23, 1919, would be decidedly business as usual for the Glen Riddle superstar, as Loftus allowed Upset a brief early lead, a temporary glimmer of hope, then dashed it by sending his mount into a lead that rapidly became insurmountable. Loftus damped down the afterburners when the race was won, and in the end, Man o' War's margin over his erstwhile conqueror was a deceptive one length.

Man o' War next annexed Saratoga's Hopeful Stakes on a track that was virtually "a river of soup . . . almost ankle deep in mud," enriching Riddle's bankroll with the $24,600 winner's purse and leading home a cavalcade of Saratoga's other top 2-year-olds: by four lengths over the filly Cleopatra, who was four lengths ahead of Constancy, another filly, who was followed by Hasten On, two lengths farther back, then a length to Upset, then three to Dr. Clark and two more to Ethel Gray, with Captain Alcock trailing another two lengths back.

And still the flying son of Fair Play wasn't done. Now racing moved back to Belmont Park, and Man o' War remained unconquerable, winning the rich Futurity and its $26,650 winner's purse over the Whitney Stable's promising John P. Grier, with Upset fifth and the following year's

Derby winner, Paul Jones, sixth over the Belmont Park straightaway. With this win, Man o' War's trainer, Louis Feustel, became the youngest man ever to have conditioned a winner of the Futurity, a race that had first been contested in 1888.

And thus ended Man o' War's 1919 season, with nine wins in ten starts and earnings of $83,325 (equivalent to approximately $1.3 million in 2024 currency), the most for any 1919 juvenile and more than any 2-year-old had earned since 1907, when undefeated Colin reeled off twelve consecutive victories (including two over Man o' War's sire, Fair Play) and brought home $131,007 in purse money. Loftus, the leading rider of 1919, would finish the year with sixty-five wins in just 177 starts, 37 percent winners. His total purse earnings for the year were $252,707 (approximately $4.5 million in modern-day funds).

Man o' War had carried 130 pounds in a race six times while still a 2-year-old, which in today's racing environment seems less a racing secretary's tool to bring about close finishes than a form of animal abuse bordering on the criminal. At the time, though, 130 pounds was not even the top weight assigned to juveniles. Combing through the history books, one discovers that Hall of Famer Billy Kelly, who in 1918 won fourteen of seventeen starts as a 2-year-old, carried 135 pounds to victory in the Eastern Shores Stakes.

But it did not require Hall of Fame–caliber talent for a 2-year-old to earn a 130-pound impost. Among other juveniles who carried 130 pounds were the following, a few of whom earned lasting acclaim, but most never became household names: Burning Blaze, Campfire, Dice, Dominant, Domino, Equipoise, His Highness, Jamestown, Ladysman, Martingale, Master Charlie, Mohawk II, Morvich, Nassak, Novelty, Papp, Pebbles, Peter Pan, St. James, Sun Briar, Tryste, and War Pennant. This is not necessarily a complete list.

If the owners and trainers of the season's next-best 2-year-olds harbored hopes that their juvenile colts and fillies might mature over the winter into legitimate challengers for Man o' War, they were to be sorely disappointed. As Edward L. Bowen noted in his book, *Man o' War: Racehorse of the Century*, in the autumn and winter of 1919–1920, Man O' War's trainer, Louis Feustel, *was saying back at [the Glen Riddle training facility in] Berlin, Maryland . . . that he had never seen a horse come forward as much from two to three as Man o' War. The recorded facts bore out his awe: At Saratoga, Man o' War had weighed 970 pounds. Over the winter, he filled out to 1,150.*

And despite the hard work and fervent dreams of those seeking to dislodge Man o' War from the pinnacle of the 1917 crop, the son of Fair Play would spend the 1920 season further distancing himself from his peers.

There was virtually no winter racing season in those days; racing began in the springtime, and among the first key races on the calendar was the Kentucky Derby. Riddle chose not to enter his colt in the race, believing that its demanding mile-and-a-quarter distance was too long, too early in the season, for a young 3-year-old. Man o' War, Riddle announced, would make his initial 1920 start ten days later, in the mile-and-an-eighth Preakness (which would be increased to its current one-and-three-sixteenths miles in 1925).

And so it was that on May 8, 1920, as Riddle and Feustel watched from the clubhouse and Man o' War lounged in a stall in Maryland, the gelding Paul Jones, who the previous year had won five times in ten tries while earning $6,404, led wire-to-wire to win the forty-sixth Kentucky Derby and its $30,375 winner's purse, at odds of 16-to-1. In Paul Jones's stirrups was jockey Ted Rice, one of the top horsemen of the era, who three years later would die at New York's Jamaica racetrack when thrown by a horse named McKee. Second in the Kentucky Derby, a head behind the winner, was Man o' War's Sanford Memorial nemesis, Upset.

Forever since, 1920 has been known in the Bluegrass as the year Man o' War did not win the Kentucky Derby. In fact, Man o' War, who was bred and foaled in Kentucky, and would retire there and die there, would never race in his native state. But of course, in 1920 there was no notion of an American "Triple Crown"; the Kentucky Derby was an important race with a distinguished history and a large purse, but it was not yet part of any more significant combination of races.

And Riddle's strategy succeeded. Beginning with the Preakness, Man o' War would go about humiliating his cropmates and smashing his sport's records, in the process cementing his place in the annals of sports history.

Perhaps Riddle's fellow owners sensed an opportunity in the Preakness to confront Man o' War at a vulnerable point in the season, making his first start in over eight months and with a new jockey, Clarence Kummer, in the irons. This may be why eight sprightly 3-year-olds were sent postward to challenge the colt on a day that Riddle later described as "very hot," but that the Department of Agriculture Weather Bureau pegged at a moderate seventy-five degrees. The crowd at Pimlico, described in one report as "enormous," expressed their confidence in the reigning supercolt, sending him to the starting line as the odds-on 4-to-5 favorite, and would be rewarded for their faith with $3.60 for each $2 win bet—an 80 percent profit, the largest return on investment anyone wagering on Man o' War would experience for the remainder of his career.

The race was over almost before it began. Man o' War was two lengths ahead after the first quarter-mile, and from that point on there was always daylight between the big colt and his closest pursuers. Upset, under a powerful whip ride by jockey Joseph Rodriguez, the first Hispanic rider to compete in a Triple Crown race, pulled to within a length-and-a-half at the finish; the remainder of the field was strung out more than forty lengths behind. The winner's purse was $23,000, the winning time 1:51⅗, just three ticks slower than the track record for the distance.

And now, with Man o' War's first start as a 3-year-old in the sport's official records, something unusual began to happen. The Glen Riddle Farm colt having won impressively in his return to the races, owners and trainers of other 3-year-olds began avoiding him in droves. Perhaps it was time to face reality, send their colts and fillies elsewhere, and employ a strategy of fighting battles on the racetrack with a reasonable possibility of being won.

There may be no clearer way to describe Man o' War's effect on the 1920 racing calendar: He scared the opposition into abandoning the sport's classic races.

The nine-horse Preakness would mark the last time Man o' War would face more than three opponents in a race, and he would be challenged by as many as three only once. On three occasions, he would be taken on by just two other starters; six times he would face just one rival. Perhaps history's greatest match racer, Man o' War would win all six of these two-horse contests, recording an average winning margin of 25¼ lengths.

Following his Preakness romp, Belmont Park's Withers Stakes, which required all starters to carry the same weight, 118 pounds, was little more than an exercise run for Man o' War—except that the Glen Riddle Farm colt earned a $4,825 winner's purse for his owner and shattered Fairy Wand's world record for the one-mile distance, recording a 1:35⅘ clocking.

Here was Man o' War's first official record time, and according to the official *Daily Racing Form* chart, which recorded that he had "displayed wonderful speed under restraint" and "won under a stout pull," the 3-year-old set his record without any urging whatsoever from Kummer.

The Belmont Stakes, next on Man o' War's agenda, became a near walkover when only one runner, his frequent rival Donnacona, could be found to contest the mile-and-three-eighths event. Donnacona, a stakes winner with a third-place finish in the Preakness, was no pushover, but he had faced Man o' War once as a 2-year-old and would try him three times at age three without ever mounting a serious challenge. On Belmont Stakes Day, Man o' War quickly disposed of his rival, opening a lead that would eventually reach twenty lengths. He crossed the finish line in 2:14⅕, obliterating by three and one-fifth seconds the American record set the previous year by Sir Barton. The Belmont Stakes would be run until 1925 at the eleven-furlong distance, but Man o' War's record for the classic would endure. No one would ever approach his clocking.

Man o' War next surfaced at Jamaica Park for the one-mile Stuyvesant Stakes, in which he would carry his highest impost yet, 135 pounds, and be offered at odds of 1-to-100—the bettor who risked $100 on him would receive $101 following the almost inevitable Man o' War victory. Only one runner, Yellow Hand, could be found to take him on, offering a 60-to-1 payoff to the rare on-site bettor who cared to make so forlorn a gamble.

As was the case for Donnacona, Yellow Hand was an excellent racehorse, for the times. He would win twenty times in forty-nine career starts and would record multiple stakes victories, setting track records for seven furlongs at Saratoga and one-and-one-eighth miles at Empire City. Following Man o' War's retirement, the colt would emerge as the best remaining 1917 foal, topping the nation's 4-year-olds with earnings of $42,271. In the Stuyvesant, he was receiving a 32-pound pull in the weights, carrying 103 pounds to Man o' War's 135, but both the bookmakers and the crowd believed that in this company he was hopelessly overmatched, out for some exercise and a quick $700 in runner-up money.

Which proved precisely the case. Man o' War broke on top, was five lengths clear after the first quarter-mile and was ahead by four at the half-mile. Then he was let loose for a few strides, and left Yellow Hand eight lengths behind while jockey Clarence Kummer eased his mount through the final furlongs.

To this point in the season Man o' War had been winning on sheer power, going directly to the front at the break and overpowering the opposition. The Dwyer Stakes, contested on July 10, 1920, at Aqueduct, was another sort of race entirely—and the first time ever in which it appeared, for a stunning moment, that the son of Fair Play might be defeated by another horse on their relative merits. Here, for the first time, Man o' War would be tested for courage.

As was now so often the case, the nine-furlong Dwyer Stakes drew just Man o' War and a single challenger, a colt called John P. Grier, named for a financier of the period. Trainer James Rowe, who over the course of his long career conditioned more champions than any other trainer in the history of the American turf, had been pursuing Man o' War doggedly with colts owned by leading breeder Harry Payne Whitney—Upset and Wildair and Dr. Clark, as well as John P. Grier—seeking either the strategic two-horse combination of speed and closing kick to tag-team Man o' War into a loss, or the one colt who might have the ability to defeat the champion on his own, with help, of course, from the scale of weights.

It was Rowe who had trained Upset to the Sanford Memorial victory, and his reward for dethroning the champion, if only for a day, was a series of newspaper articles unanimously portraying the victory as a fluke, to be blamed on a terrible start by an incompetent substitute starter and a horrendous ride by a usually reliable jockey. The articles were about Man o' War's abysmal racing luck, not about Rowe's training prowess.

John P. Grier, Rowe believed, might be the best of the Whitney string. He had already finished second to Man o' War the previous year in the Belmont Futurity, and now, with Grier having won two races already at age three, the day had come for a very fast colt to apply more pressure than even Man o' War could withstand. John P. Grier would challenge Man o' War from the start, and Rowe would hope that the combination of Grier's class and an eighteen-pound weight advantage—Grier carried 108 pounds, Man o' War 126—might win the day.

The starter pulled the string, and for the first time in 1920 an opponent jumped to the lead. Man o' War was quick to correct this oversight, and the two colts—big Man o' War and the more compact John P. Grier—raced through the early stages as a team, so much so that some of the estimated crowd of 25,000 might have believed that Grier had been left at the start, so perfectly was he concealed on the outside of his adversary.

They continued this way down the backstretch and to the final turn—Man o' War in full flight, conceding nothing; John P. Grier refusing to yield—and at the top of the stretch, both Clarence Kummer on Man o' War and Eddie Ambrose on John P. Grier believed that for a brief moment Grier thrust his head into the narrowest of leads. This was echoed in the next day's *Daily Racing Form* chart call: "JOHN P. GRIER . . . had a slight lead between calls in the homestretch." One can only imagine Rowe's jubilation as the colt's flaring nostril showed in front.

It was at this point, however, that John P. Grier gave way, his immense store of energy and will finally depleted by the unyielding presence of a runner whose endless power seemingly knew no bounds. As John P. Grier finally fell back, Man o' War found a gear that no other horse had yet discovered and surged away, reaching the finish a length-and-a-half ahead. Nothing—not John P. Grier's heart nor his unmistakable talent nor Rowe's unequaled training skills—could tip the scales in the Whitney colt's favor. John P. Grier would win ten starts in his seventeen-race career, win stakes races and set track records, but he would never defeat Man o' War, whose time for the Dwyer's nine furlongs, 1:49⅗, was yet another American record.

Given nearly a month to recuperate from his most testing challenge, Man o' War next surfaced at Saratoga for the Miller Stakes, where an outsized crowd approaching 35,000 and a new jockey—the great Earl Sande replacing the injured Clarence Kummer—awaited him. Donnacona and the overmatched King Albert would be Man o' War's adversaries.

The result, however, was unchanged. Man o' War, under 131 pounds and backed down to 1-to-30 in the odds, quickly left Donnacona, carrying 119 pounds, and King Albert, under 114, respectively six and ten lengths behind. The son of Fair Play fell three-fifths short of the American record this time, but following the all-out finish of the Dwyer, the Glen Riddle contingent was taking it easy with Man o' War. The official *Daily Racing Form* chart noted that the victor was "never fully extended."

Two weeks later, Man o' War was back in action, in the fifty-first running of Saratoga's historic "Midsummer Derby," the Travers Stakes. The Travers could boast a succession of winners over the years as impressive as that of any race: Kentucky and Ruthless and Glenelg and Kingfisher and Harry Bassett and Joe Daniels and Tom Bowling and Baden Baden and Duke of Magenta and Falsetto and Hindoo and Henry of Navarre and Hermis and Broomstick and Roamer and Omar Khayyam and Sun Briar and more. Surely 1920 would be the year in which Man o' War would append his name to this illustrious company, despite his second new jockey in two starts, as the capable Andy Schuttinger subbed for the unavailable Earl Sande.

Going to the post with the Glen Riddle colt were Upset and John P. Grier, as James Rowe had yet another try at defeating his stable's archrival. As even the obsessed Rowe must have realized, a six-pound pull in the weights would do little to advance Upset's agenda—Man o' War had defeated the son of Whisk Broom II by a length-and-a-half with "abundant speed in reserve" when Upset was given a four-pound advantage in the Preakness. And a fourteen-pound pull in the weights surely must have seemed inadequate for John P. Grier, who had just fallen short with an eighteen-pound edge.

This proved an accurate assessment. Man o' War took the early lead and Grier, perhaps still recovering from his supreme effort in the Dwyer, attempted to force the pace, lasting six furlongs before falling back, leaving Man o' War coasting on a four-length lead. When Upset was unable to make an impact, Schuttinger began easing his mount down the stretch, settling for a confident two-and-a-half-length victory. Man o' War had reached the mile marker in 1:35⅗, one tick faster than his own existing record for the distance, and his 2:01⅘ clocking for the mile-and-a-quarter equaled the track record for the distance.

Man o' War would next race in Belmont Park's one-and-five-eighths-mile Lawrence Realization Stakes, and when no other runner could be found to oppose him, it appeared that this would become a walkover. For both racetrack management and Riddle, this was an outcome to be avoided if possible: A "race" featuring a lone runner would be a non-wagering event that would cost the track money, and since walkovers pay the winner only 50 percent of the purse, Riddle would forfeit half of the $15,000 winner's share. The fans would lose, too; they would lose the opportunity to see Man o' War conquer another equine challenger.

This was avoided at nearly the last moment, when Mrs. Walter Jeffords, the Riddles' niece, stepped forward to offer her colt Hoodwink as an added starter, a gesture that both solved the immediate issue and, though perhaps no one expected it at the time, created in the Lawrence Realization a race that would add considerably to Man o' War's rapidly growing legend.

Shockingly, it was Hoodwink's nose that showed in front when the starter released the barrier, but this was merely a momentary snag, quickly set straight as Man o' War tossed in a few gigantic strides and bolted to the lead. After this, the substantial difference in talent between the two starters rapidly asserted itself, and Man o' War began pulling away, opening immense tracts of space between himself and Hoodwink, who, as the *Daily Racing Form*'s official chart would note, "made no effort to keep pace with the leader."

Perhaps it would be more instructive, more dramatic, simply to reprint Man o' War's progression, as reflected in the *Daily Racing Form* chart, than to attempt to wring a paragraph out of the numbers. The chart call, reflecting Hoodwink's surprising opening few strides and the non-contest from that point forward, read:

Table 1-1: Man O' War, Hoodwink, and the Lawrence Realization

	St.	¼ mi.	½ mi.	¾ mi.	Stretch	Finish
Man O' War	2	1-20	1-20	1-30	1-50	1-100
Hoodwink	1	2	2	2	2	2

A hundred lengths is a sizable margin. Some spotted Hoodwink, who would finish his career with just a single win in eleven starts and minuscule earnings of $2,753, galloping slowly into the stretch at the moment Man o' War was blazing past the finish, stopping the judges' watches in 2:40⅘. Here was yet another record for Man o' War, eclipsing by more than four seconds the American standard for the distance set by Fitz Herbert in 1909. It was perhaps Man o' War's most impressive record, having been earned with absolutely no challenge from a rival.

A week later Man o' War was entered in the Jockey Club Stakes, a weight-for-age twelve-furlong affair for 3-year-olds and up. There was hope that this might be Man o' War's first experience tangling with older horses; perhaps even Derby-Preakness-Belmont-winner Sir Barton would be entered. But no entry forms would be filed for good older runners, whose owners were understandably disinclined to send their handicap specialists to the track while conceding weight to Man o' War.

Moreover, with rumors swirling about a possible season-ending race featuring the best runners of all ages for a purse that might exceed $50,000, nobody was sending a top older horse into a race with a winner's purse of just $5,850. To avoid a walkover, Harry Payne Whitney offered his 3-year-old colt Damask as an added starter, earning the runner-up's $1,000 share of the purse.

Damask was what might be termed a "nice colt." At three he had won the nine-furlong Louisiana Derby, at four he would win the mile-and-five-sixteenths Aqueduct Handicap, at five he would gallop home first in Jamaica's mile-and-a-sixteenth Flight Handicap. By age seven, he was competing over the jumps and was good enough to win Belmont Park's Corinthian Steeplechase at two-and-a-half miles.

Against 3-year-old Man o' War, Damask was a hopeless 60-to-1; Man o' War's odds, for the third time in 1920, were 1-to-100. Under a snug hold by jockey Clarence Kummer, Man o' War opened a substantial early lead over the springy Belmont Park surface that grew steadily larger, crossing the finish fifteen lengths ahead and earning yet another new American record with his 2:28⅘ clocking. This record would remain on the books for seven years, until Handy Mandy, carrying a feathery 109 pounds at the Latonia racetrack, edged it by one-fifth of a second in 1927. Ten years later, Man o' War's best son, War Admiral, would complete his Triple Crown, clinching the Belmont Stakes in 2:28⅗ and earning a share of the record his sire had once held.

Man o' War's next race was scheduled for September 18 at the Havre de Grace racecourse in Maryland. The Potomac Handicap was a mile-and-a-sixteenth test for 3-year-olds that would allow the track handicapper to pile weight on Man o' War in the effort to create, at least theoretically, an incentive for on-track gamblers to open their wallets. When Man o' War was assigned a career-high 138 pounds, trainer James Rowe sent out H. P. Whitney's Metropolitan Handicap winner Wildair, assigned just 108, in yet another effort to earn a second victory over the champion. Ral Parr's Blazes (104½ pounds) and Kentucky Derby winner Paul Jones (114) also received substantial weight concessions.

But Riddle and Feustel were less concerned about weight assignments than about the problematic track at "the Graw," which was known to have a cuppy surface that tended to break out from under long-striding horses like Man o' War. The risk of injury was a legitimate concern, and as post time approached the two men considered scratching the colt. But ultimately the decision was made to send Man o' War after the $6,800 winner's purse, and Kummer was directed to forego records, to win the race and get his mount home safely.

Kummer followed his instructions nearly perfectly. Man o' War gained the lead at the start and maintained a sensible length-and-a-half advantage virtually from flagfall to finish, withstanding an early challenge from the speedy Blazes, and then, when that one faded at the race's midpoint, holding Wildair safe the rest of the way. Paul Jones never caught anybody, running in fourth position all the way around the track.

But despite Kummer's instructions, Man o' War ran fast enough to set a new track record for the eight-and-a-half-furlong distance, arriving at the finish in 1:44⅖. And Man o' War did incur a minor injury, what Dorothy Ours in *Man o' War: A Legend Like Lightning* described as "a swelling spot on Red's right foreleg, where a bruised tendon now threatened his racing career."

The swelling was treated and subsided, and Man o' War was declared safe to race again. And now it was announced that he would next meet Sir Barton, with Exterminator one of the two best older horses in training. Racetracks were invited to bid on the race, and in the end Kenilworth Park, a Canadian track, offered the high bid: $75,000 plus a $5,000 gold cup. "The Race of the Century," as it was coined, would take place north of the border.

As plans for the race moved forward, Riddle was considering Man o' War's future. The minor injury had concerned the colt's owner, and he recognized that purses for 4-year-olds were less lucrative than those for younger horses. Legend has it that Riddle made his decision after a conversation with Walter S. Vosburgh, the official handicapper for the New York tracks. "How much weight," Riddle (or perhaps it was trainer Louis Feustel) asked Vosburgh, "would you assign Man o' War if he raced as a 4-year-old?"

Vosburgh pondered, perhaps considering the additional fans Man o' War, with his towering reputation and nearly pristine record, might draw to New York tracks in 1921, and how much wagering money those fans might pour into the association's coffers. But Vosburgh's role as official handicapper was not to enhance funding streams; it was to create close finishes by adjusting the weights carried by the entrants, and he was considered the best anywhere at this painstaking task.

He gave the only appropriate answer: "If Man o' War wins his first race as a 4-year-old, I'll assign him the highest weight any horse has carried in my lifetime." With visions of imposts starting at 140 pounds and proceeding upward from there, Riddle announced that his colt would be retired following his match with Sir Barton.

Man o' War's early retirement, however, may not have been a unanimous decision. Reporter George Buchanan Fife, writing in the October 31,

1920, edition of the *Atlanta Journal,* suggested that forceful opinions may have been heard on both sides of the issue:

> *Man o' War . . . is practically worshipped by two women. One of them is Mrs. Samuel D. Riddle, the wife of his owner, and the other Mrs. Walter Jeffords, their adopted niece . . . when [Man o' War] is entered in any event there is a family council over him, a very earnest discussion as to his programme, the jockey who is to be up and how he should be ridden. . . . Recently the council met to discuss sending Man o' War to England to compete for the Ascot [G]old [C]up. Both Mrs. Riddle and Mrs. Jeffords were for entering him, certain that he would capture this turf classic. . . . But Mr. Riddle and Louis Feustel, Man o' War's capable trainer, were opposed, for a variety of reasons. And at this writing [eighteen days following the Sir Barton match race at Kenilworth Park] it seems quite a settled thing that this great horse has run his last race.*

Man o' War's final race proved anticlimactic. There was drama on race day, as Sir Barton's owner, Commander J. K. L. Ross, replaced Earl Sande aboard Sir Barton with journeyman rider Frank Keogh, and the human entourages of both contestants concerned themselves with the hardness of the track surface, but in the end it proved to be just another Man o' War triumph—a front-running, seven-length romp that pushed Man o' War to the top of America's all-time leading earners.

Man o' War's 2:03 clocking for the mile-and-a-quarter was another track record for the champion, this one by a monumental six and two-fifths seconds, but then, Kenilworth did not attract top-flight Thoroughbreds, and its track records were correspondingly slow. For Man o' War not to have run faster than the existing record, 2:09⅖, would have been unthinkable.

And with that, Man o' War was done. Plans were made—other people's plans, never Riddle's—that would have him challenge Exterminator at age four, that would send him to Europe to demonstrate that American Thoroughbreds could outrun the haughty Europeans, even on their own tracks. But Riddle would not be swayed. Man o' War would race no more.

The sporting press challenged Riddle's decision, some with headlines bordering on the insulting. The day after the Riddle colt's victory over Sir Barton, Vreeland had proclaimed Man o' War "king of kings." With Man o' War now relegated to the sidelines, a more acerbic Vreeland emerged, bluntly asking in a *Brooklyn Daily Eagle* headline, "Is Mr. Riddle Afraid to Race Man o' War Next Year?"

There were plans for a national tour, discussions of sending Man o' War to Hollywood to star in a movie, other proposals, perhaps, so outlandish that they were never made public. As Palmer wrote, "[A]t all such propositions Mr. Riddle snorted, and when Mr. Riddle snorted at a proposition, then that proposition lay dead and partly decomposed."

As he went to stud, Man o' War had won twenty times in twenty-one starts, and the one loss was universally dismissed. The Glen Riddle Farm colt set track, stakes, American, and world records with impunity, most often while under a stout pull. There were times during his races when his chin was literally on his chest.

Man o' War dominated at distances from five furlongs to one-and-five-eighths miles, and without exception defeated every runner who dared to take the track with him. He won on fast tracks and in the mud, and he lugged weights that few horses of the era were asked to carry. He won only once against an older opponent, but given that the opponent was future Hall of Famer Sir Barton and the winning margin was seven emphatic lengths, this is hardly an issue.

He seemingly accomplished every goal set for him, and in doing so impressed fans, racing writers, and horsemen with long, hard-won knowledge of the Sport of Kings that this was indeed a one-of-a-kind Thoroughbred, a generational or perhaps multi-generational talent. He brought fans to the races in droves, and the positive publicity he brought to a sport badly in need of it was priceless. Even into the twenty-first century, his impact on the sport continues.

Was this, indeed, the most outstanding racehorse in our history? Was Man o' War the greatest horse ever to race in America?

Let's ponder the possibilities.

Secretariat going to the post in the Whitney Stakes. (Bob Coglianese)

CHAPTER 2

Dominance

Man o' War vs. Secretariat

A SON OF THE GREAT STALLION BOLD RULER, SECRETARIAT WAS A MILD 3-to-1 favorite when first sent postward, in a five-and-a-half-furlong Aqueduct maiden race on Independence Day 1972. It was not an encouraging outing. Under jockey Paul Feliciano, the Lucien Laurin trainee was bumped hard leaving the starting gate, then raced in a cluster of horses down the backstretch before finding racing room. Secretariat closed with a rush, but could manage only fourth, a length-and-a-quarter behind a colt named Herbull. It may have been the Fourth of July, but there were no fireworks that day for Secretariat. His record stood at one start, once out of the money.

Eleven days later, Secretariat raced as a champion-to-be should, leaving Master Achiever and nine others six lengths behind in a six-furlong maiden race. Once again, Feliciano was in the stirrups, but that was about to change. Adding Ron Turcotte in Feliciano's stead, Secretariat proceeded to stride away by a length-and-a-half in an allowance race. He then sampled stakes competition at Saratoga, winning by three lengths over the previously undefeated Linda's Chief in the Sanford Stakes, the event that had denied Man o' War a perfect career. Watching Secretariat run past Linda's Chief was like watching "a Cadillac pulling away from a Ford," exclaimed a clocker in the press box.

From this point, Secretariat would win by daylight in every remaining race at age two. He blazed from last to first to crush Flight to Glory and Stop the Music by five in the Hopeful, was a length-and-a-half better than Stop the Music in the Futurity, overcame a slow start to win by two lengths over Stop the Music in the Champagne, and demolished Stop the Music and fellow Lucien Laurin trainee Angle Light by eight in the Laurel Futurity. He closed his season with a three-and-a-half-length drubbing of Angle Light and Step Nicely in the Garden State, rallying from fifteen lengths behind to blow past yet another outclassed field. He was denied the trophy only in the Champagne, when he was disqualified and placed second for interference during the stretch run.

It was an impressive enough performance that year-end voters named Secretariat not merely the season's champion 2-year-old but Horse of the Year. Secretariat is one of only four 2-year-olds to have received this honor, along with Alfred G. Vanderbilt's Native Dancer in 1952 (co–Horse of the Year with One Count), Claiborne Farm's Moccasin in 1965 (sharing the award with Roman Brother), and Joseph LaCombe's Favorite Trick in 1997.

Selecting a 2-year-old as Horse of the Year can be dicey. Runners who seem unbeatable as juveniles sometimes fail to mature over the winter and come abruptly back to the pack as 3-year-olds. As is always the case with a highly regarded 2-year-old, the racing world held its collective breath, awaiting Secretariat's 3-year-old debut. The son of Bold Ruler and Somethingroyal had earned an impressive collection of hardware for the Meadow Stable's trophy room, and his $456,404 led all 2-year-olds in seasonal earnings. But he still had much to prove.

Secretariat began the task of defending his title on a sloppy Aqueduct track on March 17, 1973. Bulling his way between tightly packed rivals in the seven-furlong Bay Shore Stakes, he kicked clear for a four-and-a-half-length victory over Champagne Charley and Impecunious, and despite the contact during the stretch run, his season-opening triumph was allowed to survive another foul claim. Returning three weeks later in the one-mile Gotham Stakes under a 126-pound impost, the big chestnut equaled Aqueduct's mile record, set five years earlier by 4-year-old Plucky Pan carrying 115 pounds, with a 1:33⅗ clocking. He was favored at 3-to-10 odds for the nine-furlong Wood Memorial but could manage only a third-place finish behind Laurin's other starter, Angle Light, with California's Sham second.

And now the whispers began. One heard rumblings that Secretariat's Bold Ruler breeding, which had never produced victory in a Triple Crown race, would be his undoing at the Kentucky Derby's classic mile-and-a-quarter. Even the mile-and-an-eighth of the Wood Memorial, a furlong shorter, had been beyond Secretariat's comfort zone.

A lively rumor as Derby Day approached had Secretariat's knees failing him. It was reported that one visitor to Lucien Laurin's barn said that he was sorry for the trainer. "I asked him why," said Laurin. "He said because he'd heard we had to scratch Secretariat." This was news to Laurin, whose daily contact with the colt predicted nothing but victory.

The mile-and-a-quarter Kentucky Derby proved Laurin correct. Away last, Secretariat was content to race near the rear of the pack for his first time under Churchill Downs' twin spires, then moved quickly into contention on the backstretch. Turning for home, Secretariat ran past first the fading Shecky Greene and then Sham, pulling away down the stretch to win by two-and-a-half lengths, with Sham second, Our Native eight lengths farther back in third, and future three-time Horse of the Year Forego another half-length away. Secretariat's time, 1:59⅖, was three ticks faster than the Derby record established by Northern Dancer in 1964. More than a half-century later, it has never been bettered.

Secretariat's record-shattering Derby performance—and the continued presence on the Triple Crown trail of the game and gritty Sham—sent owners and trainers scurrying for less daunting company, and by Preakness Day, just two weeks later, the thirteen-horse Derby field had been whittled to six.

At Pimlico, Secretariat went to the starting gate as the odds-on choice at 3-to-10; Sham was 3-to-1. The rest of the Preakness field was more or less disdained by the betting public: Derby third finisher Our Native and expected front-runner Ecole Etage at 11-to-1, Deadly Dream at 35-to-1, and Torsion the longest shot at 39.

Secretariat was again slow to find his best stride, but when he did find it he did so explosively, shifting to the outside on the clubhouse turn and passing rivals with a surge that catapulted him into the lead midway down the backstretch, with Sham once again his closest pursuer. Sham remained in striking position to the top of the stretch, at which point jockey Laffit Pincay Jr. unlimbered his whip and took aim on the leader.

Interviewed after the race, Turcotte described the stretch run vividly. He recalled listening to the repeated cracks of Laffit Pincay Jr.'s whip on "that poor Sham" as horse and rider struggled vainly to gain any ground during the stretch drive. Turcotte, however, was still hand-riding Secretariat. "I didn't even turn my stick up," he reported, and he had no need to. After three-quarters of a mile, Secretariat's margin was two-and-a-half lengths; at midstretch it remained two-and-a-half lengths. At the wire, the results were a rare carbon copy of the Derby finish: Secretariat by that same, immutable two-and-a-half lengths, Sham by eight, Our Native third.

Secretariat's Preakness time was captured by the track timer at 1:54⅖, two-fifths of a second slower than the mark set by Cañonero II in 1970, but this was disputed by the *Daily Racing Form*, whose clockers had caught the winner in 1:53⅖, race record time. When technicians created side-by-side films of the Preaknesses of Secretariat and Cañonero, Secretariat reached the finish comfortably ahead. The controversy regarding Secretariat's Preakness clocking persisted until May 11, 1991, when Farma Way won the mile-and-three-sixteenths Pimlico Special in 1:52⅖, forever erasing both Cañonero II and Secretariat from the record books as Pimlico's track record holders. It is now generally conceded that Secretariat did set a new stakes record in his Preakness.

Secretariat's Belmont Stakes was, of course, a race for the ages. "Moving like a tremendous machine," in the undying words of race caller Chic Anderson, the Meadow Stable colt ran a gallant but overmatched and probably exhausted Sham into the ground on Belmont Park's long backstretch, then stopped the official timer in 2:24 flat, some two and three-fifths seconds faster than Gallant Man's existing track record.

There was astonishment throughout the racing world. Racing fans knew that on those rare occasions when racetrack records were broken, it was usually by fractions of seconds, not multiples of them. When the 200th anniversary of Ruthless's victory in the first Belmont Stakes is celebrated in 2067, it is likely that whatever version of popular media exists at that time will still be showing replays of Secretariat's miraculous, Triple Crown–clinching victory and expressing awe at his seemingly impossible 2:24 clocking.

Secretariat had been syndicated by Meadow Stable co-owner Penny Tweedy for a record $6.08 million as a 3-year-old, the money needed to provide a quick and substantial boost to a stable that was experiencing financial challenges. The syndication agreement specified that Secretariat would not race beyond his 3-year-old season, and so, at year's end, racing's greatest drawing card would be relegated to the relative anonymity of the breeding shed.

But before that sad day arrived for the millions who saw in Secretariat the reincarnation of that once-in-a-century Thoroughbred who had redefined the word "racehorse" in 1919 and 1920, Secretariat would race six more times in the next four and a half months. He would win the Arlington Invitational, a race created expressly to lure the champion to Chicago, then would lose the Whitney Stakes at Saratoga—"The Graveyard of Champions" indeed—to nondescript Allen Jerkens trainee Onion. He would defeat the nation's best older horses, Onion included, in the first Marlboro Cup, then would lose the muddy Woodward Stakes to 16-to-1 shot Prove Out, another from the giant-killing Jerkens Stable.

He would then conclude his career as few champions ever have, switching to turf and defeating the continent's best grass horses twice at their own game, winning by five lengths in the Man o' War Stakes and then, just to confirm that that one was legitimate, winning by six-and-a-half lengths in the Canadian International Championship Stakes.

And then it was over. Like Man o' War, Secretariat would never see racing action as a 4-year-old. His place in the pantheon of America's favorite racehorses was assured, his second Horse of the Year title a mere formality.

As the world looked back upon his historic career, Secretariat was recognized by racing people as something truly phenomenal, a runner whose exploits raised him above the terminology reserved for Thoroughbreds whose accomplishments were merely outstanding. Summarizing the 1973 racing season in the *American Racing Manual*, longtime racing journalist Charles Hatton expressed the adulation this once-in-a-lifetime equine engendered:

> *Secretariat was a Superhorse, rather than a transient Horse of the Year. . . . Veteran turfmen, sophisticates of deep experience and broad, informed tastes pronounced him "The Horse of the Century."*

He will likely be the only Thoroughbred ever to appear simultaneously on the covers of three major national magazines: *Time, Newsweek,* and *Sports Illustrated.* In 2010, the feature-length movie *Secretariat* was seen on movie screens nationwide. The US Postal Service released a Secretariat postage stamp. Racing fans across the nation wept when nineteen-year-old Secretariat, suffering the painful ravages of laminitis, was mercifully euthanized on October 4, 1989.

Additional tasks awaited Secretariat, had financial necessity not prevented his racing at age four. The highest weight he was asked to carry was just 126 pounds, and he certainly would have been assigned more as a handicap horse. The Jockey Club Gold Cup remained a two-mile race in Secretariat's day, and it would have been fascinating to observe whether his once-maligned Bold Ruler breeding would carry him a half-mile beyond the Belmont Stakes distance. He never had the opportunity to face Forego as an older horse, when the formidable three-time Horse of the Year was at his peak of power and stamina.

But all of this seems trivial in light of Secretariat's accomplishments. Yes, Secretariat was among the very best racehorses ever produced in America. If we know nothing else about Thoroughbred racing, we most assuredly know that.

DOMINANCE

We begin with the fact that neither Secretariat nor Man o' War raced beyond their 3-year-old seasons. Secretariat was retired for financial reasons, Man o' War, by one account, to spare him the high weights racing secretaries would have assigned him as a 4-year-old; by another, to place him forever beyond the reach of gamblers who might injure him in their attempts to cash a big winning ticket.

For our purposes, the two retirements, more than fifty years apart, provide a level playing field for the consideration of two of the most charismatic Thoroughbreds in racing history. The question then becomes how to measure their dominance, given the vastly different eras in which they performed.

I began by analyzing every past performance record in the most recent edition of the *Daily Racing Form*'s incredibly detailed book *Champions*, which provides a race-by-race record for every American Thoroughbred champion from the 1890s through 2010. I wanted to know: When these horses, representing perhaps the top 1 percent of the top 1 percent of Thoroughbreds, won a race, how far did they tend to leave their opponents behind? How thoroughly, in other words, did they dominate their rivals?

Obviously, winning margin is not the only factor to be considered in assessing dominance, but it did, at the least, provide a baseline indicating which runners, when asked to defeat a field of top Thoroughbreds, did so with the sort of power and equine enthusiasm that leads to dominant, overwhelming victories. I performed this analysis for 107 runners that I considered particularly noteworthy, and by this measure, average winning margin, the most dominant horses ever to tread the American turf were:

Table 2-1: Largest Average Winning Margins

	Horse	Average Winning Margin (lengths)
1	Man o' War	9.43
2	Landaluce	9.30
3	Ruffian	8.28
4	Count Fleet	6.91
5	Rachel Alexandra	6.75
6	Heavenly Prize	6.36
7	Chris Evert	6.23
8	Inside Information	6.05
9	Secretariat	6.02
10	Spectacular Bid	6.01

Interestingly, fillies and mares filled six of the top ten slots. When a distaffer is good, she is *really* good!

It is not enough, of course, to proclaim, based on these very raw numbers, that Man o' War was the most dominant Thoroughbred ever to race in America. For starters, we can note that when the next edition of *Champions* is published, Man o' War will no longer be the name at the top of this list. In 2021 and 2022, a new superstar, Flightline, blazed across the American racing scene, winning his races by distances that led viewers to compare him to the historic greats of the sport. He raced only six times before being retired to stud with a projected value that might rival the gross national product of some small nations, and in those six races his average winning margin was 11.83 lengths.

But digging just slightly more deeply into the pre-Flightline numbers, Man o' War becomes a more difficult horse to back as the most dominant of all time. The problem is (and we'll spend more time on this in chapter 4) that Man o' War did not race against particularly compelling competition. He is, as we have noted, the only horse in the 1917 foal crop to garner a Hall of Fame plaque, and the one opponent he faced from outside that 1917 crop, Sir Barton, was known to have sensitive hooves that probably affected his performance on a Kenilworth Park oval that had been honed and hardened in the hopes of creating a fast time for Man o' War's historic final race.

Then there was a fact of life of racing at the time: fewer horses. The number of runners being produced in the period 1910 to 1920 was small, and the result was both fewer horses available to fill races and, once Man o' War's exceptional quality was recognized, fewer horses yet whose owners were willing to challenge their overpowering cropmate.

There were also fewer races. In 1919, a total of 3,531 starters competed in 4,408 races nationwide; in 1920 the numbers were 4,032 starters in 6,897 races. Fewer starters and fewer opportunities to compete meant that one outstanding horse could run off and hide from runners that were simply not good enough to create a legitimate challenge. Man o' War faced a total of just eighty-three other horses, many of which—all but Upset, in fact—lost to him repeatedly.

With just eighty-three challengers in twenty-one races, Man o' War faced an average of only 3.95 starters per race. In eleven races at age three, he averaged just 2.09 opponents.

Secretariat did not race in a day of small foal crops. In his twenty-one races, Secretariat faced 138 rivals, 6.57 per race. For Secretariat, whose 1970 foal crop totaled 24,361—fourteen-and-a-half times as many as Man o' War's—there was no lack of challengers. And unlike Man o' War, who faced only one older horse over the course of his career, Secretariat took home the Triple Crown against the best of his own crop, then challenged—and, for the most part, overpowered—the best of previous crops, winning three of five races against older horses.

Unlike Man o' War, who raced six times against only a single opponent, Secretariat never had the luxury of competing in a two-horse race, certainly not one involving a single opponent he could defeat by 100 lengths, as Man o' War defeated Hoodwink. Secretariat's average winning margin against multiple rivals was 6.02 lengths. Man o' War's was 2.64 lengths.

The quality of Secretariat's older rivals must also be considered. Man o' War defeated Sir Barton, one of the finest colts of his era. Secretariat took on and defeated Hall of Famers Riva Ridge and Cougar II on dirt, then beat everyone who could be found to challenge him on their favored grass surface.

By sheer numbers, by quality of opponents, Secretariat faced a tougher task than Man o' War, but it was Secretariat who produced the bigger margins. Unless he was in a two-horse match race, Man o' War won his typical start by less than three lengths; Secretariat won his by more than six, over larger fields of better horses.

The judgment here can only be that Secretariat was the more dominating racehorse.

Affirmed (right) and Alydar battle it out again. (Bob Coglianese)

CHAPTER 3

Gameness

Man o' War vs. Affirmed

AFFIRMED VS. ALYDAR IS THE GREATEST RIVALRY IN THE HISTORY OF the American turf.

The reader may find it strange to see this statement presented as a simple declarative sentence, without the word "perhaps" somewhere among those fourteen words. Surely, one must imagine, there must have been rivalries reaching the level of Affirmed vs. Alydar. What about Seabiscuit vs. War Admiral? Lexington vs. Lecomte? Nashua vs. Swaps? Colin vs. Fair Play? Damascus vs. Dr. Fager? Secretariat vs. Sham? Gun Bow vs. Kelso? Citation vs. Noor? Man o' War vs. Upset? Bold Ruler vs. Gallant Man? How, you might ask, can any one rivalry be declared categorically greater than these historic rivalries?

Well, fine. Let's get those out of the way, and then we can consider what you will soon agree was unquestionably a greater rivalry than any of them.

We can begin with Seabiscuit and War Admiral, the former a grandson of Man o' War, the latter his most successful son. They competed exactly once, on November 1, 1938, when Seabiscuit won their Pimlico match race. Lexington faced Lecomte only twice before failing vision forced his retirement, a not altogether unfortunate event, since after ending his racing career early, Lexington went on to become the greatest sire ever seen in America. "The Blind Hero of Woodburn Farm" led the General Sire List sixteen times, fourteen of them in succession.

Nashua and Swaps also squared off only twice, once in Swaps's 1955 Kentucky Derby victory, once when Nashua earned his revenge in a match race for the ages. Fair Play chased Colin home all four times they raced, but Fair Play would eventually make amends by siring Man o' War, a horse more celebrated than either himself or his four-time conqueror. Damascus raced four times against Dr. Fager—they split the four meetings—and Secretariat won three of his four outings against Sham.

Gun Bow and Kelso competed on five occasions, as did Citation and Noor; Man o' War faced Upset seven times, five times at age two and twice at three, defeating his rival in all but one. Bold Ruler competed against Gallant Man on seven occasions, finishing ahead of his rival three times but losing four.

Now, let's consider Affirmed and Alydar, who raced against one another ten times. That's not a typographical error, it's t-e-n, 10. Alydar raced a total of twenty-six times in his career, so in nearly 40 percent of his outings he faced a rival who would earn the juvenile championship, win the Triple Crown, top the nation's 3-year-olds, lead the handicap ranks, and win two Horse of the Year trophies. Anything written about Affirmed is necessarily also about Alydar—their rivalry was that important.

It is instructive to consider what Alydar's record might have been, had the Racing Gods not consigned him to the same crop as a runner of Affirmed's unique quality. With Affirmed in the picture, Alydar won fourteen of his twenty-six starts, was second nine times, third once, and twice out of the money.

In a world with no Affirmed, Alydar would have won twenty of twenty-six, run second three times and third once. He would have amassed an eight-race winning streak as a 2-year-old, an eleven-race streak at age three. Instead of finishing his career with purse money of just under a million dollars, Alydar's earnings would have been stratospheric.

Today, we would view him as a superhorse.

Subtract Affirmed from the 1975 foal crop, and Alydar wins the 2-year-old championship. He is undefeated at age three, winning all ten of his starts, wins the Triple Crown and also takes the Travers—becoming only the second runner, after another Calumet powerhouse, Whirlaway, to accomplish this. He is the unanimous choice as Horse of the Year for 1978.

But Alydar, perhaps the unluckiest Thoroughbred ever to contest a stretch run, never won so much as a divisional championship. Affirmed would not permit it. And Alydar has a place in racing's Hall of Fame in spite of it all, as quite possibly the most talented racehorse never to be a champion.

In their ten faceoffs, Affirmed finished in front eight times, racing against one of the best second-best Thoroughbreds ever. He was disqualified from one of those wins, so the official record shows Affirmed with seven victories, Alydar with three. Affirmed defeated Alydar sprinting and routing, at ages two and three. Their races usually had championship implications and were almost always close, often to the point of qualifying as nail-biters.

As it had since 1933, The Jockey Club concluded the 1977 through 1979 racing seasons by compiling the Experimental Free Handicap, a weight-based assessment of the previous year's best runners, with separate rankings for 2-year-olds, 3-year-olds, and older runners. Even in these purely theoretical assessments, Affirmed and Alydar were adjudged by far the best and next-best runners of their age, with the ranking tight but Affirmed the clear victor. In 1977, as 2-year-olds, Affirmed was rated at 126 pounds, Alydar at 125; the following year Affirmed was assigned 136 pounds, Alydar 135. Finally, in 1979, Alydar suffered a season-ending injury and Affirmed, assigned 136 pounds for his second Horse of the Year season, topped his rival by eight theoretical pounds.

And that, readers, is a rivalry.

Conditioned by Lazaro "Laz" Barrera, who in 1976 had coaxed Derby and Belmont Stakes wins out of the distance-challenged Bold Forbes, Affirmed started his career about three weeks ahead of Alydar, carrying Harbor View Farm's flamingo, black, and white silks to a four-and-a-half-length victory in a Belmont Park maiden event. Affirmed's workouts in preparation for his maiden voyage must have seemed unimpressive; he was offered at odds of 14-to-1 that day, returning $30.60 for each of his rare backers' $2 win wagers.

His victory propelled him into the Youthful Stakes and his first encounter with Alydar, who under the tutelage of confident trainer John Veitch would be attempting to win his first race in stakes company.

Rarely does a Thoroughbred debut in a stakes race, more rarely yet at 9-to-5 odds, but the Calumet Farm entourage evidently knew the sort of colt they had on their hands and wagered accordingly. But while Alydar was breaking flat-footed and finding his best stride far too late, the speedier Affirmed was untroubled on the lead, ultimately prevailing over 45-to-1 shot Wood Native, with Alydar five lengths back in fifth. This time, Affirmed paid $8 to win.

Alydar broke his maiden nine days later, scoring by six-and-three-quarter lengths over the highly regarded Believe It, and now the rivalry was ready to resume. Next for Affirmed and Alydar was Belmont Park's Great American Stakes. Alydar was odds-on at 4-to-5; the public remained skeptical of Affirmed, who was a lackluster 9-to-2, and this time the horseplayers got it right, as Alydar tracked his rival early, then took command, winning by three-and-a-half widening lengths. The score so far: Affirmed 1, Alydar 1.

Now the rivals took separate paths. Affirmed headed west to win a division of the Hollywood Juvenile Championship under Laffit Pincay Jr.; Alydar, with Eddie Maple aboard, scored as the odds-on favorite in the Tremont and then the Sapling. When Affirmed returned to the East Coast, it was with a new rider, seventeen-year-old Steve Cauthen, in the irons. The Harbor View colt promptly won Saratoga's Sanford Memorial Stakes as the 6-to-5 favorite, then Affirmed and Alydar faced off in a rapid-fire succession of encounters in which:

- Affirmed won Saratoga's six-and-a-half-furlong Hopeful by a half-length over Alydar.
- Affirmed won the seven-furlong Belmont Futurity by a nose over Alydar, with Nasty and Bold eleven lengths back in third.
- Alydar won the one-mile Champagne by one-and-a-quarter lengths over Affirmed.
- Affirmed won the one-and-a-sixteenth-mile Laurel Futurity by a neck over Alydar, with the rest trailing so far behind they were virtually in a different time zone.

With seven wins in nine starts, and four in six tries against the colt that was already his archrival, Affirmed now went to the sidelines, while Alydar started once more, losing Aqueduct's one-and-an-eighth-mile Remsen to Believe It. At season's end, as the long winter commenced, Affirmed was awarded the juvenile title. And speculation had already begun as to which of the two might be the superior Triple Crown candidate.

But Affirmed and Alydar would begin their 3-year-old seasons on different shores, and their human contingents would allow the suspense to build over the months leading to the First Saturday in May. While Alydar was reeling off a series of impressive victories in the East—by two lengths in a seven-furlong Hialeah allowance race, by four-and-a-half in the Flamingo, by two in the Florida Derby, and by thirteen in the Blue Grass—Affirmed and Cauthen were in California, disabusing the locals of any misguided notion that the local Derby-aged colts might contend at Churchill Downs. Affirmed began with a five-length Santa Anita allowance win, followed by a two-length triumph in the mile-and-a-sixteenth San Felipe, an important prep race for the $195,300 Santa Anita Derby, which attracted more than 48,000 fans to Affirmed's eight-length victory. And since the $284,750 Hollywood Derby was scheduled three weeks in advance of the Run for the Roses, Affirmed was sent down the freeway to Hollywood Park for that one, too, running off with it by two lengths as the odds-on 3-to-10 favorite.

As Derby Day approached, Affirmed and Alydar were unquestionably the leaders of their crop. All that remained was for the Kentucky Derby, Preakness, and Belmont Stakes to test them at the classic distances.

The Churchill Downs faithful anointed Alydar the Derby favorite, sending him out at 6-to-5 odds, with Affirmed the 9-to-5 second choice. The speedy Sensitive Prince had his backers at 9-to-2 odds, and Wood Memorial winner Believe It, at 7-to-1, also had some believers.

The day, however, belonged to Affirmed, who tracked Sensitive Prince through blistering :45⅗ and 1:10⅖ early fractions, and then, when the front-runner proved more sensitive than princely, opened a two-length lead at midstretch. Alydar, who had dallied some seventeen lengths behind in the early going, charged furiously but too late down the stretch, running out of real estate a length-and-a-half before the finish.

This earned Affirmed the grudging respect of the handicappers, who bet him down to 1-to-2 for the Preakness; at 9-to-5, Alydar would be the second choice, and Believe It was the third pick of the horseplayers at 6-to-1. Beyond those three were Noon Time Spender, Indigo Star, Dax S., and Track Reward, all available at odds in the 80-to-1 to 90-to-1 range but best left alone; they would comprise the out-of-the-money contingent of Preakness finishers.

Since Sensitive Prince was no longer on the Triple Crown trail, Affirmed set the early Preakness pace, with Alydar looming ever nearer through the race's middle furlongs. The big Calumet colt made a determined stretch run, but the game Affirmed held him safe, hanging on by a neck in a rapid 1:54⅖, with third finisher Believe It seven-and-a-half lengths farther back.

Three weeks later, only three could be found to challenge Affirmed and Alydar in the Belmont Stakes, with Affirmed sent off the 3-to-5 favorite, Alydar the 11-to-10 second choice, and Darby Creek Road, Noon Time Spender, and Judge Advocate quite rightly dismissed as largely irrelevant.

This one proved to be a race for the ages. Cauthen shepherded the front-running Affirmed through a relaxed half-mile in :50 while Alydar worked his way into the second spot, a length behind the leader. When jockey Jorge Velasquez asked Alydar for more, the Calumet colt quickly engaged Affirmed, the two colts battling head-and-head through the final turn and into the stretch. The huge Belmont Park throng roared as Alydar poked his nose ahead for a few strides at midstretch, but this was answered by another roar as Affirmed battled back, regaining the lead nearing the wire.

At the finish, it was Affirmed by a head, Alydar second, Darby Creek Road thirteen lengths farther back. Judge Advocate and Noon Time Spender were along later. For the eleventh time—and the second consecutive year—racing had a Triple Crown winner. It would not have its next until American Pharoah ended a thirty-seven-year drought in 2015.

Neither colt returned to competition for over a month. Alydar surfaced on July 22 in Chicago, facing four opponents in the Arlington Classic, and, finding Affirmed not among them, made a shambles of the event, powering to a thirteen-length victory as the 1-to-20 favorite. He next took on older horses in the Whitney, which a few years earlier had eluded the mighty Secretariat. Alydar left Buckaroo and Father Hogan some ten lengths behind while conceding the second and third finisher eleven and nine pounds, respectively.

Alydar appeared to be at an absolute peak, and the timing could not have been more perfect, for next on both his and Affirmed's agenda was Saratoga's historic Travers Stakes.

Affirmed had made a less splashy return to the races following his Belmont Stakes victory. In the traditional forerunner to the Travers, the Jim Dandy, he allowed Sensitive Prince a seven-length lead, then reeled him in, winning by a restrained half-length. Perhaps not as visually impressive as Alydar's two triumphs, Affirmed's Jim Dandy victory would nevertheless have him on his toes for the Travers.

And so the two rivals went postward together again—Affirmed at 7-to-10, Alydar at even money, Nasty and Bold and Shake Shake Shake striving for third money in a classic race. Cauthen was not available that day to ride Affirmed, so Laffit Pincay Jr., who had ridden the colt to two smashing victories in California, was summoned eastward; Velasquez would again ride Alydar.

Affirmed, as usual, made good use of his speed, tracking the early pace of Shake Shake Shake, then taking over as Alydar moved willingly along the rail. The two were on nearly even terms when Velasquez abruptly stood up in the irons, pulling Alydar back into third place. The Calumet colt regained his stride quickly and retook second, but Affirmed could not be caught, finishing a length-and-a-half clear. Following a stewards' inquiry, Affirmed was found to have impeded his rival, and Alydar was awarded the victory by disqualification. The long-running Affirmed-Alydar rivalry had captivated racing fans for the better part of two seasons, but the tenth and final installment would prove a most unsatisfactory conclusion to their drama.

Alydar was later found to have sustained a tendon injury and was done for the year. He would never again achieve the same level of excellence, returning after seven and a half months away from the races to win two of his six starts at age four. He was retired to stud following a third-place finish in the July 4, 1979, Suburban Handicap. Affirmed, his nine-race victory streak ended with the Travers disqualification, would not win again in 1978.

The Triple Crown winner's next start was the Marlboro Cup at Belmont Park. Affirmed was the 1-to-2 favorite; the second choice in the race was defending Horse of the Year and 1977 Triple Crown winner Seattle Slew, a colt with both the speed to run with Affirmed early in a race, and the stamina to battle him late. In history's first-ever meeting of two Triple Crown winners, 4-year-old Seattle Slew bolted to the early lead and never looked back, finishing three lengths clear of his younger challenger.

The two met again four weeks later in the mile-and-a-half Jockey Club Gold Cup. It was to have been a glorious two and a half minutes of reckoning between two of America's Triple Crown immortals, but what will always be remembered is the stretch-long battle between future Hall of Famers Exceller and Seattle Slew, with Exceller prevailing by a nose in a racing epic. Affirmed, whose saddle slipped shortly after the start under jockey Steve Cauthen, finished fifth, his chances lost before the field had covered a mile.

Affirmed retired to the sidelines for the winter, his Triple Crown having long since assured him the Horse of the Year title, to prepare for one more campaign. It was decided that the colt would begin his 4-year-old season in California, and he promptly sent shock waves through the sport with back-to-back losses, to Little Reb in Santa Anita's seven-furlong Malibu Stakes and to Radar Ahead in the mile-and-an-eighth San Fernando. With Cauthen mired in one of the worst riding slumps in memory, Barrera made a difficult decision, replacing Affirmed's Triple Crown companion with Laffit Pincay Jr., whose last ride aboard Affirmed had resulted in his Travers disqualification.

But that wouldn't happen a second time. Pincay guided Affirmed to a ten-length victory in the $100,000-added Charles H. Strub Stakes, completing the mile-and-a-quarter in a sensible 2:01, then added the Santa Anita Handicap by a comfortable four-and-a-half lengths, setting a track record with a sensational 1:58⅗ clocking. This earned Affirmed a two-and-a-half-month respite and his first-ever 130-pound weight assignment, and he responded with an authoritative five-length, wire-to-wire victory under 130 pounds in Hollywood Park's one-and-a-six-teenth-mile Californian. To prove unquestionably that his colt was back on track, four weeks later Barrera saddled Affirmed for a professional half-length victory in the Hollywood Gold Cup. Racing over a light-ning-fast track, Affirmed covered the mile-and-a-quarter in 1:58⅖.

Now Affirmed made his final return to New York. He was six lengths the best in a one-mile Belmont Park exhibition race, running 1:34 in the slop, then passed on the Marlboro Cup when Barrera objected to his 134-pound weight assignment. Instead, the trainer opted for the weight-for-age Woodward, and Affirmed carried 126 to a two-and-a-half-length victory over Belmont Stakes winner Coastal. Affirmed's final start, it was announced, would be in the mile-and-a-half Jockey Club Gold Cup, in which he would take on the season's Derby-Preakness winner, Spectacular Bid.

Affirmed in his Jockey Club Gold Cup victory was the essence of the professional racehorse. The defending Horse of the Year assumed the lead after a half-mile, with Spectacular Bid poised menacingly on his outside and Coastal not far away along the rail. And now, here came their challenges: first Spectacular Bid, then Coastal, then Spectacular Bid again. But each time, Affirmed found another gear, holding his adver-saries safe as he continued his relentless front-running journey. At the wire, Affirmed was three-quarters of a length clear of Spectacular Bid, with Coastal a fading third. One had the feeling that if they went around the long Belmont Park oval another time, they'd pass under the wire in precisely the same order. With that, Affirmed was retired from the sport he had dominated for three seasons. He would shortly be voted Horse of the Year for the second time.

Affirmed had raced brilliantly in the toughest of company. He won championships every season he raced, while competing against Hall of Famers Alydar, Seattle Slew, Exceller, and Spectacular Bid; Belmont Stakes winner Coastal; Seattle Slew's conqueror, J.O. Tobin; and the excellent but never quite competitive Believe It. He won at distances from five-and-a-half furlongs to one-and-a-half miles under imposts as high as 132 pounds. He was voted into the National Museum of Racing's

Hall of Fame on first eligibility. It was Affirmed who ended Kelso's reign as racing's all-time leading earner.

GAMENESS

Throughout his career, Affirmed was admired as the epitome of gameness in the Thoroughbred. Some of his most prestigious victories, most notably his Triple Crown sweep, were closely contested affairs in which Affirmed simply outbattled his rivals, refusing to yield.

The word "gameness" implies that the winner was challenged severely and emerged with a narrow victory, an issue for Man o' War supporters because the 1919–1920 superhorse was so superior physically that he was rarely required to fight a close battle.

Perhaps the Man o' War vs. Affirmed comparison for gameness can begin with races in which the result was a win or loss of a length or less. Evaluating such races results in the following:

At age two, Man o' War won by a length in Aqueduct's Tremont Stakes, lost the Sanford Memorial by a half-length at Saratoga, and won the Grand Union Hotel Stakes at the spa by a length. At age three, his closest finishes were length-and-a-half victories over Upset in the Preakness, John P. Grier in the Dwyer, and Wildair in the Potomac Handicap at Havre de Grace. Of these three, only the Dwyer was ever seriously in doubt, as Man o' War, giving his rival an eighteen-pound edge in the weights, was stalked throughout by John P. Grier and surrendered an infinitesimal lead at midstretch before powering clear in the final furlong.

At age two, Affirmed won the Youthful by a neck, the Hopeful by a half-length, the Futurity by a nose, and the Laurel Futurity by a neck. At age three, he won the Preakness by a neck, the Belmont Stakes by a head, the Jim Dandy by a half-length, and the Hollywood Gold Cup and the Jockey Club Gold Cup each by three-quarters of a length.

The raw numbers, then, show Man o' War winning twice and losing once in efforts requiring some exercise of gameness, while Affirmed won nine times in tight finishes and never lost. Even more impressive, on five of those occasions the narrowly defeated challenger was Alydar, and on another it was Spectacular Bid.

We always knew Affirmed was an incredibly game runner, and the numbers validate that.

But was he gamer than Man o' War might have been, had he been required to compete against runners of more substantial quality? The numbers cannot provide an answer. Man o' War's one loss, as we have seen, was obviously the result of human error, but even in the Sanford Memorial, he demonstrated gameness when he nearly outran the combination of Upset (receiving fifteen pounds from that one), official starter C. H. Pettingill, and jockey Johnny Loftus, as their individual malfunctions combined to minimize the champion's winning probabilities. In other races, Upset was an occasionally annoying presence, rather than a worrisome challenger. On the other occasion in which Man o' War was called upon to demonstrate gameness, he outfinished the courageous but outgunned John P. Grier in what was assuredly a game victory. Man o' War absorbed his rival's challenge for the full first mile of the race and still had enough left at the finish to win.

Affirmed was perhaps as game as any Thoroughbred has ever been; Man o' War seldom needed to call upon his innate gameness, but when he did so it was there in abundance. The Dwyer and John P. Grier merely proved what had already been demonstrated—that when Man o' War needed to be game, the quality was there for him.

Man o' War demonstrated enough gameness to avoid being defeated in this category. In the gameness contest between Man o' War and Affirmed, we declare the result a draw.

Count Fleet after winning the Preakness. (Keeneland Library Cook Collection—4379)

CHAPTER 4

Beating Good Horses

Man o' War vs. Count Fleet

"He was a titan among minnows."

—THE 1954 EDITION OF THE *AMERICAN RACING MANUAL* BEMOANS THE LACK OF COMPETITION DURING TOM FOOL'S UNDEFEATED 1953 SEASON.

AT THIS POINT, AS WE BEGIN DISCUSSING COUNT FLEET AND MAN O' War, and the importance of beating good horses as a demonstration of equine quality, I believe I should confess a fact that the reader may find relevant as this discussion moves forward. It concerns my personal feelings about Count Fleet, the 1943 Triple Crown winner.

It is my intention to be as objective in this book as humanly possible, presenting verifiable facts about Man o' War and the horses I've selected to challenge him in the various categories of racehorse excellence. My goal, upon consideration of the relevant facts, has been to determine whether the runner I've chosen to typify a particular category either succeeds in their challenge to Man o' War, or doesn't.

But with this category, Beating Good Horses, and my selection of Count Fleet as Man o' War's rival, I find it particularly difficult to maintain my vow of objectivity. Quite frankly, I have never understood the adulation racing fans and historians seem to hold for Count Fleet, who is almost universally placed among the top 10 American Thoroughbreds whenever anyone seeks to establish such a ranking.

Top 10? Having won sixteen times in twenty-one lifetime starts, against competition from only his own foal crop, one from which he was the only representative voted to the Hall of Fame, Count Fleet is typically ranked with the likes of five-time Horse of the Year Kelso, who defeated champions from multiple crops of Thoroughbreds, and with Dr. Fager, who battled the likes of Hall of Famers Damascus and Gamely and Buckpasser, among others. He is rated at least even, and often ahead of, such clearly (in the author's view) superior runners as Forego, Seattle Slew, Spectacular Bid, Affirmed, Round Table, Swaps, and John Henry. And to that list I would add Nashua, who defeated Hall of Famer Swaps and went on to a superb 4-year-old season; two-time Horse of the Year Whirlaway, who raced into his 6-year-old season after winning the Triple Crown as a 3-year-old; and Alydar, who tested and occasionally defeated a runner as brilliantly talented as Triple Crown winner Affirmed.

It defies logic—again, in my opinion—that Count Fleet would rank ahead of any of these, let alone all of them.

But let's consider this logically. Count Fleet was unquestionably a phenomenal Thoroughbred, who accomplished even more in the breeding shed than he did in his unfortunately brief time on the racetrack, and was particularly important as a broodmare sire. He sired a total of thirty-eight stakes winners; his female offspring produced 119 more. He is the maternal grandsire of Kelso, of Kentucky Derby winner Lucky Debonair, of champions Quill and Lamb Chop. His impact on the sport has been ongoing and profound. Let's give credit where credit is due.

But let's also not get carried away. Yes, Count Fleet is deserving of a spot in the top 30, maybe even among the top 20. Anything higher than that, the rater must demonstrate that this colt defeated rivals of substantial quality. And anyone who attempts to make this case will quickly find that the facts don't support the contention.

Count Fleet came into the world in 1940, which, but for his own towering presence, would probably be considered an off year for the breeding industry. The United States was already formally at war as Count Fleet was about to become a racehorse, and the war would lead to restrictions on both horses and people attempting to travel to race venues, particularly Churchill Downs, leading to fields too small to seriously test a truly excellent colt.

He faced only one other champion over the course of his twenty-one races. In the Futurity, conducted at Belmont Park on October 10, 1942, Count Fleet took on 2-year-old filly Askmenow, who at season's end would be voted the championship of her division while Count Fleet was being declared the top 2-year-old colt. On Futurity Day, Askmenow out-finished Count Fleet by a head, as both came home five lengths in arrears of Occupation, who had already defeated Count Fleet two months earlier in the Washington Park Futurity.

And thus it was that Count Fleet never defeated a champion. Had he survived another year of racing, perhaps even another month, he might have been matched with Alsab, Market Wise, Devil Diver, perhaps even Whirlaway, all of them champions, but it was not to be. Count Fleet had suffered an injury in his Triple Crown–clinching Belmont Stakes, and when the injury did not respond to treatment as readily as his veterinarians had hoped, it was determined that he should be retired, rather than being risked in possibly reduced circumstances.

By this time, the venerable jockey Johnny Longden, who rode 32,413 races in his forty years in the saddle and won a then-record 6,032, had stated that Count Fleet was the greatest horse he ever rode. And with those numbers, no one will deny that Longden was entitled to his opinion.

Count Fleet won races by twenty and twenty-five lengths; he set stakes and track records. He ran faster in morning workouts than his opponents did in races. There can be no question that he was one of the speediest runners to compete on the American turf.

Count Fleet began his career with a pair of losses, to Dove Shoot in a five-furlong Belmont Park maiden race and then, two weeks later, to Supermont, going a half-furlong farther at Aqueduct. These were not defeats to highlight a showy curriculum vitae for a Thoroughbred. Before he was done, Dove Shoot raced 177 times and won $41,370, suggesting a lengthy career in racing's claiming ranks; the highlight of his career was a third-place finish in the National Stallion Stakes. Supermont's eleven-year career produced twenty wins in 111 starts, including victory in the Tremont Stakes. He earned a total of $43,655.

It is on June 19, 1942, in a $1,500 Aqueduct maiden special weight event, that Count Fleet first carries Mrs. John Hertz's yellow silks with black circles into a winner's circle, with a four-length romp at the expense of Seaward Bound and Crest. Clark Gable happened to be in attendance at Aqueduct that day—"the recipient of many admiring eyes, mostly from the weaker sex," noted one article—but little did Gable know that he had observed the maiden victory of a future superstar whose accomplishments in the Sport of Kings might one day be considered more important than even he could claim to be in the world of entertainment.

On Independence Day 1942, two weeks after his maiden triumph, Count Fleet would win his next race, a five-length thrashing of five other 2-year-olds, in a five-and-a-half-furlong allowance race at the Empire City track. By this time, the knowledgeable New York fans had recognized that this colt might be a good one; he had been sent off at 4-to-1 odds in his first outing, but by his fourth start he was the heavy favorite at 6-to-5 odds, and ran like it, winning by five wide-open lengths. Another Triple Crown winner, Whirlaway, was defeated in the following race, the Butler Handicap, losing in track record time under a 132-pound impost to Tola Rose, carrying just 103. The 1941/42 and 1943 Horses of the Year may well have crossed paths, Count Fleet on the way back to the stable, Whirlaway on his way to the saddling enclosure. It was as close as Count Fleet would ever come to a championship-quality racehorse.

Next on Count Fleet's agenda was the East View Stakes, a five-and-three-quarter-furlong event at Empire City, and the son of 1928 Derby winner Reigh Count made a big stretch run but ran out of ground before catching Gold Shower, with the third finisher, a colt called Rurales, another seven lengths back. A week later, Count Fleet reversed that outcome with emphasis, winning the not-quite-six-furlong Wakefield by four lengths, with Rurales second and Gold Shower third.

This performance earned him a spot three weeks later in Chicago's Washington Park Futurity, but he was first sent after a six-furlong, $1,800 Washington Park allowance race. Here he would have his first encounter with Blue Swords, whom he would defeat six times over the remaining fifteen races of his career. Count Fleet won his allowance race by a neck, with Blue Swords charging "like a locomotive" at the end but swerving erratically nearing the wire when victory was within his reach.

Neither Count Fleet nor Blue Swords could outfinish Occupation four days later in the $69,875 Washington Park Futurity, although Count Fleet, storming belatedly from post position eleven, made a race of it, getting to within a neck, five lengths clear of Blue Swords. Occupation would win nine of thirteen starts as a 2-year-old and flirt with the $200,000 earnings mark, leading all juveniles for the year.

Returned to New York, Count Fleet won consecutive prep races for the Futurity and was sent to the post as the 3-to-2 favorite to Occupation's 5-to-2. He worked for the Futurity in a blistering 1:08⅕ for six furlongs, which, had he accomplished this in a race, would have shattered Belmont's track record by a full second.

Count Fleet's trainer, Don Cameron, was reportedly less than thrilled, and the result was a rare bad performance for Count Fleet, who never did catch the victorious Occupation despite carrying seven fewer pounds. Among the beaten runners in the Futurity was a colt whose photo, to this day, hangs on many a racing aficionado's wall: Bossuet, one of three noses on the wire (with Brownie and Wait a Bit) in the rare 1944 Carter Stakes triple dead heat. Count Fleet would face Bossuet twice at age two and again at age three, never losing to the son of Boswell.

Though no one knew it at the time, the 31,805 in attendance on Futurity Day had just witnessed the final defeat of Count Fleet's career. In his remaining 236 days as a racehorse, he would win ten times in ten trips to the post, his average winning margin more than nine lengths.

In fact, the average may have been more than ten. While the *Daily Racing Form*'s records reflect a thirty-length victory for Count Fleet in Pimlico's Walden Stakes, the *Baltimore Sun*'s chart shows twenty, and while there is a temptation to attribute the difference to a typo in *The Sun*, turfwriter Don Reed's report in the newspaper's sports section states that Count Fleet's margin at the end "was estimated at 20 lengths or more." Eight decades after the fact, there is no reconciling the difference.

Next on Count Fleet's agenda was the Champagne Stakes at Belmont Park, and it was among the easiest victories of his 2-year-old campaign.

The colt was assigned 116 pounds to 119 for Blue Swords, whom he had defeated just two months earlier while giving his rival eleven pounds. Count Fleet went directly to the front and widened throughout, increasing his bankroll by $9,375 with his six-length win in 1:34⅖, reported at the time to be the fastest mile ever raced by a 2-year-old. This was followed by an impressive victory in a Jamaica tightener for the Pimlico Futurity, and eleven days later Count Fleet and Occupation entered the starting gate once again to battle for the juvenile championship. One other colt, Vincentive, joined the field, third-place money assured.

It would not be a close race. Breaking just off the pace, Count Fleet quickly assumed the lead and widened as Longden pleased, reaching the finish five decisive lengths clear of Occupation in 1:43⅗ for the mile-and-a-sixteenth, equaling the track record for the distance. Next came Count Fleet's twenty- or thirty-length victory in the Walden, and the colt was sent to the sidelines for the winter with a 10-for-15 record, more than good enough for championship honors.

Based on the end-of-year polls, Count Fleet was considered more than merely a run-of-the-mill 2-year-old titlist. He was awarded an unprecedented 132 pounds on the 1942 Experimental Free Handicap, and with this honor in place, he entered his winter break as the clear-cut favorite for the following year's Kentucky Derby—if, that is, World War II would not force the cancellation of the 1943 Run for the Roses.

Count Fleet emerged from winter quarters as the shortest-priced Derby winter book favorite in memory, quoted at 5-to-2 by at least one oddsmaker. With the Santa Anita Derby and the Flamingo Stakes cancelled due to the war, there would be no new challengers from those sources. Count Fleet's Derby rivals would be known quantities, runners he had already vanquished, some of them multiple times. All he needed to do, it appeared, would be to avoid injury on the way to Derby Day.

As he began his Derby quest, all went well. Entered in a $3,000 Jamaica Park allowance race two and a half weeks before the Derby, Count Fleet returned in mid-season form, winning by three-and-a-half lengths over Bossuet and Towser. His future book odds shifted abruptly downward, to 4-to-5.

The Wood Memorial, just four days later, would be his final Derby prep, and before a crowd of more than 24,000, Count Fleet was again an easy winner, opening four lengths almost at the start while carrying 126 pounds for the first time, then maintaining a safe three-and-a-half-length margin to the finish.

When he returned to the winner's circle, however, it was seen that he had suffered a gash on his left hind leg that was spurting blood. Amid concern that the favorite might be forced out of the Derby, oddsmakers shortened the odds on a number of the lesser lights, and Count Fleet was increased to even money. This seemed a bargain to one enterprising handicapper, who promptly registered a $1,000 win bet on the favorite.

This proved an excellent investment, as Count Fleet recovered quickly. He was given a clean bill of health the next day and was shipped to the Bluegrass State for a race whose only remaining drama was the possibility that it might be cancelled, to conserve precious fuel for the war effort. Asked to assure the racing world that the race would go forward, Matt Winn, president of Churchill Downs, was emphatic: "The Kentucky Derby" he said, "will be run in 1943, even if there are only two horses in the race, and only a half dozen people in the stands. And the money added by Churchill Downs will be the same as in previous years—$75,000—and a $5,000 gold cup."

The government responded by prohibiting auto traffic to the racecourse, and Winn countered by chartering dozens of streetcars to shuttle racegoers to the track. The reported attendance for what would forever be called the "Streetcar Derby" was 66,000. In his autobiography, *Down the Stretch*, Winn, who saw the Derby with the eye of both a racing historian and a masterful promoter, called the 1943 edition "the greatest Derby of them all."

The Derby's outcome was never in question. As was his habit, Count Fleet assumed the early lead and was never headed, prevailing as the 2-to-5 favorite by three lengths over Blue Swords, with Slide Rule another six lengths back in third. The Derby winner's questionable left hind leg was never a problem, and the slow clocking, 2:04, was surely more a reflection of the lack of competition than of Count Fleet's obvious quality. He and Blue Swords shipped to Maryland for the Preakness; Slide Rule, nominated for the Withers, was sent to Belmont Park to prepare for another confrontation with the champion. The other runners were shipped anywhere Count Fleet was unlikely to turn up.

From this point, Count Fleet's Triple Crown was a virtual walkover. Bet down to fifteen cents on the dollar in the Preakness, the Derby winner finished eight lengths ahead of Blue Swords, who had three lengths on Vincentive, who in turn had twenty on New Moon. The track was labeled "good" rather than "fast," which may explain the race's lackluster 1:57⅖ clocking.

One evidence of the increasing respect for Count Fleet is that none of his Preakness foes was sent after him again. Blue Swords, who had finished second to the champion on three successive occasions—by three-and-a-half, three, and eight lengths—was pulled from the Triple Crown trail, as was Preakness third finisher Vincentive, whose closest approach to Count Fleet at Pimlico had occurred in the walking ring.

This was the era when the gap between the Preakness and the Belmont Stakes was four weeks, and it was considered wasteful to keep a healthy runner on the sidelines for so long a stretch of time. Count Fleet was therefore entered in Belmont's Withers Stakes, where he finished five lengths ahead of Slide Rule despite racing wide throughout, with Tip-Toe another dozen lengths in arrears. His 1:36 was not a particularly noteworthy time for the mile, but under the muddy track conditions, the *New York Daily News* described it as "remarkable."

It was so clear that Count Fleet had no real competition among the 3-year-old ranks that the *Baltimore Sun*'s Don Reed, covering the Withers, noted:

> *[F]or those who like to see a champion put to a real test instead of being conceded races before he gets onto the track, there's a ray of hope with the coming of the combined Arlington-Washington meetings at Washington Park in Chicago. There, for the first time since last season, Count Fleet may be called upon to meet . . . Occupation, while Calumet Farm's [Derby Trial winner] Ocean Wave, forced to pass up the Kentucky Derby at the last minute, may also be on hand.*

But it was not to be. The Belmont Stakes drew only two overmatched rivals, Fairy Manhurst and Deseronto. The former would win four of twenty-one lifetime starts (including a Count Fleet–less Lawrence Realization Stakes) and a total of $34,212; the latter would conclude his career with four wins in forty-six starts and earnings of $9,540.

Racing before a tote board that reflected Count Fleet's 1-to-20 odds and displayed a sign warning racegoers, "In case of air raid, keep calm. Obey orders of wardens and police. Follow directional signs. Walk, do not run," Count Fleet ran off with a twenty-five-length win in 2:28⅕, taking two ticks off the stakes record set in 1937 by War Admiral.

With the Triple Crown swept and no worlds left to conquer among the season's 3-year-olds, plans for bigger races against seasoned horses with championship credentials were suggested, but suddenly, Count Fleet's career was over. Cameron had authorized Longden to push Count Fleet during his Belmont victory, hoping to thrill the crowd and bring home the stakes record, and in making this extreme effort the colt injured a hoof. When it became clear that this injury, unlike the open wound sustained in the Wood Memorial, would not be transitory, retirement was the inevitable decision.

In June 1943 Grantland Rice suggested that "Count Fleet's injured hoof may be far more serious than it first looked to be," and by late July turfwriter Jim McCulley in the *New York Daily News* could report that "the news that Count Fleet will race no more came as no great surprise to insiders of the turf world."

Count Fleet ended his career with sixteen wins in twenty-one starts, the least competitive Triple Crown in the history of the event, and a reputation for blazing speed, in both races and morning workouts, that on at least one occasion left his trainer in the throes of frustration.

BEATING GOOD HORSES

Some will recognize the irony of matching Man o' War and Count Fleet in this category. The two extraordinary colts compiled brilliant records and impressed horsemen of their day immeasurably, while defeating, in Man o' War's case, only one worthy contender, and in Count Fleet's, none at all.

Man o' War earns credit for having defeated Sir Barton, who would become a Triple Crown winner when the racing world finally got around to recognizing the Kentucky Derby, Preakness, and Belmont Stakes as a grouping of important races. Sir Barton has received the sport's ultimate recognition, a plaque in the Saratoga Springs home of the National Museum of Racing and Hall of Fame, and he deserves the recognition, having defeated Exterminator and Billy Kelly and Mad Hatter, and carried as much as 134 pounds to victory.

Thoroughbreds who had appeared hopelessly inferior prior to Man o' War's retirement suddenly sprouted wings when the champion was no longer a factor. Blazes won the Delaware Handicap; Captain Alcock won the Suburban, the Bowie, the Havre de Grace Handicap, and the Pimlico Cup; John P. Grier won the Queens County Handicap and ran second in the Brooklyn. Wildair won a Delaware Handicap; Paul Jones won the Suburban and was second in the Pimlico Cup; Constancy ran second in the Carter; Damask won the Aqueduct Handicap at age four, the Flight Handicap at five; Dominique was still racing, and earning stakes placings, at age eight. Sandy Beal won the Chesapeake Stakes; Yellow Hand won the Empire City Handicap, the Excelsior Handicap, and the Saratoga Handicap.

The same held true for Count Fleet. Runners he routinely left in the dust became world-beaters when injury forced the champion off the track. Slide Rule won the Arlington Classic, the Westchester, the Jerome, the Peter Pan, the Interborough, the Swift, and the Experimental; Four Freedoms won the Brooklyn, the Widener, the Tropical, the Palm Beach; Bossuet was in the famous Carter triple dead heat; Vincentive won the Dwyer and was second in the Peter Pan; Famous Victory was second in the Dwyer and third in the American Derby, the Havre de Grace, the Jerome, the Lawrence Realization, the Peter Pan, and the Travers. Eurasian won the Gallant Fox, the Jersey Handicap, and the Travers; Bankrupt won the Manhattan Handicap; Fairy Manhurst won his depleted Lawrence Realization.

None of this, however, is a particularly positive reflection on either horse. The traditional races were offered, as always. Somebody had to win them.

What is more telling is that neither runner's cropmates earned a spot in racing's Hall of Fame. Man o' War raced in the days before official championships were tendered; of Count Fleet's opponents, the filly Askmenow was awarded championship honors as the leading 2-year-old filly. As noted, she outfinished Count Fleet by a head the one time they met.

"Beating Good Horses?" Man o' War beat every runner he faced, and avenged the one loss to Upset by leaving that colt behind every other time they met. Count Fleet, on the other hand, lost two of three to Occupation and lost to Askmenow. He lost to Dove Shoot and Supermont and Gold Shower. And Count Fleet met nothing during his Triple Crown sweep that might have warmed up Sir Barton when the Derby-Preakness-Belmont winner was at his peak.

Count Fleet represents a very low bar for Man o' War to surmount, and Man o' War, given his victory over Sir Barton, clears it easily. Perhaps Count Fleet, had he remained healthy, might have defeated the likes of champions Whirlaway, Alsab, Market Wise, or Devil Diver. All were active during the 1943 season. But he didn't, leaving us to muse about what might have happened had the colt stayed healthy, while admitting that Count Fleet earned his 16-for-21 record against a supremely unimpressive group of rivals.

We award a sizable edge in this category to Man o' War.

Forego winning the 1974 Gulfstream Park Handicap. (Keeneland Library Raftery Turfotos Collection)

CHAPTER 5

Winning Major Races

Man o' War vs. Forego

AMERICA'S 1970 THOROUGHBRED FOAL CROP WAS, AT THE TIME, THE largest in history, some 24,361 potential racehorses. There had been more or less steady growth in the number of Thoroughbreds produced each year in this country, beginning with the conclusion of World War I. The count of Thoroughbred foals would continue to grow steadily into the 1980s. Big crops are more likely than small ones to produce good horses, and there were world-beaters on the horizon, as racing expanded and the breeding industry grew to meet the demand for ever more horses.

That big 1970 crop was not merely good; it was sensational. Ponder three years forward, to the 1973 group of 3-year-olds, and the adjectives that come to mind are majestic, resplendent, historic, all-conquering. The National Museum of Racing and Hall of Fame has seven plaques honoring 1970 foals, tied with 1966's crop for the most from one year. No other foal crop has produced more than four.

Moreover, there are no near things, no skin-of-the-teeth inductees among the 1970 group, which includes Ancient Title, winner of twenty-four races and $1.25 million over a fifty-seven-race career; Dahlia, 1974's turf champion and winner of $1.5 million on the international stage; Desert Vixen, champion 3-year-old filly who repeated at age four; La Prevoyante, undefeated champion 2-year-old filly of 1972 with twelve wins in twelve starts; Secretariat, two-time Horse of the Year, champion

2-year-old, champion 3-year-old, champion turf horse; and two-time champion steeplechaser Café Prince.

And, not even close to the least of these, Forego: three-time Horse of the Year and four-time champion older horse. Forego might well have earned a fourth Horse of the Year title had 1977 not been the year 3-year-old Seattle Slew emerged from the Triple Crown trail as history's only undefeated winner of the Derby, Preakness, and Belmont Stakes. Forego's 1977 was plenty good—four wins in seven starts, a Metropolitan, a Nassau County, a Woodward—but Triple Crown winners hold a special place in our sport, and nobody was going to deny Seattle Slew his Horse of the Year title.

The most important moment of Forego's brilliant career was probably one that concerned another horse. The day Meadow Stable owner Penny Tweedy signed the syndication papers for Secretariat, calling for him to be retired to the breeding shed at the conclusion of his 3-year-old campaign, Forego was removed forever from the shadow of his one-of-a-kind cropmate. And for the next three years, as his trio of Horse of the Year awards will attest, there was no better racehorse in America than Martha Gerry's big son of the outstanding Argentinian stallion Forli.

But perhaps this is giving too little credit, for Forego was a brilliant racehorse in his own right. Given time to grow into his large, muscular frame at ages two and three, he then dominated the four subsequent crops, confronting and overpowering the likes of True Knight, Mr. Prospector, Arbee's Boy, Big Spruce, Stop the Music, Wajima, Ancient Title, the two Pleasures (Foolish and Honest), Master Derby, Great Contractor, and Dr. Patches.

Forego had been so awkward and ungainly at age two that he was gelded before making it to the track and was held out of racing altogether as a 2-year-old. He began his career at age three, in a Hialeah seven-furlong maiden event, and as has so often been the case for runners who would prove to be exceptional, his abilities were not immediately clear to the horseplayers, who sent him off at 10-to-1 odds. With Pete Anderson aboard, Forego endured some bumping and raced evenly in his maiden voyage, finishing fourth to future stakes winner Buffalo Lark. From there, however, the Sherrill Ward trainee moved forward fast, winning his second start by eight lengths and following this with a two-and-a-half-length victory in a six-furlong allowance race.

Forego was now deemed ready for stakes competition and was entered in Gulfstream Park's seven-furlong, Grade 3 Hutcheson Stakes, which unfortunately also drew the season's eventual sprint champion, Shecky Greene, named for a popular comedian of the day. Shecky proceeded to cover the seven-eighths of a mile in a track-record-equaling 1:20⅘, leaving runner-up Forego three-and-a-half lengths behind. It was another nine lengths back to the third finisher.

Perhaps there were comments that Shecky Greene's performance was anything but funny, but no one believed that his speedy seven furlongs were a demonstration of Derby-worthiness. Forego continued on, winning a seven-furlong Gulfstream Park allowance race, and found himself on the Derby trail. Unfortunately for Forego's Triple Crown aspirations, Secretariat and Sham were already there.

And Forego was not yet a Derby horse. Favored in the Florida Derby, he finished second behind Royal and Regal; favored in the Blue Grass, he struggled home fifth to My Gallant. Entered anyway in the Kentucky Derby, he was 28-to-1, finishing a creditable fourth, eleven lengths behind Secretariat, with Sham and Our Native earning the minor awards.

Forego was held out of the Preakness, but five weeks after the Derby, on June 9, 1973, he again found himself on the same Belmont Park card with Secretariat—but not in the same race. About a half-hour before Secretariat won his historic Belmont Stakes, Forego, now ridden by Heliodoro Gustines, who would pilot him for much of the next three years, won a Belmont Park allowance race by nine lengths, covering the mile-and-a-sixteenth in 1:40⅘, just one tick off Pass Catcher's track record. Clearly, the big gelding still had great potential.

From here, Forego pursued a quirky and arduous path to his first stakes victory, winning four of five allowance races, in the process setting or equaling two track records. His one race versus older horses resulted in a loss to Prove Out, who would later play a major (if negative) role in Secretariat's story. Sent back into stakes competition, the big gelding lost narrowly in the Grade 2 Jerome to Step Nicely while carrying 124 pounds to the winner's 118. He then ran fourth in yet another Aqueduct allowance race before finally earning back-to-back black type with victories in Aqueduct's mile-and-three-sixteenths Roamer Handicap under 123 pounds and, two weeks later, in the nine-furlong Discovery under 127.

Over the next four seasons, the big gelding would win twenty-four of thirty-seven starts, with ten more in-the-money performances and only three times off the board. During those four years, he brought home $1,735,008, drawing to within shouting distance of Kelso's all-time leading earnings mark. He gave weight when he won, and, when he lost, it was usually the weight differential that allowed lesser horses to overcome his might.

He carried 125 and gave True Knight two pounds in winning the 1974 Donn Handicap; carried 127 and gave True Knight four in winning the Gulfstream Park; carried 129 and gave True Knight five in the Widener, his first Grade 1 victory. Returning to New York, he carried 129 and gave Mr. Prospector five while winning the Carter, and now the racing secretaries got serious. Forego was assigned 134 pounds and lost to Arbee's Boy (carrying just 112) in the Metropolitan; carried 132 and gave Timeless Moment twenty pounds while losing the Nassau County.

Weight differentials of this magnitude would become a hallmark of Forego's career as a handicap horse. He carried 130 pounds or more twenty-five times and won fourteen of them. It was very nearly the case that *only* high weight could prevent another Forego winner's circle ceremony: From his 4-year-old season until the end of his career, Forego won twelve of fifteen races when assigned 129 pounds or less. It was nearly a sure thing.

Forego also showed the racing world a sequence of victories that we had never seen before and almost certainly will never see again.

It began on September 28, 1974, when Forego, carrying a rare 126 pounds in the weight-for-age Woodward Stakes, charged from seventeen lengths behind to nail a stubborn Arbee's Boy on the wire, winning by a neck at a mile-and-a-half. Three weeks later, the big gelding again charged from off the pace, blowing past Stop the Music in the Grade 2, seven-furlong Vosburgh to win by three-and-a-half rapidly expanding lengths. And three weeks later, Forego was best once again, this time in the Grade 1 Jockey Club Gold Cup, which in those days was contested at two grueling miles.

Forego may have blossomed tardily, but the blossom was truly a brilliant one. What other horse might have accomplished this unique and nearly miraculous sequence: consecutive victories at twelve furlongs, then seven, then sixteen?

And Forego earned his three Horse of the Year trophies, and his four handicap championships, primarily in the seething cauldron of American racing: New York's spring, summer, and autumn classics.

He won thirteen Grade 1 races in twenty-five tries, was six times second and three times third. Twenty-two of those contests were in New York, and he won eleven of them: was 4-for-4 in the Woodward, 2-for-4 in the Metropolitan, 2-for-4 in the Brooklyn. He won his only try in the Jockey Club Gold Cup. He was 1-for-3 in the Marlboro Cup, 1-for-4 in the Suburban, and never out of the money in all seven. He met with failure in both of his Governor's Handicap tries, carrying 128 pounds and giving Big Spruce ten in 1974, then lugging 134 and conceding nineteen to champion Wajima in 1975.

And then there was Forego's 1976 Marlboro Cup, surely one of the most spectacular come-from-out-of-the-clouds races any horse has ever won, in this country or any other.

Having won his third Woodward under 135 pounds two weeks earlier, it was conceded that the now 6-year-old would be assigned even more weight in the Marlboro Cup. The racing secretary, through whatever complex calculus determines such things, settled on 137, and assigned the speedy Honest Pleasure 119, with the remainder of the field weighted downward from 114 to 109. By now, the great Frank Whiteley was training Forego and the phenomenal Bill Shoemaker was his regular rider, but the rest of the race's script came up negative: The track was sloppy and Forego, not a fan of the mud, drew post position ten in the eleven-horse field.

Forego broke well enough, but then dropped well off the pace, seemingly anchored by the highest weight he had ever carried. Somehow, ever so slowly, he began to close laboriously on the front-running Honest Pleasure, who had been allowed to canter unchallenged on the lead through a leisurely half-mile in :47⅖. But now Forego's long stride began to assert itself, and as the field neared the top of the stretch he came into view of the television cameras, struggling, working hard, racing on the extreme outside of the field.

Forego was still fourth, four lengths back, with a furlong to the finish, but he was pulling closer to Honest Pleasure, and as the two passed under the wire, it was Forego, almost unthinkably, who pushed his nose into the clean, fresh air breathed only by winners. Even Shoemaker had had his doubts, commenting after the race, "I never thought we could catch up. For a while, I didn't think we'd even be in the money." Even with the photo finish results reflected on the tote board and the flash of the winner's circle camera still blurring her vision, owner Martha Gerry admitted, "No, I didn't think we won it."

Describing the race in the 1977 *American Racing Manual*, turfwriter Joe Hirsch wrote:

> *How great is great? Are there degrees of greatness? Was Secretariat, on the day he won the Belmont Stakes by 31 lengths, a greater horse than Native Dancer when he came from so far back to win the Metropolitan Mile? Was Citation, in soundly whipping his brilliant stablemate, Coaltown, in the Kentucky Derby a greater horse than Count Fleet when that speedster completed an undefeated 3-year-old campaign by winning the Belmont Stakes by 25 lengths? These were all memorable moments of racing by truly great horses. Forego belongs with these superstars in any assessment of outstanding American thoroughbreds, and his Marlboro Cup will be the race for which he is always remembered.*

Forego had clinched 1976 Horse of the Year honors, his third consecutive championship, but he was beginning to show the strain of carrying all those top weights, and while he was still a commanding presence at age seven, he was not quite as good. He won a second Metropolitan Handicap and a fourth Woodward but narrowly missed under a career-high 138 pounds in the Suburban, came up empty under 137 in the Brooklyn Handicap, and never made an effort under 136 in the sloppy Whitney.

By age eight, it was clear that the gelding had had about enough. He edged Dr. Patches in a June allowance race at Belmont Park, then lost by fourteen lengths in the July 4 Suburban, and trainer Frank Whiteley suggested to owner Gerry that the time had come. Forego had just failed to catch Kelso on the all-time earnings list, but it would have to do. Forego was enshrined in the Hall of Fame in 1979 and spent many of his remaining years at the Kentucky Horse Park in a stall adjoining that of another one-of-a-kind gelding, John Henry. Forego fractured a leg at age twenty-seven and was mercifully put down.

WINNING MAJOR RACES

Beginning with the 1974 racing season, North American racing authorities began classifying stakes races in accordance with the system still in use today. The most important races on the calendar were classified as Grade 1, the next level was Grade 2, a level down was Grade 3, and further down the ladder were other races, still considered stakes events but not of sufficient importance to merit a "Grade" classification.

At this writing, the all-time leaders in Grade 1 victories are:

- 16—John Henry
- 14—Affirmed, Forego, and Goldikova
- 13—Bayakoa, Spectacular Bid, and Zenyatta

With no system for grading races in place in 1919 and 1920, we are left to find other criteria for judging the importance of Man o' War's races. One might be by value: Among his age two races, the Hopeful and Belmont Futurity, two of the season's richest contests, would surely have been Grade 1, and one might assign a high level of importance to Saratoga's

United States Hotel Stakes and Grand Union Hotel Stakes, both of which provided a substantial $7,600 to the winning owner, suggesting that these were intended to be more than bottom-rung stakes events.

This is not an ideal method for determining the importance of a horse race, but with no other available it seems reasonable to award Man o' War four "Grade 1" victories for his 2-year-old campaign.

We are on somewhat firmer footing with Man o' War's 3-year-old season. The Preakness, Withers, and Belmont Stakes are surely deserving of Grade 1 status; the Dwyer remains an important race today and would have been at least a Grade 2; the Travers would certainly have been Grade 1; the Jockey Club Stakes would eventually grow into the Grade 1 Jockey Club Gold Cup; and Man o' War's match race with Sir Barton would surely deserve Grade 1 status. That's seven "Grade 1" victories in seven tries at age three, coupled with four as a 2-year-old. By this decidedly unofficial and arbitrary method, we can award Man o' War eleven "Grade 1" wins in twenty-one lifetime starts.

Forego was a mainstay in New York's most prestigious races for four solid years, turning up every season to contest the Woodward and the Suburban, the Brooklyn and the Metropolitan. He left his imprint permanently on the Marlboro Cup and, when not in New York, worked his way up twice to the Grade 1 Widener Stakes by prepping in Grade 2 and 3 races, which he always won. At age three, he had raced in the Florida Derby, the Blue Grass, the Kentucky Derby, the Withers, the Jerome, the Roamer, and the Discovery.

No one demands perfection in Grade 1 races, particularly when a horse is routinely carrying the sort of weights Forego was asked to tote around the track while giving substantial weight to good opponents. But fourteen wins in twenty-five tries in these circumstances at age four and older, with only three races out of the money, can hardly be disparaged.

In some ways, Man o' War and Forego defy comparison. Man o' War was all but unbeatable as a 2-year-old, racing at Saratoga, the sport's hotbed, and dominating the era's most important juvenile stakes. Forego never raced at two and was a late bloomer who earned his first stakes victory at age three on November 24, 1973. By November 24, 1920, Man o' War had already been retired for more than a month.

But both Man o' War and Forego ran in major races whenever they were asked to do so, and both acquitted themselves as champions. Forego won more important races because he raced for more years; nothing on four legs can ever overcome Man o' War's "Grade 1" winning percentage, a perfect 100 percent.

Here is a contest with no runner-up. We declare Man o' War vs. Forego a draw.

Seattle Slew wins the Marlboro Cup. (Bob Coglianese)

CHAPTER 6

Precocity and Staying Power

Man o' War vs. Seattle Slew

EVEN THE MOST TALENTED OF 2-YEAR-OLDS SOMETIMES FALL BACK TO ordinariness at age three. We remember well the seemingly limitless ability of Moccasin, undefeated and unchallenged in eight 1965 starts, so outstanding a 2-year-old that in one poll she was named Horse of the Year, the only juvenile filly to earn this honor. But we also recall that she came back to the pack with a vengeance as a 3-year-old, then won only three times in thirteen, with almost uniformly disappointing efforts over the next two seasons.

How much more respect we have for Seattle Slew, unbeatable at age two and nearly so at three, and continuing to race brilliantly at age four against the likes of Hall of Famers Affirmed and Exceller. Here is the epitome of the ideal Thoroughbred: a champion at age two, a Triple Crown winner, a major stakes winner at four, finally retired to one of the most productive stud careers in history. Seattle Slew's career arc included all of that.

As history's first undefeated Triple Crown winner, Seattle Slew brought to the sport a special and, until the short reign of undefeated Justify in 2018, unique achievement. [*Author's Note: as this is being penned, an investigation of Justify's first-place finish in the Santa Anita Derby is proceeding, and his win has been vacated. Should this result stand, Seattle Slew may again be recognized as the only runner ever to emerge undefeated from a Triple Crown sweep.*]

But an undefeated sweep of the Triple Crown was far from the son of Bold Reasoning's only important achievement. In fact, it could be stated that this equine superstar's finest moment occurred during his 4-year-old season—in a race he lost.

Bold Reasoning sired only three crops before a breeding shed accident at age seven fractured his hip, leading to a fatal case of colic. He survived long enough, however, to be bred to My Charmer, a daughter of Poker, and the mating produced a racy-looking dark bay or brown colt. Sold as a yearling for $17,500 to Seattle residents Karen and Mickey Taylor, the colt, given the name Seattle Slew, would earn $1.2 million on the track, then achieve one of history's most successful stud careers. Quite possibly, the Taylors' modest investment may have represented the greatest bargain in the history of Thoroughbred racing.

Seattle Slew would be tardy in joining his cropmates on the track. Suffering an injury in his stall, the colt did not make it to the races until September 20 of his 2-year-old season. In the fifth race at Belmont Park that day, the colt broke slowly as the modest 5-to-2 favorite under jockey Jean Cruguet, then quickly made up the lost ground and blew past the ten other entrants. He made the lead before the first quarter-mile was complete and drew away from that point to win by five lengths. Returning two weeks later in a seven-furlong allowance race, this time as the odds-on 2-to-5 favorite, Slew and Cruguet registered a three-and-a-half-length victory, checking in with a rapid 1:22 clocking.

The Taylors and trainer Billy Turner now sent their undefeated and as yet unchallenged 2-year-old after a major prize, the Grade 1, $137,250 Champagne Stakes. Helping to comprise a highly accomplished field were Futurity winner For the Moment, Sapling champion Aly Oop, Cowdin Stakes winner Sail to Rome, and Tremont winner Turn of Coin. Seattle Slew, the 6-to-5 favorite, treated them as nonentities, drawing off by nine-and-three-quarter lengths in a blistering 1:34⅖, missing Belmont's track record, held by Forego and Stop the Music, by less than a second. Contested at the one-mile distance since 1940 by the likes of Count Fleet, Never Bend, Buckpasser, Riva Ridge, Secretariat, Foolish Pleasure, and Honest Pleasure, no renewal of the Champagne had ever been run in a faster time than Seattle Slew's. With three overpowering wins in three starts, Seattle Slew was awarded the juvenile championship and made the instant future book favorite for the 1977 Kentucky Derby.

The newly turned 3-year-old next came to the races in early March, in a seven-furlong Hialeah allowance race that also drew the exceptional sprinter White Rammer, who had won his last three starts. Once again, Seattle Slew drew away emphatically, tossing in a :21⅘ second quarter after the two favorites had blazed the first quarter-mile in :22⅕. Not many runners could continue slugging it out following a forty-four-second half-mile, but Seattle Slew kept to his task, reaching the six-furlong marker in 1:08 (three-fifths of a second faster than the track record). By this time, White Rammer was in full retreat and the rest of the starters were well behind, and Seattle Slew finished nine lengths clear, in track record time of 1:20⅗. It was, to say the least, an encouraging start to a Derby colt's season.

The Taylors' 3-year-old had raced just four times, but already he was drawing headlines that some might view as grandiose. "Seattle Slew Super Horse?" asked one headline writer; "A Healthy Seattle Slew Just Might Be Unbeatable," proclaimed another. To some, it may have seemed too much hype, too early in the colt's career. But even better was yet to come.

Seattle Slew was next sent after Hialeah's Flamingo Stakes, and at 1-to-5 odds the colt dominated, blazing the distance in 1:47⅖ and finishing four lengths clear of Giboulee and Fort Prevel. Only Bold Ruler and the wickedly fast Honest Pleasure had ever run the Flamingo in a faster time.

In today's world, with fewer starts demanded of Derby hopefuls, Seattle Slew would likely be prepared for the First Saturday in May with a series of workouts designed to have him at absolute peak form on Derby Day. But this was 1977, when horses were expected to race if they were able, and Seattle Slew was shipped to New York, where he made a triumphant parade of the nine-furlong Wood Memorial, scoring by three-and-a-quarter lengths at 1-to-10 odds. He covered the distance in 1:49⅗, and if challenged might have run it a good deal faster.

And now one began to hear whispers that this might be a one-of-a-kind Triple Crown. Secretariat, of course, had won the first Triple Crown since Citation's day just four years earlier, but even the immortal son of Bold Ruler had accumulated a few losses along the way to Derby Day, including a third-place finish in the Wood Memorial. With six wins in as many starts, Seattle Slew had experienced no such temporary derailments. And one veteran turfwriter was already proclaiming, "It's Foolhardy to Run Against Seattle Slew."

One verity of the sport, however, is that races must be run in the flesh, not merely on paper, and one profound truth about every Kentucky Derby is that no one really knows that the winner can handle the classic mile-and-a-quarter until the winner's circle photo is taken. Almost anything can happen in the Derby, as Native Dancer and countless others had learned over the years, and fate nearly toppled the Derby hopes of Seattle Slew. Let's let the *Daily Racing Form*'s official chart caller describe Seattle Slew's eventful Derby start:

> *SEATTLE SLEW swerved sharply to the outside into GET THE AXE, after failing to break smartly, was rushed to the leaders early placing SIR SIR in slightly close quarters, continuing through tight quarters, nearing the end of the opening quarter. SEATTLE SLEW forced his way through moving FLAG OFFICER, AFFILIATE, and BOB'S DUSTY out.*

Having finally worked himself clear of this nightmarish traffic jam, the 1-to-2 Derby favorite collared For the Moment going around the first turn, then finally took command on the turn for home and powered into a three-length lead by midstretch, at which point he was geared down by Cruguet, who hand-rode him to a length-and-three-quarters victory. The final time was a businesslike 2:02⅕. Seattle Slew had now been tested for distance and certainly for toughness, and had not been found wanting.

Two weeks later, Seattle Slew faced a new challenge in the Preakness in the form of the speedy Cormorant, who had been held out of the Derby to prepare for the Triple Crown's second jewel. The new challenger drew post position one, and prognosticators across the country began warning about Pimlico's powerful and often decisive rail bias. Could this be the combination of factors—a fast horse with a built-in track advantage—to end Seattle Slew's Triple Crown bid?

What happened instead was that Seattle Slew, favored at 2-to-5, allowed 9-to-2 Cormorant a three-length head start, and then, after six strong furlongs in 1:09⅘, ran his rival into the ground and sped away. The lead was three lengths by midstretch, and once again Cruguet allowed his mount to coast to the finish. Seattle Slew hit the finish a relaxed length-and-a-half ahead of Iron Constitution and Run Dusty Run, with Cormorant a tired fourth and J.O. Tobin, who would soon play an outsized part in the Seattle Slew saga, fifth. The final time was 1:54⅖—fast, but not in the ballpark with Secretariat's unofficial but widely accepted 1:53⅖ from four years earlier.

The Belmont Stakes was now all that stood between Seattle Slew and the Triple Crown, and the mile-and-a-half classic proved to be the least trying of the three contests. The heavy favorite at odds of 2-to-5 on a track labeled muddy, Slew shook off early challengers Spirit Level and Run Dusty Run with six slow furlongs in 1:14, pulled clear with a fourth quarter-mile in :24⅘, and breezed down the lane, Cruguet jubilantly standing in the stirrups and waving his whip as the pair passed under the wire four lengths clear of any alleged challengers.

And with Seattle Slew's ninth consecutive win, Thoroughbred racing could celebrate its first undefeated Triple Crown winner. But the end of the winning streak was imminent, and changes were coming, both to Seattle Slew's health and to his human retinue.

The Taylors and trainer Billy Turner had planned to give Seattle Slew a post–Triple Crown vacation from racing. He would be shipped to the West Coast and paraded at the Taylors' home track, Longacres, near Seattle, then begin preparation for Saratoga's classic Travers Stakes.

But there was an offer on the table for Seattle Slew to race in Hollywood Park's $200,000 Swaps Stakes, which would be increased in value to $300,000 should the newly minted Triple Crown winner be entered. The Taylors and their superstar 3-year-old were heading west anyway, and with confirmation that Seattle Slew had exited the Belmont Stakes in good condition, the decision must have seemed an easy one. Seattle Slew would be sent to California for one more race, one more payday.

It proved to be one race too many. With a massive crowd of 68,115 looking on in disbelief, jockey Bill Shoemaker broke Preakness also-ran J.O. Tobin on top and outran the Triple Crown winner throughout, turning in sensational fractions of :22⅖, :45⅗, 1:09⅕, and 1:33⅗ on the way to an eight-length victory in 1:58⅗, three-fifths faster than the previous stakes record, and just two-fifths off the existing world record. For the first time, Seattle Slew simply didn't fire, finishing a distant fourth.

Veterinarians examined the champion and pronounced him sound, and plans were changed: Following the planned journey to Washington, Seattle Slew would be retired for the season as 1977's 3-year-old champion and Horse of the Year.

Over the winter, the Taylors decided to make a change. Billy Turner, Seattle Slew's conditioner throughout his juvenile and sophomore seasons, would be released, to be replaced by Doug Peterson. And under Peterson, Slew prepped eagerly for his return to the races, scheduled for January 1978.

But an early return to competition would not happen. Over the winter, the champion spiked a fever, which increased dangerously. When one of the horses in Peterson's stable with similar symptoms succumbed to illness, Colitis X, a serious equine malady, was suspected. Seattle Slew recovered gradually from his illness, and when he was determined to be out of danger, it was announced that he had been syndicated for a record $12 million. He would, it was announced, resume racing if and when his condition allowed.

It was on a rainy May 14, 1978, that Seattle Slew, the odds-on 1-to-10 favorite, grabbed the early lead in a seven-furlong Aqueduct allowance race, then drew off from five outclassed rivals to win by eight-and-a-half lengths in a restrained 1:22⅘. Plans were made for a return in the Metropolitan Mile, New York's traditional Memorial Day feature, but when a minor leg injury was detected, he was forced to the sidelines again.

He next returned in August at Saratoga, again at seven furlongs, again at 1-to-10 odds, and again in the slop. The allowance conditions of the race somehow assigned Seattle Slew 119 pounds to 115 for his nearest rivals, and Seattle Slew scored almost effortlessly, defeating Proud Birdie by six lengths, Capital Idea by eight-and-three-quarters. This time, his 1:21⅗ clocking missed the track record by just three-fifths of a second.

Slew seemed as good as new, but it was decided that one more prep race might be desirable before sending him after New York's important autumn stakes, particularly given that 3-year-old Affirmed had swept the Triple Crown and would likely be a particularly difficult rival for the defending Horse of the Year. The Meadowlands' Grade 3 Paterson Handicap was chosen for Slew's next appearance, and the field entered the starting gate with the reigning champion the 1-to-5 favorite.

Slew seemed well on his game, blowing out of the gate and assuming a three-and-a-half-length lead almost before the echoes of the starting gate bell had faded. This time, however, 9-to-2 shot Dr. Patches, who would share the season's sprint championship with Slew's other con-queror, J.O. Tobin, gradually closed the gap, finally edging past his rival nearing the finish. Slew never stopped trying, but at the wire it was Dr. Patches by a neck. Perhaps Seattle Slew had needed the prep race more than anyone had realized.

With the Marlboro Cup just eleven days away, the Seattle Slew camp made another change. Jockey Jean Cruguet, who had ridden the colt in each of his races, was replaced in the saddle by perennial East Coast jockey champion Angel Cordero Jr. And with Affirmed and teenage riding sensation Steve Cauthen also likely Marlboro Cup entrants, what seemed an epic battle was joined. This would be history's first race to feature two Triple Crown winners.

Not surprisingly, with Affirmed's Triple Crown sweep and Seattle Slew's recent loss fresh in the horseplayers' minds, the 3-year-old was made the even money favorite, while Slew's odds drifted to 2-to-1. But Seattle Slew was ready now, and the Marlboro Cup became nothing less than a tour de force for the older colt. Carrying 128 pounds to his rival's 124, Seattle Slew exploded out of the gate into a lead that quickly became two-and-a-half lengths down the backstretch and grew to three on the final turn. From there Seattle Slew maintained his margin, never allowing Affirmed to get close. The time for the mile-and-an-eighth,

1:45⅘, fell two ticks short of the record Secretariat had established in 1973, carrying four pounds less.

Two weeks later, the mile-and-a-quarter Woodward Stakes drew a new and dangerous rival, Mrs. Charles Engelhard's distance-loving Exceller. The Woodward was a weight-for-age contest, requiring both colts to carry 126 pounds, and it proved to be yet another wire-to-wire romp for Seattle Slew, who raced without challenge for the entirety of the contest. Slew's 2:00 clocking was a track record for a ten-furlong race starting on the turn, but for Cordero, records were but a secondary concern. "If I rode him harder we might have broken Forego's record," said the jockey in the race's aftermath, "but they don't pay for records."

The Jockey Club Gold Cup, which two years earlier had been reduced from two miles to a mile-and-a-half, was next on Seattle Slew's agenda and was to prove a historic battle of Thoroughbred titans. Seattle Slew and Affirmed would reprise their Marlboro Cup face-off, and would be joined by Exceller, this time racing at his favored mile-and-a-half distance. Affirmed having merely followed Slew around the track in the Marlboro Cup, trainer Lazaro Barrera also entered the filly Life's Hope to run with the 1977 Triple Crown winner in the race's early furlongs, in the hope of blunting Seattle Slew's late kick.

But all strategy was made meaningless when Affirmed's saddle slipped, costing jockey Steve Cauthen any hope of controlling his mount. With Cauthen now essentially a passenger, Affirmed battled head-and-head with Seattle Slew and his own stablemate through the early furlongs and onto the backstretch, using his energies prematurely in a suicidal speed duel. Affirmed eventually retreated to a fifth-place finish.

This left Seattle Slew blazing along on the lead, with a hard-charging Exceller relentlessly closing ground down the backstretch and onto the final turn, and what followed was a historic stretch drive between two hugely talented and dead-game champions. Somehow, Slew was still running strongly after a half-mile in :45⅓, then three-quarters in what race caller Chic Anderson called a "very unbelievable" 1:09⅖, but early fractions that swift had to make themselves felt eventually, and with Exceller now at his hip, now at his throatlatch, Cordero pushed Slew hard.

And Slew responded. A head in front at the top of the lane and seemingly on his way to victory, Exceller opened a half-length, and Seattle Slew called on what was left of his reserves and re-rallied. He was still a neck behind with a furlong to run, a head behind with a sixteenth left, and regained all but the final few inches before running out of ground. As Seattle Slew's wistful owner Mickey Taylor commented later, "Slew won everything but the money." If anyone had questioned Seattle Slew's gameness before, that question had been emphatically answered.

Seattle Slew's final start could be nothing but an anticlimax. Carrying a career-high 134 pounds in the one-and-an-eighth-mile Stuyvesant Handicap, the reigning Horse of the Year was first out of the gate and first at every furlong marker, outclassing Jumping Hill (in receipt of nineteen pounds) by three-and-a-quarter lengths and Wise Phillip (receiving a twenty-one-pound edge) by six.

And with that, Seattle Slew's seventeen-race career was over. He would be awarded the championship of the handicap division, while Triple Crown winner Affirmed, despite losing both times to his older rival, was named Horse of the Year. As the *American Racing Manual's* summary of the season proclaimed with understated simplicity about Slew, "This was a racehorse."

Retired to stud, Seattle Slew proved to be a phenomenal stallion, siring more than 1,100 foals, of whom 111 were stakes winners. He led the sire list in 1984, when one son, Swale, won the Kentucky Derby and the Belmont Stakes, and another, Slew o' Gold, won the Whitney, Marlboro Cup, Woodward, and Jockey Club Gold Cup. Seattle Slew was inducted into the National Museum of Racing and Hall of Fame in 1981, and subsequently two of his offspring, Slew o' Gold and A.P. Indy have also been enshrined. Stated in its baldest terms, Seattle Slew did everything— *everything*—that was asked of him.

PRECOCITY AND STAYING POWER

Seattle Slew's three seasons as a racehorse were among the most successful ever seen in America. He was undefeated as a 2-year-old; lost but once at age three, when he was, perhaps unwisely, sent to California for an additional race rather than being rested following the Triple Crown races; and lost twice at four, to champion Dr. Patches at The Meadowlands and to champion Exceller in the Jockey Club Gold Cup. Seattle Slew's near-legendary Gold Cup performance, following early fractions that would have left virtually any other Thoroughbred gasping for breath at the top of the stretch, will stand forever as an example of Thoroughbred gameness and resilience.

He was brought back to the races for his 4-year-old season after overcoming a troubling illness that some sources declared threatened the colt's life, and there is an injury gap of nearly three months in his 1978 record. Having begun his season with a seven-furlong Aqueduct allowance victory in the mud, he was brought back some ninety days later in another muddy seven-furlong sprint, this time at Saratoga, as conditioner Doug Peterson attempted to train him up to the Marlboro Cup and the other fall fixtures. Perhaps Slew was not quite fully cranked up for his loss to Dr. Patches, who was, one might note, carrying 114 pounds to 128 for Slew, and defeated his Triple Crown–winning rival by just a neck.

Syndicated for $12 million, Seattle Slew was not going to race at age five, and his retirement as an extremely successful 4-year-old would have been expected by anyone with knowledge of the sport. He is the personification of a horse whose juvenile championship demonstrated his precocity, whose Triple Crown and Horse of the Year trophy at age three and whose victories at age four in the Marlboro Cup and the Woodward proved beyond doubt his staying power. His glorious near-miss in the Jockey Club Gold Cup and career-ending victory in the Stuyvesant proved beyond question that he retained his high quality to the end of his racing career. He is the equine embodiment of both precocity and staying power.

Man o' War was, of course, a brilliant 2-year-old and an unbeaten—and perhaps unbeatable—3-year-old. At the very least, he matches Seattle Slew in precocity and, for one season, in staying power. He was, however, retired following his 3-year-old season and was not permitted to demonstrate his staying power in the longer term.

As we have noted already, Man o' War's retirement after his 3-year-old campaign was seen as almost a matter of necessity by owner Samuel Doyle Riddle. Man o' War would have carried historically high weights as a 4-year-old, and rumors of wagering coups involving threats to his champion were credible enough to be taken seriously. Riddle took the safest path, exiting the sport while his colt was sound and all but undefeated.

And thus, while we cannot blame Man o' War for being retired at age three and therefore not matching Seattle Slew for staying power, Seattle Slew earns a tenuous victory in this category. Both Big Red and Seattle Slew were outstanding horses, but Slew's owners permitted him a 4-year-old season; Riddle chose a safer program for his superstar.

It leaves us only one course: The vote here, with a nod to what Man o' War might have accomplished with one more year on the track, goes narrowly to Seattle Slew.

Dr. Fager winning the World's Playground Stakes. (Keeneland Library Raftery Turfotos Collection)

CHAPTER 7

Versatility

Man o' War vs. Dr. Fager

IN ITS EARLIEST DAYS, THOROUGHBRED RACING HAD AN IMPORTANT role in military preparedness. Thoroughbreds were expected to carry soldiers into battle, bearing weapons and encased in protective gear that was both heavy and bulky. One goal of racing, then, was the production of steeds that possessed not only fleetness but also great muscle power and unbounded stamina. The best of these war horses were intended to return to the stud barn to become the progenitors of even faster, even more powerful offspring.

Early racing reflected this. The best racehorses were expected to win at distances up to four miles; they were also required to win two of three heat races in one day in order to claim a victory. Soldiers going into battle would certainly demand mounts with power, resilience, and speed, and the most prized runners might win not only at extensive distances and in multiple heats but over jumps, too. Life was not a cakewalk for an eighteenth-century Thoroughbred.

Winning at extremely long distances was so important a factor that Ten Broeck, a Hall of Famer of the late nineteenth century, earned his greatest acclaim for eclipsing the American four-mile record, covering the distance in what was, in the 1870s, the scarcely-to-be-believed time of 7:15¾. The *New York Times* headlined this feat as nothing less than "The Greatest Event in the History of the Turf." The sporting publication

Turf, Field and Farm enthused that Ten Broeck's accomplishment represented "the acme of equine power."

Four-mile heat races were on their way into racing's past tense with the turn of the nineteenth century into the twentieth, as the mass production of motor vehicles with internal combustion engines began rendering equine-mounted soldiers increasingly obsolete—too slow-moving, too ill-protected, and a horse presenting all too large a target for the era's increasingly sophisticated and powerful machine guns and other technologically improved weaponry.

With the gradual transition from equine-based cavalry and a horse-based economy to a mechanized military and a society dependent on internal combustion engines, the sport of racing also changed. We no longer ask our Thoroughbreds to demonstrate their versatility by winning at distances from a few furlongs to four miles. Today's Thoroughbred is faster, lighter, and, sadly, more fragile than the beasts that could rarely get a mile in a hundred seconds but could leap a wall—or, if circumstances so demanded, quite possibly run through it—at the rider's command.

Today, we define versatility in the Thoroughbred in other ways. Can the horse win at sprint distances and routes (defining a route, increasingly, as not much more than a mile)? Can it handle both dirt and turf and, should it ever chance to encounter one, an artificial surface? Can it win at various tracks, or, in the vernacular of the racetrack, must it "carry its track with it?" Can it win on fast surfaces and in the mud?

If the answer to all the above is yes, you're talking about a racehorse that shares some qualities with Dr. Fager.

He was as fiery and headstrong as he was fast, a raging blur daring the other runners to catch him, just try it. He concluded his career with eighteen wins in twenty-two starts, and on those occasions when he didn't vanquish the opposition, it was not because another horse was speedier than he was, and certainly not because he was outclassed, but because his insatiable urge for speed left him vulnerable to strategies and human machinations. The 1968 Horse of the Year was one of the most impressive of Thoroughbreds, a racehorse that was never defeated one-on-one by any rival. Perhaps he never could have been.

Dr. Fager, with jockey David Hidalgo aboard, first faced the starter on July 15, 1966, at Aqueduct Racetrack, and apparently did not particularly impress the day's racegoers, who dismissed the strapping son of Rough'n Tumble at odds of nearly 11-to-1. It required a minute and five seconds and a seven-length thrashing of his ten would-be challengers to demonstrate the error in the handicappers' calculations. For runner-up Lift Off, finishing within seven lengths of a future Horse of the Year and consensus Hall of Famer was a career highlight—he wound up 0-for-15 with lifetime earnings of $5,375—but third-place Rising Market, who finished another four lengths back, would eventually become a popular, hard-knocking stakes horse on the West Coast.

New York horseplayers would not be caught unawares again; the next time Dr. Fager appeared he was 9-to-10 in a $5,500 Saratoga allowance race. After coasting through a :46⅖ half-mile, he tossed in a casual twenty-four-second final quarter, which brought him to the finish in a sprightly 1:10⅖, more than fast enough to dispose of his seven rivals by eight lengths.

The Atlantic City track was chosen by trainer John Nerud for the good Doctor's first stakes engagement, and Dr. Fager, again the odds-on 9-to-10 favorite, made short work of the World's Playground Stakes. Rocketing to the lead out of the starting gate under a new jockey, Manuel Ycaza, he was four lengths up at midstretch, but Ycaza, as fiery a rider as his mount was a runner, neglected to take his foot off the gas pedal, and Dr. Fager added another eight lengths to the eventual winning margin, reaching the wire twelve lengths clear of future stakes winner Glengary.

This earned Dr. Fager a three-and-a-half-week respite and an introduction to jockey Bill Shoemaker, who would pilot him in Aqueduct's $88,000 Cowdin Stakes. The two teamed up splendidly, running Dr. Fager's record to four wins in as many starts as the colt came from just off the pace to defeat two of the season's top 2-year-olds, In Reality and eventual juvenile champion Successor. With the $208,000 Champagne Stakes next on his calendar, it appeared that Dr. Fager could do no wrong.

In the Champagne, however, Dr. Fager would experience double-teaming, a time-tested method for derailing brilliant speed horses.

Successor, who had finished two-and-a-quarter lengths behind Dr. Fager in the Cowdin, was provided extra ammunition for the Champagne in the person of a speedy stablemate, Great White Way. As turfwriter Charles Hatton subsequently noted in the *American Racing Manual*, Dr. Fager "could never tolerate following a rival or stalking the pace once his blood was up," and it was the colt's own temperament that would cost him the juvenile championship.

Bold Hour, with Johnny Rotz in the irons, ran head-and-head with Great White Way and jockey Eddie Belmonte, beating Bill Shoemaker and a rank Dr. Fager to the Champagne's midway point, the half-mile covered in a suicidal :44⅘, with Successor, under a cool Braulio Baeza, tracking in fifth position. Then the two pacesetters stopped and Dr. Fager kept going, building a three-length lead with six furlongs in 1:09⅖. At that point, however, Dr. Fager had nothing left, and Successor passed him easily nearing the wire, pulling away to win by a length in a rapid 1:35.

With this surprising defeat—Dr. Fager had gone to the post as the even money favorite, Successor the 3-to-1 second choice—Successor clinched the championship, while Dr. Fager, owner William McKnight, and trainer John Nerud adjourned to the sidelines to plan better things for the good Doctor's 3-year-old campaign. But even the best-laid plans . . .

Dr. Fager's naming was a fine story in its own right. In the fall of 1965, Nerud had taken a fall off a horse and suffered a head injury. At the Lahey Clinic in Boston, Dr. Charles Fager, a prominent neurosurgeon, had performed the series of delicate surgeries that saved Nerud's life. When Nerud asked to have a horse named in honor of the lifesaving Dr. Fager, McKnight chose the big Rough'n Tumble-Aspidistra colt who had shown some speed in morning workouts. Asked whether he wagered on the races, Nerud responded, "Are you kidding? If Doc Fager found out I was betting horses, he'd have me back on the operating table."

As 1967 dawned, Nerud found himself in charge of a brilliantly speedy colt who was fighting a stubborn infection and had developed sore knees. When it became clear that Dr. Fager would not be ready for a Triple Crown campaign, Nerud exercised patience. He mapped a less urgent course for the newly turned 3-year-old, taking on shorter races in the hopes that a fresh and healthy Dr. Fager might ambush the runners who had depleted their energies competing in the Derby, Preakness, and Belmont Stakes.

Dr. Fager's first 1967 start was delayed until Aqueduct's one-mile Gotham Stakes in April, and he justified Nerud's strategy by rallying from off the pace under Manuel Ycaza to defeat the highly regarded Damascus and Bill Shoemaker by a half-length in what would be the first of four epic confrontations between the two. Dr. Fager returned four weeks later and shattered stopwatches in a six-length thrashing of then-undefeated Tumiga in Aqueduct's one-mile Withers Stakes, run in 1:33⅘. Dr. Fager's time for the Withers missed Bald Eagle's track record by one tick of the stopwatch, but it was lauded by racing writers as the fastest mile by a 3-year-old in New York's racing history.

With Belmont Stakes weekend dead ahead, Dr. Fager was now ready for an additional furlong or two but not yet for the daunting one-and-a-half miles of the Belmont Stakes. Nerud opted instead for Garden State's mile-and-an-eighth Jersey Derby, which would serve as the Doctor's second loss—but not because opponents In Reality, or Air Rights, or certainly Gallant Moment, could outrun him. To the contrary, Dr. Fager, with Ycaza again in the saddle, assumed the early lead and went on to win by six-and-a-half lengths. Unfortunately, as the field had banked through the first turn, the eventual first-place finisher bore in on In Reality and jockey Earlie Fires, herding them and the rest of the field against the rail.

By the time Dr. Fager and Ycaza returned to the unsaddling area the "Inquiry" sign was already lit, and despite the choruses of boos raining down from the stands, the stewards had no choice but to disqualify the 3-to-10 favorite. Dr. Fager was forced to settle for the $5,900 fourth finisher's purse, and, just as importantly for the colt's future, for all but two of the colt's remaining races, Braulio Baeza would be in the saddle.

Returning to the races in Chicago three weeks later, the Tartan Stable colorbearer was on his best behavior in the sloppy Arlington Classic, forging to the lead following a swift :45 half-mile and completing the journey in 1:36, ten lengths clear of runner-up Lightning Orphan, with Diplomat Way third. Next followed the Rockingham Special, in which Dr. Fager won a wire-to-wire romp by four-and-a-quarter lengths in track record time, and then the mile-and-a-quarter New Hampshire Sweeps Classic, by a length-and-a-quarter over In Reality, in a time three full seconds faster than the track record. If there had been any concern that Dr. Fager could not win at ten furlongs, he had now demonstrated that America's classic distance was well within his scope.

At this point, Dr. Fager had won nine of eleven lifetime starts, all of which could be considered a prequel to the classic race that would capture the nation's attention four weeks later. Aqueduct's Woodward Stakes would draw Preakness-Belmont Stakes winner Damascus and defending Horse of the Year Buckpasser, as well as the speedy Brooklyn Handicap winner Handsome Boy. Presented to a nationwide television audience as nothing less than "The Race of the Decade," this meeting of champions would serve, in those pre–Breeders' Cup days, as the season's highlight.

But it would not be a case of three or four outstanding horses testing their abilities in laboratory conditions. In a harkening back to Dr. Fager's first loss, Damascus and Buckpasser would be accompanied by speedy stablemates—"rabbits," in the parlance of the track—whose sole purpose would be to compromise the chances of likely front-runners Dr. Fager and Handsome Boy. Frank Whiteley, Damascus's trainer, entered Hedevar; Buckpasser's conditioner, Eddie Neloy, added Great Power. Neither would be expected to win; indeed, neither would be *wanted* to win. Their role would be to improve their stablemates' chances by denying Dr. Fager and Handsome Boy an easy lead.

As is often the case, these time-tested tag-team tactics proved effective. Great Power broke slowly and never saw the lead, but Hedevar pushed Dr. Fager from the beginning, forcing him through rapid-fire fractions of :22⅖, :45⅕, 1:09⅕, and 1:35⅗. Hedevar then disappeared from the lead, and Dr. Fager all but spit out the bit. And now Damascus came to the fore and began pulling clear of the field, ultimately crossing under the wire with a ten-length victory. Buckpasser, making the final start of his Hall of Fame career, closed belatedly in the final furlong to wrest second from Dr. Fager, who outlasted Handsome Boy for the show. It would be a while before Hedevar and Great Power galloped past the finish.

Dr. Fager started twice more in 1967, winning the mile-and-a-quarter Hawthorne Gold Cup by two-and-a-half lengths and the seven-furlong Vosburgh by four-and-a-half, and his Vosburgh victory earned him the trophy as champion sprinter, but Damascus had clinched Horse of the Year honors for 1967 with his spectacular Woodward victory. Dr. Fager and Damascus would take separate paths during the early part of the following year: Dr. Fager remaining on the sidelines until early May, Damascus beginning his season in January in California.

There have been few seasons on the American turf to match Dr. Fager's 1968. His eight starts would result in seven wins, his single loss as excusable as Man o'War's much-lamented loss to Upset. He would begin the season carrying 130 pounds and would receive no breaks from the racing secretaries, never once racing under less than 130. He would cover tens of thousands of miles, racing in California, New York, Chicago, and Atlantic City, taking on all challengers. By the end of the season, he had demonstrated, as few horses ever have, that this was not merely a run-of-the-mill Horse of the Year but a champion for all times.

He began the season in Aqueduct's seven-furlong Roseben Stakes, a race named for a horse New Yorkers had admiringly nicknamed "The Big Train." Dr. Fager, sent postward at 1-to-5 odds, led wire-to-wire, finishing three lengths clear of Tumiga, who in some seasons might have been a candidate for leading sprinter, but not in 1968, when nobody was within twelve pounds of Dr. Fager. The good Doctor's clocking, 1:21⅖, missed the track record by a fifth of a second. Two weeks later, on the other side of the continent, he again hefted 130 pounds, giving future Hall of Fame mare Gamely fourteen pounds and old rival Rising Market, now a stakes star, nine. He held off all challenges while winning Hollywood Park's eight-and-a-half-furlong Californian Stakes by three emphatic lengths.

A month and a half later, Dr. Fager was back at Aqueduct for the Suburban Handicap, hoisting 132 pounds and jockey Braulio Baeza while Damascus was assigned a pound more, with Manny Ycaza, Dr. Fager's former escort, in the saddle. Hedevar was not entered, and in the absence of a partner for Damascus, it was no contest. Dr. Fager was the crowd's choice at 4-to-5 odds, Damascus the 7-to-5 second choice, and when Dr. Fager broke cleanly, the battle was for second money, which fell to Bold Hour, receiving seventeen pounds from third-place Damascus. Dr. Fager's 1:59⅗ clocking equaled Gun Bow's four-year-old track record for the mile-and-a-quarter distance. Sports page scribes were quick to note that Gun Bow, who in 1999 would be elected to the Hall of Fame, had carried 122 pounds in achieving the record; Dr. Fager equaled it under 132.

And now, Dr. Fager would experience the final defeat of his career, his lone loss of 1968. Trainer Frank Whiteley, noting that Damascus at virtually level weights in the Suburban had been unable to cope with Dr. Fager, decided that in the Brooklyn Handicap, he would again employ the tag-team tactics that had been the only consistently successful strategy against his speedier rival. And so Dr. Fager found himself bedeviled from the start of the Brooklyn by the speedy but distance-challenged Hedevar, who ran full-out for as long as he could, tiring his stablemate's only real rival to add oomph to Damascus's closing charge.

The result, once again, was a rabbit-aided Damascus victory. Dr. Fager, this time the 3-to-5 favorite, carried 135 pounds; Damascus, the 7-to-5 second choice, had been assigned 130, and the weight differential plus Hedevar's annoying presence meant a two-and-a-half-length victory for Damascus, who set a new track record for ten furlongs at Aqueduct and in the process became history's sixth equine millionaire, his earnings pushed to $1,025,526.

The two champions, Damascus and Dr. Fager, would not meet again on the track. Nerud insisted that Dr. Fager would not race if Whiteley entered a rabbit; Whiteley demanded the right to employ any means necessary to maximize his charge's chances. The two magnificent colts concluded their rivalry tied at two wins apiece.

Dr. Fager was next shipped to Saratoga, where he would reign as the 1-to-20 favorite despite being assigned 132 pounds and giving eighteen pounds apiece to thoroughly outgunned rivals Spoon Bait, Fort Drum, and Fast Count. With nothing in the field that could begin to match strides with Dr. Fager, the Tartan Stable superstar was allowed to lope through :23⅖, :47⅕, 1:11⅗, and 1:36⅗ fractions on the way to a 1:48⅘ final clocking and an eight-length win.

The Doctor's next stop was the one-mile Washington Park Handicap at Arlington Park in Chicago, where under 134 pounds he stopped the clock at 1:32⅕, submerging by two stopwatch ticks the mile record Buckpasser had set two years earlier.

On May 7, 2003, multiple stakes winner Najran, carrying just 113 pounds, ran a mile at Belmont Park in 1:32.24, technically equaling Dr. Fager's one-mile record. In the fifty-six years since Dr. Fager's lightning-fast mile at Arlington Park, no horse has run the distance faster.

Dr. Fager was not going to race beyond age four, and the plan was to conclude his career with three important turf races: the United Nations, the Man o' War, and the Washington, D.C. International. Dr. Fager was shipped to Atlantic City, where he was assigned 134 pounds for the United Nations Handicap; defending turf champion Fort Marcy would carry just 118.

Dr. Fager delivered, defeating Advocator, carrying 112, by a neck, with Fort Marcy another length-and-a-half back in third. But it was a near thing, and jockey Baeza, who had needed to re-rally the Doctor when Advocator threatened, reported that Dr. Fager had disliked the grassy surface. At season's end, his lone grass effort would earn him the turf championship, but he would not be subjected again to turf. Instead, the seven-furlong Vosburgh Stakes, to be run at Aqueduct on November 2, would be Dr. Fager's farewell to racing.

Throughout the history of the Sport of Kings, there are a handful of races that have become iconic: Man o' War's 1920 victory over Sir Barton certainly qualifies, as does Seabiscuit's 1938 match race victory over War Admiral. Secretariat's 1973 Belmont Stakes win and Zenyatta's 2009 Breeders' Cup Classic victory were instantly iconic. Perhaps one day Flightline's 2022 Breeders' Cup Classic win will join the mix.

Dr. Fager's 1968 Vosburgh victory must surely qualify. Carrying 139 crushing pounds, the Rough'n Tumble colt faced off against California's brilliant Kissin' George, under 127, and top East Coast sprinters Jim J. (125) and R. Thomas (122). By any standard it should have been a sensational horse race, but the others never had a chance. Dr. Fager attended the early pace, accelerated away from the competition when jockey Baeza so directed, and won going away, six lengths clear, in 1:20⅕, obliterating the track record by a full second.

With this ultimate victory of his career, Dr. Fager's earnings inched above the million-dollar mark, settling at $1,002,642. His status as Horse of the Year was unquestioned. He was also voted top handicap horse and best sprinter, as well as turf champion for winning the United Nations Handicap while giving the previous year's champion a sixteen-pound edge.

Dr. Fager, in summary, won every year-end award for which a male handicap horse might be eligible. As the *American Racing Manual* summed up a campaign unique in the history of the sport, Dr. Fager "excelled in more departments and [earned] more divisional titles than any horse since the *Daily Racing Form* and the *Morning Telegraph* poll was instituted in 1936."

VERSATILITY

But excellence is more than mere numbers, more than handfuls of seasonal titles. Dr. Fager proved to be one of the most versatile Thoroughbreds ever to grace the sport. He defeated opponents on both coasts and at stops in between. He handled fast tracks and off surfaces, won on dirt and on the grass. He won seven times in eight tries under 130 pounds or more, and his one loss, to Damascus and Hedevar in the Brooklyn Handicap, was accomplished through double-teaming tactics. And, one might add, it was no disgrace to lose to Damascus, a deserving member of racing's Hall of Fame.

It is possible that only Dr. Fager's unwillingness to tamp down his speed when challenged early prevented him from being considered the best Thoroughbred ever to tread the American turf. His rabbit-aided losses and his Jersey Derby disqualification were all that stood between him and a perfect 22-for-22 record.

Man o' War cannot challenge Dr. Fager for versatility; the conditions of his day did not permit it. Turf racing was not widely available in the 1920s, and the technological advancements that enabled Dr. Fager to jet around the country, dominating in New York one day, in California two weeks later, then in Chicago, were largely not yet invented during Man o' War's era.

Man o' War does gain an edge as a superior distance racer. Dr. Fager was never tried beyond a mile-and-a-quarter, presumably because there were enough races available at his preferred shorter distances that it was never necessary to send him longer. Man o' War won the mile-and-a-half Jockey Club Stakes and the mile-and-five-eighths Lawrence Realization, and probably would have won going even longer if anyone had asked him to.

But while we can believe that Man o' War, given the opportunity, might have matched, perhaps even exceeded, Dr. Fager's feats in many areas of racing, Dr. Fager actually did these things. In our opinion this rates the edge. Through demonstrated accomplishments, Dr. Fager proved himself the more versatile of the two phenomenal racehorses.

Citation with jockey Eddie Arcaro. (Keeneland Library Cook Collection—14002)

CHAPTER 8

Overcoming Adversity

Man o' War vs. Citation

CALUMET FARM, WHICH WAS TO RACING IN THE 1940S AND '50S WHAT the New York Yankees of the 1920s and '30s were to America's National Pastime, was led by a pair of trainers, both of whom would become members of racing's Hall of Fame, accompanied by a cascade of runners of top quality and championship-winning accomplishments.

Between 1941 and 1961, a period of twenty-one years, Calumet earned more money in a season than any other stable twelve times, a skein of excellence that stands out, both for dollar earnings and length of time atop the leader board, among the many successful owners and stables that have dominated American racing.

In six of those years—1947, 1948, 1949, 1952, 1956, and 1957—Calumet both led all owners and banked more than a million dollars. A million dollars in earnings is commonplace today for a reasonably successful owner—in 2023, a total of 133 owners earned purses totaling seven digits—but was still an accomplishment of note in those pre-inflation days. The five previous years had seen Greentree Stable lead all stables in 1942 by banking $414,432; Calumet topped the standings in 1943 with $267,915 and repeated as leading owner with $601,660 in 1944. They then lost the top spot to Maine Chance Farm with $589,170 in 1945, and regained it with $564,095 in 1946. Even two decades later, when Marion H. Van Berg led all owners with $895,246 in 1965, a million in earnings for the leading earner was not necessarily a sure thing.

But 1947 was a different sort of year. Calumet introduced juvenile champion Citation and champion 2-year-old filly Bewitch, sent out a Horse of the Year in Armed, added to the mix a rising star in Coaltown, and with so many superstars on their roster they blew up the paradigm. Here was a new financial world of great possibilities—if the other stables could produce, or buy, or conjure by any other means a windfall of championship-quality horses, a million dollars in earnings was no longer an impossible dream.

And Calumet did produce the horses, starting well ahead of 1947. The string begins with Triple Crown winner Whirlaway, champion 3-year-old male of 1941 and Horse of the Year in 1941 and 1942. There is Mar-Kell, champion handicap mare of 1943; and Twilight Tear, champion 3-year-old filly of 1944, top handicap mare of 1944, and that season's Horse of the Year.

The superb gelding Armed was leading handicap horse of 1946 and '47, Horse of the Year in the latter year; Bewitch, top 2-year-old filly of 1947 and leading handicap mare of 1949; and Coaltown, champion sprinter of 1948 who stretched his blazing speed to become the champion handicap horse of 1949. There were Two Lea, top 3-year-old filly of 1949 and best handicap mare of 1950, and Wistful, even better than Two Lea in 1949 according to one poll, and awarded a separate trophy as champion 3-year-old filly. Search as you will, you will never again find a single stable sending forth two champion 3-year-old fillies in the same season.

Then there was Real Delight, top 3-year-old filly of 1952; and Tim Tam, best 3-year-old male of 1958 and, but for an injury incurred in the Belmont Stakes, very possibly another Calumet Triple Crown winner. There were Our Mims in 1977 and Davona Dale in 1979 and Before Dawn in 1981 and Horse of the Year Criminal Type in 1990, but those were earned for a different Calumet, led by different owners, some even ridden by jockeys clad in silks bearing no resemblance to Calumet's traditional devil's red and blue.

History takes some strange turns, and those who have read Ann Hagedorn Auerbach's *Wild Ride* and other volumes that purport to tell the tragic story of Calumet's fall will know that the farm's history has taken some of the strangest. Suffice it to say, however, that for a period of time unmatched in the sport's history, Calumet could be counted on to bring into the sport some of its brightest equine lights.

And for four memorable years, 1947 through 1951, with 1949 lost to injury, the brightest light was Citation. Indeed, for the first two of those years, he might have been the brightest light of any that has ever shone upon the world of Thoroughbred racing.

Citation, a member of the 1945 foal crop, entered the sport at a time when memories of the Great Depression and the deprivations of the Second World War were still vivid, and his race record may in some ways have mirrored those difficult times. Racing stables had for decades participated in the sport under the assumption that their horses were expendable resources that should earn their keep as soon as possible and be kept to the task for as long as they could be expected to earn a check. Some had held to this philosophy even before the Depression, and for some, the hard years beginning with "Black Tuesday," October 29, 1928, may have exacerbated the belief that earning as much as possible, as quickly as possible, was the key to avoiding a descent into poverty.

Horses, even horses of evident quality, were raced with what today might be seen as alarming frequency, even at ages two and three, when skeletal and muscular systems are still developing. And in a few cases, they would be raced almost until the specialness they could once claim had been thoroughly raced out of them.

To name just a handful, all of them future Hall of Famers:

- The grand mare Imp (whose career lasted from 1896 to 1901) ran eleven times as a 2-year-old, fifty times at age three.
- Pan Zareta, also a female (1912–1917), raced a total of fifty-two times at ages two and three.
- Grey Lag (1920–1931), winner of the 1921 Belmont Stakes and many other important races, finished his career in cheap claiming races, finishing far behind as an elderly 13-year-old.
- Seabiscuit (1935–1940) went to the post thirty-five times at age two and twenty-three more as a 3-year-old.

- Alsab (1941–1944), a champion at ages two and three who might have earned Horse of the Year honors with better timing—Calumet's enormously popular "Mr. Longtail," Whirlaway, was his chief rival for the award—raced twenty-two times as a 2-year-old and twenty-three more at age three.
- Stymie (1943–1949) raced twenty-eight times at age two, twenty-nine more at age three, continuing on for four additional years and ending his career with 131 lifetime starts.

Citation, born at the tail end of this mindset but not before memories of the great economic downturn had completely faded, would be both a reflection and a victim of Depression thinking. He was raced nine times as a 2-year-old, certainly a reasonable enough season for a top juvenile, but at age three made twenty appearances, just one fewer than Man o' War, nearly three decades earlier, had made in his two-year career.

Citation's were arguably the best combined 2- and 3-year-old seasons in the history of the American turf.

A son of the imported stallion Bull Lea, Citation began his career on the Maryland circuit, breaking his maiden first time out under jockey Al Snider, who would play a pivotal, if tragic, role in the Citation saga, then prevailing over some long-forgotten juveniles in allowance races at Havre de Grace and Pimlico. In his fourth start, an otherwise forgettable five-furlong Arlington allowance event known as the Sealeggy Purse, Citation gave notice that he might be something out of the ordinary, sprinting the distance in :58, two ticks faster than Arlington Park's track record for the distance. Rather shockingly in light of subsequent developments, Citation was the 2-to-1 second choice in the Sealeggy to a filly called Kandy Comfort, who would ultimately face the starter sixty-four times without ever winning a stakes race.

Six days later came Washington Park's $24,550 Elementary Stakes at six furlongs, and here the future Triple Crown winner earned his first stakes victory, scoring by two lengths under 122 pounds.

Now Calumet entered both the eventual champion juvenile colt and the top juvenile filly in the $78,050 Washington Park Futurity, with another promising Calumet juvenile, Free America, there to ensure that third money did not escape without a struggle. Citation lagged early in the six-furlong event while Bewitch charged to a lead that she would never surrender, earning her eighth consecutive victory, with Citation closing tardily for second and Free America annexing third. Sent away at 1-to-5 odds, the Calumet trio created a minus pool of over $23,000. Even at the minimum legal payout for winning wagers, it had cost Washington Park $23,000 in lost profits to present its 1948 Futurity.

Now the Calumet runners were shipped to New York, their goal Belmont's rich $50,000-added Futurity, scheduled for October 4, 1947, but first Calumet would run Citation in the $10,000 Futurity Trial. As the 2-to-1 second choice to favored My Request, Citation lagged early under Snider, then blew by everybody to win by a length. Calumet trainer Jimmy Jones allowed Bewitch to sit out the Trial, but she would be very much in evidence on Futurity Day.

Indeed, the presence of Citation's erstwhile conqueror was virtually the contest's sole hint of drama. Carrying 123 pounds to her stablemate's 122, Bewitch could not match Citation's blistering :44⅘ half-mile and was three lengths back at the top of the stretch. From there, it was a relaxed canter to the wire, and in 1:15⅘, Citation avenged his only loss of the season. The victory was worth $78,430 to the winner, with an additional $6,800 for Bewitch's third-place efforts.

The 1-3 finish skyrocketed Calumet's seasonal earnings to $1,239,021, far beyond the stable's own previous record of just over $600,000. Citation finished his season with a length-and-a-half victory as the 2-to-5 favorite in the muddy Pimlico Futurity, adding another $36,675 to Calumet's seasonal revenues and bringing the champion's record to eight wins in nine starts. Although Citation had long since clinched the juvenile championship, he finished well behind Bewitch in total seasonal earnings, bringing home $155,680 in purse money to the filly's $213,675.

Citation was returned to the farm as the early choice to win the 1948 Kentucky Derby, but, of course, at this point virtually no one outside the boundaries of Calumet had even heard the name of Coaltown, a late-blooming but sensationally fast colt who would emerge as the champion's greatest Derby Day threat.

Merely winning eight of nine races and a divisional championship did not earn Citation the right to lollygag through the winter of his 3-year-old season, however. Emerging at Hialeah on February 2, 1948, Citation, favored at 1-to-5 odds, raced close to the pace in a six-furlong, $5,000 allowance race for 3-year-olds and up, winning by a restrained three-quarters of a length in a professional 1:10⅖.

This was far from a routine belt-tightener for a putative Derby favorite. Runner-up Kitchen Police was a 5-year-old who had been a stakes winner at age three; third finisher Say Blue was a 4-year-old mare who would finish her career with multiple stakes wins and earnings of more than $100,000. Citation conceded them weight and defeated them handily.

This highly competitive first seasonal start, however, was merely a prelude. Citation was returned to the races nine days later in Hialeah's seven-furlong Seminole Handicap, once again taking on older horses. These were not just any older horses, however; among his rivals were Calumet's reigning Horse of the Year Armed; Delegate, who would become 1949's champion sprinter; and Faultless, the previous year's Preakness winner.

It was an amazingly difficult task for a colt who had officially turned three less than a month-and-a-half earlier, and, having been foaled on April 11, 1945, was still nearly two months shy of his actual third birthday. But Citation was up to the task, winning by a length over Delegate, with Armed another neck behind.

And now, with Florida's Derby prep races next on his agenda, Calumet could actually look forward to Citation facing fields of his own cropmates—less stressful competition.

A week after the Seminole, Citation was 15-to-100 when he ran down 3-year-old Hypnos by a length in the mile-and-an-eighth Everglades; returning ten days later, he won by eight in the Flamingo. In the modern day, of course, a Derby contender with four wins before the first of March, including a Flamingo victory, would have earned a guaranteed spot in the Churchill Downs starting gate, but the 1948 Derby was still more than two months away, guaranteed Derby spots were a half-century in the future, Citation was a Calumet colt, and there was money to be earned. Surely a race could be found somewhere.

But here fate intervened. Al Snider had been Citation's primary rider during 1947 and had been aboard for all four Florida wins. On March 5, Snider went fishing in the Florida Keys and was never seen again. It was theorized that a sudden, violent storm had capsized the jockey's skiff, sending Snider and two companions to the bottom.

It was a respectful six weeks before Citation was again entered to race, at Maryland's Havre de Grace. Eddie Arcaro, who had been in the saddle for Whirlaway's Triple Crown sweep seven years earlier, would take over for Snider. Arcaro, one of the greats of the game, would guide Citation through the vast majority of his East Coast races for the remainder of his career, with Steve Brooks or Gordon Glisson assuming the task when the colt was raced elsewhere.

Citation's goal at Havre de Grace was the mile-and-a-sixteenth, $25,000-added Chesapeake Stakes, but first, of course, there would be a $10,000 formality known as the Chesapeake Trial, a six-furlong race that, as fate would have it, would be run in the mud. Citation went to the post as the 3-to-10 favorite.

Citation broke from the outside post and stalked the early leaders from a length-and-a-half away. Turning for home, he had only the front-running Saggy to catch. But here, as Citation was carried wide by a tiring runner, Arcaro decided that putting the Calumet colt to a hard drive in a $10,000 race would use up physical resources that might be better saved for a more important, higher-value future contest. He allowed Citation an easy run to the wire, in second place.

And Saggy had his moment of glory. Interviewed afterward, Arcaro declared, "If Citation had had a recent race under his belt I would have given him a harder ride in the stretch, but I didn't want to knock the horse out and I'm sure [Citation's trainer, Jimmy Jones] didn't want me to do so."

Perhaps that was a prudent call, although in retrospect Arcaro's decision was all that stood at year's end between Citation and a unique 20-for-20 season. Arcaro's split-second decision also had a completely unanticipated consequence: Thirteen years later, the racing world would celebrate an enormously popular Kentucky Derby-Preakness winner named Carry Back, who happened to be Saggy's son. And how likely is it that Saggy, with his unimpressive $62,340 in lifetime earnings and handful of minor stakes victories, would even have had a stud career without this shocking win over a future Triple Crown winner? It is questionable.

Citation and Saggy renewed their rivalry five days later in the $25,000 Chesapeake Stakes, and now the stars aligned properly. The distance increased from the Trial's six furlongs to a mile-and-a-sixteenth, the track was good rather than muddy, and Citation won by four-and-a-half lengths, with Saggy trailing the entire field, fifteen lengths back.

With the Kentucky Derby now two weeks away, there was still time for Jones to get more work into Citation—and inject some additional cash into Calumet's coffers. And so the soon-to-be Derby favorite was entered in the one-mile Derby Trial, which preceded the Run for the Roses by just four days and offered a winner's purse of $8,525. Arcaro launched Citation into the lead after the first half-mile and brought the 1-to-10 favorite home by a sensible length-and-a-quarter. And the following Saturday was Derby Day.

On May 1, 1948, a two-horse Calumet entry confronted the four starters who hadn't been frightened away by so awesome a show of equine firepower. Citation had won fourteen of his sixteen races; his entrymate, undefeated Coaltown, had been unraced in 1947 due to a throat abscess, but had won all four of his 3-year-old starts. These had included a track record–equaling six furlongs in 1:09⅗ in just his second race, which he won by twelve lengths, and a four-and-a-half-length romp in the Blue Grass, breaking the track record while being eased to the finish.

The Calumet pair went to the post as the 2-to-5 favorites, and on a muddy track Coaltown and jockey N. L. Pierson made every effort to outbreak the starting gate. They had jumped to a six-length lead after a half-mile and were up by three-and-a-half as the field moved down the backstretch. And then Arcaro asked Citation the question, and Citation provided the desired response. At the top of the lane, Coaltown was still a half-length to the good, but Citation was gaining with every stride, and after one more furlong, he was long gone. At the wire, the margin was three-and-a-half lengths, with Coaltown three lengths clear of third-place My Request.

Citation's $2.80 win payoff tied with Count Fleet's five years earlier as the lowest in Derby history. With oversized twenty-horse Derby fields the norm in the modern era, it is virtually certain that there will never again be a lower one.

Next on Citation's agenda was the Preakness, where trainer H. A. "Jimmy" Jones handed the colt off to his brother Ben. Citation's competition in the four-horse field was of the nominal variety, and on a track labeled heavy the 1-to-10 favorite posted a front-running five-and-a-half-length win. Citation's fractions of :50⅖, 1:16, 1:43, and a final time of 2:02⅖ suggest that the track was heavier than merely heavy. It was in 1925 that the Preakness distance had been standardized at one-and-three-sixteenths miles. Citation's 2:02⅖ remains the slowest of a century's nine-and-a-half-furlong Preaknesses.

With four weeks between the Preakness and the Belmont Stakes, the Calumet brain trust looked for another race for Citation. Garden State Park was offering the Jersey Derby and a $43,300 purse practically for the taking, and Citation was duly dispatched to New Jersey. Once again the 1-to-10 favorite, Citation shook off an early challenge and pulled away, finishing eleven lengths clear of the nominal competition. In the process, he demolished Garden State's mile-and-a-quarter track record by a second and three-fifths. Now Citation was surely ready for the Belmont Stakes.

Oh yes, he was. Arcaro sent Citation directly to the lead, and after brushing off a brief early challenge from Faraway, who would be the last colt from the Glen Riddle Farm of Man o' War's owner, Samuel Riddle, to participate in a Triple Crown race, the pair widened continuously on the field, which surprisingly included seven would-be challengers. Citation galloped to the wire eight lengths clear of Better Self, and America's eighth Triple Crown was in the books. It would, of course, be a quarter-century wait before Secretariat would thrill a nationwide television audience by sweeping the ninth.

During the remainder of 1948, Citation would race nine times in just over five months, at distances from six furlongs to two miles. His would be a cross-country journey, beginning in New York, then moving on to Chicago, back to New York, and then to Maryland, where he would be handed a walkover in the Pimlico Special.

Turfwriter Joe Palmer was on hand for Citation's walkover and observed that Citation was both an exceptionally powerful force on the track and an exceptionally difficult horse to control when it was his decision to ignore the jockey's wishes and run. As Palmer described it in *This Was Racing*:

> *In 1948, [jockey Eddie Arcaro] took Citation out for the Pimlico Special. Everything else had been scared out, and Citation had a walkover. All he had to do, for $10,000, was get around the track.*
>
> *The expectation was that Eddie would jog him a mile and then let him run a little through the stretch to please the customers. But Citation had some ideas of his own. He went over the mile and three-sixteenths in 1:59⅘. Shut Out took longer than that to win the race, and so did Challedon. If there had been another horse to run with him, Citation would have done it a good deal faster, and neither Arcaro nor that rider who was supposed to be able to hold the Twentieth Century Limited could have stopped him.*

And then, following another cross-country journey, Citation would race in northern California, obliterating another track record with a five-length cakewalk in the December 11 Tanforan Handicap.

At the end of an extraordinary racing season, Citation would have nineteen wins in twenty 1948 starts. His seasonal earnings would total $709,470, more than a quarter-million dollars beyond Assault's previous record of $424,195, set in the King Ranch star's Triple Crown year of 1946.

Could this be the best horse ever to have raced in America? Turf-writers with decades of experience—Joe Williams in the *Buffalo Evening News*, Harry M. Hayward in the *San Francisco Examiner*—were beginning to discuss the possibility in print. Frank Eck in Kentucky's *Paducah Sun* urged caution: "It will take a number of years before a true comparison can be formed between Citation, the horse of the year, and Man o' War." It was a compliment to both horses that either was being compared to the other.

But as 1948 ended and 1949 began, other headlines were surfacing, disquieting headlines. "Citation Injured, Out of Santa Anita Meet," blazed the *Los Angeles Times*. "Citation Hurt, Out for Three Months!" exclaimed the *San Francisco Examiner*, and by now Citation's reputation was so glossy that the headline demanded an exclamation point.

Eventually, Citation's absence from the races would stretch to thirteen months. He had developed an osselet, a chronic arthritic condition that can worsen over time without rest and treatment. Given the importance of this unique Thoroughbred, this malady was not treated casually. On June 10, 1949, farm manager Paul Eberhardt was quoted that "a horse of less importance would have been running again long ago, but not Citation. We gave him a full three months to recover and another three months to get ready to run again. He is in training now and looks fine."

Speculation that bids were being taken to consign the Horse of the Year to a stud farm could be ignored, according to Eberhardt: Calumet was "not soliciting them." But after three months, and then six, Citation was still not ready. His recovery would ultimately require an entire year, and the horse that was finally returned to training was a lesser one. "This was the last of the towering greatness of Citation," Kent Hollingsworth would recall in *The Great Ones*. Trainer Jimmy Jones admitted that the champion was "a shell of what he had been."

Finally, on January 11, 1950, at Santa Anita, the champion was entered in a six-furlong allowance race over a sloppy track. Citation, the heavy favorite, scored over a trio of moderate opponents, but . . . was this the same Citation? Jockey Steve Brooks had been forced to use the whip in disposing of the stubborn Bold Gallant before Citation pulled away to his final length-and-a-half margin. It was the Calumet star's sixteenth consecutive win, a string that had begun in April 1948 with his payback victory over Saggy. It was perhaps the least impressive race of the sixteen.

That this was not the Citation of 1948 became evident in his next start, a six-furlong Santa Anita overnight handicap. For the first time in his career, the Calumet superstar was asked to carry 130 pounds in a race, and while he nearly pulled it off, jockey Steve Brooks was unable to drive Citation past a colt named Miche, assigned just 114. Miche was a nice enough sort—in 1952, at age seven, he would win a shocking Santa Anita Handicap, paying $55.40 to win and defeating Horse of the Year Hill Prince—but his defeat of Citation in a common race proved that Citation's osselet was anything but a mere ailment. It was a career-altering affliction.

Reunited with Arcaro, Citation was a close second to stablemate Ponder under 130 pounds in the San Antonio Handicap, which earned him a boost to 132 for the $135,000 Santa Anita Handicap. Here, for the first time, he ran afoul of Noor, an Irish-bred carrying just 110, and fell one-and-a-quarter lengths short, with Calumet's champion mare Two Lea third. This was the beginning of a five-race winning streak for future Hall of Famer Noor, four of which would feature the remnants of Citation in the supporting role.

Noor's Big 'Cap victory earned him seven additional pounds—117 to 130 for Citation—for the one-and-three-quarter-mile San Juan Capistrano Handicap, and rarely has a racing secretary cut the margin more finely. After a prolonged stretch drive, Noor prevailed by a nose, with runner-up Citation twelve-and-a-half lengths clear of third finisher Mocopo. Noor's clocking of 2:52⅘ shattered the track record for the fourteen-furlong distance. One more pound on Noor, one less on Citation, and the nose decision might have been reversed, the track record Citation's.

Given two and a half months to regroup, Citation was shipped to Golden Gate Park in the San Francisco area. Following a near-miss six-furlong prep, as Roman In prevailed with a track record–equaling 1:08⅖, the old Citation put in an appearance with a world record 1:33⅗ clocking in the Golden Gate Mile. But as Citation was being prepared for longer distances—and the racing world was beginning to debate whether he could possibly become racing's first million-dollar earner—a daunting prospect arose. Noor had arrived in northern California.

Both runners were named for the nine-furlong Forty-Niners Handicap, Citation assigned 128 pounds, Noor 123, an eight-pound shift in Citation's favor from the pair's most recent meeting. It required a world record 1:46⅘ for Noor to prevail, this time by a neck. For their next meeting, in the $57,000 mile-and-a-quarter Golden Gate Handicap, Noor would carry 127 pounds to Citation's 126, and Noor would run a race for the history books, reaching the finish in 1:58⅕, a world record mark that would remain in place for nearly thirty years, until Spectacular Bid ran two stopwatch ticks faster at Santa Anita. This time, Noor had been the 7-to-10 favorite, Citation the second choice at 6-to-5.

Perhaps this meant that the bulk of the public had finally realized that Citation, while still a formidable racehorse, was no longer the colossus of 1947 and '48. Certainly, trainer Jimmy Jones was describing him in terms he would never have used during the colt's glory days. "Well, you know," he explained to one reporter, "Citation is a lot like an old fighter. Take a fighter like [former heavyweight champion] Joe Louis. He's past his peak and it takes a lot of work to get him into shape to meet good young fighters." And Jones added, "He's always [going to] have trouble against good young horses."

This was June 24, 1950, and it was decided that Citation would be sent to the sidelines again; he would not race until April 1951. Following five encounters with a future Hall of Famer, almost all of them close, several contested in record time, Citation needed to recuperate. He also needed to put Noor in the rearview mirror. At age five, the physical issue that had cost him more than a year away from the races likely still providing its daily dose of pain, he needed a rest. But he was not yet done. With just $61,370 remaining to the million-dollar mark, Calumet wanted him to race in 1951.

Citation's first try at age six was unpromising. For the first time in his career, he finished third, and in a Bay Meadows six-furlong allowance race against rivals—A Lark, Pancho Supreme—that he would have horrified in his younger days. His bankroll inched upward by $430 for the exercise, and eight days later Pancho Supreme outfinished A Lark, with Citation again third, adding another $400. Perhaps the Calumet executives were beginning to feel discouraged. At this pace, it might require years before Citation achieved his million.

His next start was even less encouraging. Shipped to Hollywood Park for the six-furlong Premiere Handicap, he fell behind early and could never reach contention, finishing fifth in a race that paid purse money only as far back as fourth. For the first time in his career, Citation had run a race without earning a check. His bankroll was stalled at $939,460, still $60,540 short of a million. To many, it must have seemed impossible that this aging champion—or would the proper word now be "aged?"—would ever attain Calumet's goal.

But Citation returned three weeks later in Hollywood Park's eight-and-a-half-furlong Argonaut Handicap and closed well to take second, adding $5,000 to his bankroll. Jockey F. A. Smith, who had been given the mount for this one race, was less than impressed with Citation's performance, reporting that "he sort of flattened out [in the stretch]." But the runner-up prize increased his earnings to $944,460—still a gap to be bridged, but it was growing smaller.

And now he was entered in Hollywood Park's Century Handicap. Twenty years later, the Century would be a mile-and-three-eighths turf event worth nearly enough to send Citation to millionaire's row, but in 1951 it was barely a blip on the racing calendar, a routine contest that would pay its winner only $5,000. Under just 120 pounds, Citation took charge, winning for the first time in over a year. With $952,710 now in his bank account, Citation's task was one major victory from completion. Just $47,290 to go.

With renewed hope, on July 4 Jones entered Citation and Bewitch in the $56,000 American Handicap, and now Citation was ready to run, at least as much as his age and what was left of his physical attributes would allow. With an Independence Day crowd of 54,700 screaming encouragement and stablemate All Blue forcing the pace, Citation, carrying 123 pounds, settled into a comfortable rhythm, then exploded in deep stretch to outfinish Bewitch by a half-length. Now Citation could claim total earnings of $977,510, with the $137,000, mile-and-a-quarter Hollywood Gold Cup squarely ahead.

Here was a faint memory of what Citation must have been like, back in the day. With All Blue pushing Be Fleet and the youthful Bill Shoemaker through the early stages, Citation assumed a place near the lead, then accelerated away from his rivals. He led by two lengths on the turn for home, three lengths at midstretch, and four at the finish, showing the 50,000 fans on hand that there was still some gas in the old champion's tank.

With $1,085,750 now in his bank account, Citation was led off the track, surely for the final time. He was certain to be retired to the leisurely life of a stud farm idol. Or was he?

"I wanted to run him again," recalled a wistful trainer Jimmy Jones years later. "He was just getting good again and there was a $50,000 race"—this would have been Hollywood Park's mile-and-a-half Sunset Handicap, with its winner's purse of just over $31,000—"just there for the taking." Jones raised this possibility to Mrs. Warren Wright, owner of Calumet Farm, whose firmly negative response freed Citation forever from the stress and strain of racetrack existence. Citation would come home to Calumet.

It is a nearly universal opinion that Citation is one of the best horses ever produced in America. His unparalleled record at ages two and three, his sixteen-race winning streak, his Triple Crown, and his record earnings are factors leading one to conclude that Citation was a truly exceptional individual.

This belief was echoed by horsemen of the era. Trainer "Sunny Jim" Fitzsimmons declared of the 3-year-old star, "Up to this point, Citation has done more than any horse I ever saw. And I saw Man o' War." David Alexander noted in *A Sound of Horses* that "some horsemen believed Citation was the most perfectly made colt the world had ever seen." Jimmy Jones declared, "Citation was the best horse I ever saw." After watching a future Hall of Famer, Cigar, equal Citation's sixteen-race winning streak, Jones (whose objectivity, admittedly, may be questioned in this matter) insisted that Cigar was "no Citation."

There can be no question that in any ranking of America's most outstanding racehorses, Citation's place would be near the top. It would not be without merit to suggest that this is the name that should be atop all the greats of history.

OVERCOMING ADVERSITY

There is a significant problem awaiting the analyst attempting to craft an "Overcoming Adversity" chapter in a book about Thoroughbred racing: We don't really know.

As fans, as bettors, even as writers researching the most important horses of racing's past, we have only the information that is made public, only the information that the owners and trainers and riders and administrators and news sources are willing to release, to help us decide which horses may have overcome difficulties in their careers and which were relatively unaffected by the myriad physical issues that, as much as dedicated humans may seek to prevent them, bedevil nearly every Thoroughbred.

The training profession is composed of notoriously closed-mouthed men and women who, particularly in days past, were expected to live by a virtual code of silence. Any release of information to the press might cause bettors to flock to the trainer's horses, destroying the odds available to the owners. Such a lapse in discretion could lead to the worst sort of undesired consequences, among them the firing of the loquacious trainer. And so, unless some valuable factoid nugget inadvertently emerges from the black hole of stable management, we may never learn what caused one horse to win, another to lose.

We don't know, for example, whether Sysonby, one of the Thoroughbred giants of his era, might have been drugged the day he lost the Futurity—the only loss of his career—to the filly Artful. We can suspect it, and there were strong allegations that the colt's groom had dosed him before the field went to the post. Perhaps there was even an admission of guilt by the groom—but under what duress, under what sort of harsh questioning?

We can never be certain how much greater Whirlaway might have been, had trainer Ben A. Jones been more prescient in recognizing the Calumet colt's need for the special blinkers that were applied in the days before his Triple Crown sweep; can never declare with confidence what unsuspected miseries may have been to blame for the single loss of Native Dancer's career, which unfortunately occurred in the most visible of circumstances, in the Kentucky Derby. We can never calculate with unerring precision how the results might have changed, had the brilliant 23-year-old Bill Shoemaker been assigned to ride Nashua, the more experienced Eddie Arcaro aboard Swaps, in their historic 1955 match race.

Might Damascus, as was rumored, have been drugged prior to the 1967 Kentucky Derby, costing him his opportunity to sweep the Triple Crown? What variety of blahs might have afflicted Secretariat on the days he lost to Onion and Prove Out? Should Seattle Slew have been rested, rather than being shipped to California, Hollywood Park, and his first loss? Might American Pharoah, returning just three short weeks after winning easily in the Haskell, have been feeling tired, or ill, or might he have been nursing some unsuspected ache or pain, when he lost the Travers to a runner, Keen Ice, who had certainly never troubled the Triple Crown winner in any other contest?

We just don't know. Unless we have the facts in hand, in the form of x-rays, veterinarian reports, or insider quotations from reliable sources, we can never really be sure.

This is certainly true of Man o' War, who despite being among the most imposing beasts ever to tread the American turf, was as much a flesh-and-blood creature as any equine athlete. We can know that there must have been pain in Man o' War's life, but we cannot know how that pain affected him in his races.

What we do know is that it was a rarity for a reference to injury or illness to escape the Man o' War camp. There was soreness after his Potomac Handicap victory that was said to have been treated and no longer a factor when he faced Sir Barton in his final race. If the news given to the public was true, Man o' War was among the soundest of runners, and among the most fortunate, one who seldom needed to overcome even the hint of adversity.

And we know that Citation overcame an injury that cost him a full year away from the races, at a time in his life when remaining in training might have meant hundreds of thousands of dollars in additional purse money to Calumet. Citation's affliction was, we can be certain, a serious one.

It was a long slog to Calumet's stated goal of a million dollars in earnings for Citation. To become the first to reach that exalted pinnacle, he was required to overcome the lasting effects of his injury, repeatedly challenge a powerful adversary in future Hall of Famer Noor, and lug weights, particularly at age five, that were assigned based on Citation's pre-injury exploits. But Citation surmounted all of this, and in reaching the million-dollar goal that Calumet had set for him, he will always be remembered for succeeding in particularly difficult, painful circumstances.

It certainly appears, given the inevitably limited breadth of our knowledge, that Citation overcame far more adversity than Man o' War ever faced, and he is therefore the clear winner of this category. We may not know everything about the sport, but we can unquestionably respect Citation as one of the most courageous Thoroughbreds ever to race in America.

John Henry, with Darrel McHargue up, wins the Hialeah Turf Cup. (Keeneland Library Raftery Turfotos Collection)

CHAPTER 9

Longevity

Man o' War vs. John Henry

Perhaps the reader will find it odd to compare Man o' War, in any way, with John Henry. Their career paths were so different, their achievements make such a stunning contrast, that comparisons may appear to stretch credulity. As much as any pairing of racehorses in this book, Man o' War and John Henry seem virtually different breeds of horse.

Man o' War, for example, was among the most historically brilliant of 2-year-olds, winning nine races and suffering but one debatable loss. Considered a likely superstar nearly from the first time he stepped on a track, he was saluted in the press as clearly the best of his generation as early as his third start. As far as the racing world was concerned, his record, despite the second-place finish, remained pristine.

As a 2-year-old, Man o' War raced at the prestigious New York tracks, Belmont Park and Jamaica and Saratoga and Aqueduct, dominating important juvenile races whose histories were already teeming with great names: the Youthful, the Tremont, the Hopeful, the Futurity. Had there been year-end championships in 1919, Man o' War would have been the unanimous selection as juvenile champion.

John Henry also began his career as a 2-year-old, but in far less elite company. Purchased for $1,100 as a yearling—his sire, the virtually unknown Ole Bob Bowers, had once sold for $900—the cantankerous youngster was gelded before making the first start of his career, over the three-quarter-mile track at Jefferson Downs in Kenner, Louisiana.

Entered in an eight-horse field of maiden 2-year-olds going four furlongs, John Henry won by a nose over a filly called You Sexy Thing, whose name you're likely reading for the first time. After just one start, he had repaid his minuscule purchase price, with $100 in profit.

But John Henry did not win his second start, nor did he win his third. He lost his jockey, an unfortunate lad named Munster, in his fourth outing, John Henry's minuscule 102-pound impost perhaps enabling the liftoff necessary to propel his rider out of the saddle. Munster had never before ridden John Henry in a race, nor would he ever ride him again. The gelding next won a $2,400 Evangeline Downs allowance race, enhancing his bankroll by another $1,440.

It was in his seventh start, Evangeline's $86,000 Lafayette Futurity, that John Henry earned the first of his thirty stakes victories, racing six furlongs over a sloppy track in 1:14⅖ to defeat Lil' Liza Jane by a head. His reward for the victory was a $43,225 purse; his backers at the betting windows received a generous 5-to-1 payoff.

But 1977 would see no more winner's circle celebrations for John Henry, who would complete his 2-year-old campaign with three wins in eleven starts, two seconds and two thirds, and earnings of $49,380. Affirmed was the champion 2-year-old of 1977, and if John Henry's name had received so much as a mention in the balloting, it would have been followed by a resounding "Who?"

At age three, of course, Man o' War was undefeated, unthreatened, and, after his length-and-a-half Preakness victory, largely unchallenged. John Henry's 3-year-old season was more eventful but far less successful.

On a four-race losing streak as the 1977 season ended, John Henry appended five more to the string of defeats, one a 20-length thrashing in a $20,000 claiming race. At this point, his owners, D. Lingo and C. Madere, sold the gelding to trainer H. Snowden Jr., who suffered through a nine-and-a-half-length loss in an $8,500 allowance race, then sold the ill-tempered gelding for a reported $25,000 to the Dotsam Stable of bicycle importer Sam Rubin, who was seeking a runner to enter in New York allowance races.

Once in a great while, a Thoroughbred of seemingly limited ability suddenly gains unexpected stature after being sold to a new owner.

Perhaps the classic case of this was Seabiscuit, who began his career racing indifferently for the elite Wheatley Stable and Hall of Fame trainer "Sunny Jim" Fitzsimmons, then became a champion, a Horse of the Year, and a national celebrity when sold to automobile entrepreneur Charles S. Howard.

Before being sold to Howard, Seabiscuit had won but nine of forty-seven races and finished out of the money twenty-four times while banking less than $20,000. In Howard's barn and under the tutelage of trainer "Silent Tom" Smith, Seabiscuit would—some might add the word "inexplicably"—win twenty-four of his remaining forty-two races, finish off the board only four times, defeat Triple Crown winner War Admiral in a celebrated match race, and close his career as racing's all-time leading money winner.

With some variations, this was John Henry's career arc following his purchase by Rubin. A simple chart can be prepared to demonstrate the gelding's emergence as an equine star:

Table 9-1: Race Record of John Henry Before and After Purchase by Sam Rubin

	Starts	Wins	Places	Shows	Outs	Earnings
For Others	17	3	2	3	9	$50,778
For Rubin	66	36	13	6	11	$6,541,082

The blossoming of John Henry was almost immediate. After winning a $25,000 claiming race in his first start for Dotsam, the gelding was entered for a $35,000 claiming tag in a mile-and-a-sixteenth Belmont Park turf event and won off by fourteen lengths. John Henry would face the starter sixty-four more times over the course of his long career, but never again would Sam Rubin risk him for a claiming tag. By the end of the season, the $25,000 purchase could claim two stakes victories and four more in-the-money efforts in added-money races. With five wins in nine grass starts, he had a growing reputation as a turf specialist, bolstered by a near-miss in Belmont Park's Grade 2 Lexington Handicap to turf star Mac Diarmida. His seasonal earnings totaled more than $120,000.

But John Henry was just getting started. By the close of the 1984 season, he would have earnings of nearly $6.6 million. He would be named Horse of the Year for 1981, at age six, and, unbelievably, for 1984, at age nine. He would win seven Eclipse Awards, taking home the trophies for champion grass horse in 1980, '81, '83, and '84 and earning champion older horse honors in 1981. He won the Grade 1 San Luis Rey Stakes and Oak Tree Invitational, and the Hollywood Park Invitational three times, won twice in the Santa Anita Handicap and, for variety's sake, the Arlington Million.

His victory in the 1981 Jockey Club Gold Cup pushed his earnings to $2,805,310 and vaulted him past Spectacular Bid as racing's all-time leading money earner. Amazingly, he would earn that much again, and more, over the remainder of his career. He won sixteen times in Grade 1 stakes, the most of any horse in history.

Once he had joined the Dotsam Stable, John Henry had the advantage of two excellent trainers preparing him for his races. Vernon L. "Lefty" Nickerson would take over his conditioning when John Henry was sent east to race; Hall of Famer Ron McAnally would be the trainer of record when the gelding returned to the West Coast. With Dotsam, he was ridden by a series of top-flight jockeys: Herb McCauley, Angel Santiago, Darrell McHargue, Angel Cordero Jr., Laffit Pincay Jr., Bill Shoemaker, Chris McCarron. It was a collection of good, great, and Hall of Fame caliber jockeys, riding a horse on his way to enshrinement.

If there is one negative in John Henry's resume, it is his forty-four losses, which included fifteen second-place finishes, nine thirds, and twenty times out of the money. And it is here that we confront the issues of being gelded as a young horse, never to sire foals, all of which enhances the likelihood that the runner will be kept in training and in competition for as long as he can remain healthy enough to race competently.

It is a fact of life on the racetrack that if you race often enough, you are eventually going to encounter horses who will beat you. Multiply that possibility by the number of horses a John Henry or a Forego or a Kelso or an Exterminator, for example, faces over the course of a career that covers many years and therefore many generations of challengers, and it is inevitable that the losses will accumulate in greater numbers than will be the case for a runner who races but a few times and then retires to the sidelines to attempt to re-create in the stallion barn his own characteristics of speed and power.

This can perhaps best be seen by comparing the number of starts and the distance covered by the three top selections in *The Blood-Horse's Top 100 Racehorses of the 20th Century*, and by three that were placed below them in the magazine's survey. The top three choices, all colts, were:

#1 Man o' War—20 wins in 21 lifetime starts, raced 20⅝ miles.

#2 Secretariat—16 wins in 21 lifetime starts, raced 22⅝ miles.

#3 Citation—32 wins in 45 lifetime starts, raced 45³⁄₁₆ miles.

Now compare those to these three, all of whom raced their entire careers as geldings:

#4 Kelso—39 wins in 63 lifetime starts, raced 76⅛ miles.

#7 Forego—34 wins in 57 lifetime starts, raced 63³⁄₁₆ miles.

#23 John Henry—39 wins in 83 lifetime starts, raced 96⁹⁄₁₆ miles plus 80 yards.

The three colts won 68 times in 87 starts (78.2 percent), racing a total of 89¹⁄₁₆ miles. The three geldings won 112 times in 203 starts (55.2 percent) and raced 235⅞ miles plus 80 yards. And in any rating system employed to rank-order these two types of runners, it will always be the lightly raced, heavily stage-managed careers of runners like Man o' War, Secretariat, and Citation that inevitably outrank the Kelsos, Foregos, and John Henrys.

Such runners will (a) be burdened with additional weight as racing secretaries seek to blunt the impact of their ability, and (b) likely be injured along the way, perhaps so seriously that their continuation in the sport is threatened, perhaps seriously enough that periods of recuperation are required.

And so, beloved 1918 Kentucky Derby winner Exterminator, a gelding, raced eight seasons and officially lost half of his 100 starts; Roseben raced six seasons (excluding a single losing race as a 2-year-old) and lost 59 of 111, the grand mare Imp *averaged* 28.5 starts per season over her six seasons, losing 109 of 171. Seabiscuit, who raced as a colt but was treated like a gelding over his first two seasons, lost 63 percent of his 89 starts; Stymie topped the money list at his retirement but prevailed just 35 times in 131 trips to the starting gate; Calumet Stable's mighty Armed raced 81 times in seven seasons in the 1940s and lost 40 times, including two losses to stablemate Citation and four to another Calumet star, Coaltown.

But these were all, despite the losses, outstanding racehorses. All have richly deserved plaques in the Hall of Fame, and all were awarded year-end championships, or would have been, had racing thought of creating a year-end awards program so early in its history.

All of which is to suggest that there is more than one form of excellence in the Sport of Kings. We have those precocious runners who dazzle us with their brilliance from the moment they reach the track, win important juvenile races and classic 3-year-old events, and perhaps continue on to age four, where the best of the best continue winning handicaps and traditional stakes.

But the John Henry path to glory, in which a horse is given the task of competing against the best runners of each succeeding generation, is also a valid one, although one that may not be accorded full credit. At the very least, we must always recognize that a long and productive career, despite the unavoidable defeats that come with racing so many more times, is a legitimate path to equine excellence—perhaps as much so as that chosen by Samuel Riddle and Louis Feustel in 1919 and 1920 for their emerging superhorse.

LONGEVITY

John Henry certainly wins any longevity contest with Man o' War.

At age three, when Man o' War's racetrack career was ending, John Henry's story was barely beginning. Over the remainder of his career, the gelding would run fifty-three times, winning thirty (including twenty-seven stakes), with eleven seconds and four thirds. John Henry even outlived Man o' War, lasting to see his thirty-second birthday, while Man o' War's great heart finally beat its last when the superstar was a revered thirty-year-old whose legend was already in the process of being forged and burnished.

Yes, as we have acknowledged previously, it is not Man o' War's fault that he was retired following his 3-year-old season. We can even acknowledge that given the circumstances of the time, Riddle's decision to retire his superhorse at age three was a good one.

But even giving Man o' War his 4-year-old season, and assuming he would continue to dominate whichever horses challenged him, he was surely not going to race at age five, at six, at seven, at eight, at nine. Man o' War was going to stud following his 4-year-old season at the very latest, and therefore John Henry was destined to win this longevity competition, against Man o' War, and, indeed, against every horse we have considered in this book.

There are simply no historic comparisons for a runner who earns Horse of the Year honors as a 9-year-old. At age nine, Exterminator won three allowance races under low weights, losing all four of his stakes engagements. Kelso and Forego and every other Thoroughbred of note was gone from the track at age nine or racing in dramatically reduced circumstances. A season worthy of a Horse of the Year title was well beyond their capabilities.

Man o' War and John Henry were two of the best ever to compete on the racetrack but in marvelously, almost miraculously different, ways. We may never see either's like again.

Swaps wins the 1956 Broward Handicap. (Keeneland Library Raftery Turfotos Collection)

CHAPTER 10

Record Times

Man o' War vs. Swaps

VIRTUALLY NO ONE WITH A KNOWLEDGE OF RACING WOULD DEIGN TO agree that Swaps, the 1955 Kentucky Derby winner and 1956 Horse of the Year, is in any way a challenger to Man o' War as history's most outstanding racehorse. Man o' War is, after all, a supremely daunting competitor, one whose exploits suggest that he was a singularly brilliant Thoroughbred.

But in one way, at least, Swaps was Man o' War's equal, if not his superior.

When it came to setting records, Swaps was among the most prolific Thoroughbreds in the sport's history. He towers over virtually every other Thoroughbred in this unique ability. And as we will see, this statement does not for a moment exclude the unstoppable force of nature who rewrote racing's record book during his perfect 1920 season.

Man o' War and Swaps actually had much in common. Both were red chestnut colts. They shared significant portions of their bloodlines; Man o' War, in fact, was one of Swaps's great-great-grandfathers. Both won the great majority of their races—twenty of twenty-one for Man o' War, nineteen of twenty-five for Swaps. Both were brilliant speedsters who could lead a race from flagfall to finish or come from off the pace, as needed.

Both were phenomenal sprinters who could win well beyond mere sprint distances. Both Man o' War and Swaps won at distances as short as five furlongs, as long as a mile-and-five-eighths. Perhaps, with another year of competition for Man o' War, a few more months of health for Swaps, each would have won racing even farther.

Both Man o' War and Swaps have long had plaques in racing's Hall of Fame, as have their trainers, Man o' War's Louis Feustel and Swaps's Mesh Tenney, and most of their jockeys: Johnny Loftus, Clarence Kummer, and Earl Sande, who rode Man o' War in all but one of his races; and John Longden and Bill Shoemaker, who rode Swaps to victory on seventeen occasions. "The Shoe" would occasionally declare, at least before he became the regular rider of Damascus and then Spectacular Bid, that Swaps was the greatest horse he had ever ridden. Man o' War's jockeys never bothered even comparing the great colt to their other rides; no one doubted that Man o' War was by far the best Thoroughbred each of them had had the rare good fortune to mount.

Both began their assaults on the record books during their 3-year-old campaigns, before following different paths—Man o' War to retirement and a long and successful stud career, Swaps to continue smashing records during a brilliant Horse of the Year campaign at age four.

Both Man o' War and Swaps could attribute one loss to human error. Man o' War's loss to Upset in the Sanford Memorial Stakes was attributable entirely to a terrible start and a bad ride; in Swaps's case, the culprit was Shoemaker, who in a rare lapse of racing judgment began easing his mount before the finish when victory seemed assured in Hollywood Park's 1956 Californian Stakes, allowing Porterhouse to steal the win with an unanticipated final-furlong stretch charge. The *Los Angeles Times*, which often provided fanciful headlines for the official charts of the popular colt's races—"Swaps Sparkles" and "Driving a Hard Swap(s)" are but two examples—took The Shoe to task following the Californian with a headline reading, "Shoe Blows One."

Both Man o' War and Swaps won Triple Crown races for owners who did not seek a sweep of the Derby, Preakness, and Belmont Stakes. Man o' War, of course, raced before the concept of "Triple Crown" had been coined in America. Riddle and Feustel were aware that other large purses awaited Man o' War. The Preakness, a week and a half following the Derby, would pay its winner $23,000; the Lawrence Realization would offer a winner's purse of $15,040. And the stable could cobble together a series of races that would considerably enhance Man o' War's bankroll and Riddle's prestige as the owner of a great horse.

By 1955, the Triple Crown was very much a goal for any owner of a top 3-year-old, but after Swaps won his Derby, inflicting a surprising loss on Horse of the Year-to-be Nashua, it was discovered that owner Rex Ellsworth had not nominated his colt (who had, after all, banked only $20,950 as a 2-year-old) for either the Preakness or Belmont. Learning that Swaps could not be supplemented into the Belmont and that a Triple Crown bid was therefore impossible, a chagrined Ellsworth made the decision to return the Derby winner to California, leaving Nashua to earn impressive victories, if somewhat hollow ones in the absence of his Derby conqueror, in the Preakness and the Belmont Stakes.

And both Man o' War and Swaps overturned some of racing's most hallowed records.

There are, of course, records and then there are *records*. For example, Sotemia's 7:10⅘ for four miles, set on October 7, 1912, is of historical interest but is not one to make heartbeats quicken for modern-day racegoers, since the heyday of the four-mile heat race ended over a century ago.

Records at seldom-run distances are noteworthy but not trumpeted in national headlines. Who's In Command's mile-and-eleven-sixteenths in 2:23 surely constituted a noble effort, but at a distance so seldom contested that it is more a historical oddity than a standard for greatness. Officer's Charm's three-and-a-half furlongs in 37.39 seconds, Awesome Daze's seven-and-a-half in 1:26.26, and Gold Star Deputy's mile-and-five-sixteenths in 2:07.32 may all fall one day. But will anyone notice?

But anyone who follows racing must surely respect Dr. Fager's world record mile in 1:32⅕, set at Arlington Park under 134 pounds on August 24, 1968, and now on the books for fifty-six years; no one can deny the specialness of Spectacular Bid's record 1:57⅘ mile-and-a-quarter, set at Santa Anita on February 3, 1980, and unexcelled since. We revere Secretariat's 2:24 clocking for the 1973 Belmont Stakes because we know that Triple Crown–caliber 3-year-olds have aimed at it for over a half-century without ever getting close. And we continue to marvel at Kelso's two miles in 3:19⅕, on the books since 1964 and, with two-mile races nearly gone from the calendar, increasingly unlikely ever to be excelled.

As Man o' War and Swaps transitioned from juveniles to sophomores, and then, in Swaps's case, to the age of four, the two all-time greats set those sorts of records.

Over a glorious 148-day stretch of 1920, Man o' War took his turn at rewriting the record books, and then Swaps, over a breathtaking 449 days of 1955 and 1956, rewrote them again. Racing historian William Robertson, in his monumental *The History of Thoroughbred Racing in America*, described Swaps's record-setting stretch as "the most amazing exhibition of speed in history," including in his consideration Man o' War's 3-year-old campaign.

Few racing fans, even in Swaps's home state of California, might have predicted so spectacular a career for the colt when he first stepped onto the track in 1954.

His initial start, as a 12-to-1 outsider in an otherwise nondescript Hollywood Park maiden race, had produced a galloping three-length Swaps victory, rewarding his handful of backers with a $27.20 windfall for each $2 win ticket. But despite this promising beginning to a racing career, Swaps would be favored in none of his remaining five starts as a juvenile. He was 7-to-1 when finishing third in Hollywood Park's Westchester Stakes, 9-to-2 when winning the June Juvenile, 6-to-1 when running third in the Haggin Stakes, nearly 10-to-1 when he finished out of the money in the Howard Stakes, and 5-to-1 in his final juvenile effort, winning a common Santa Anita allowance race by a matter of inches.

It was in that final Santa Anita start that Swaps first made the acquaintance of Shoemaker, then age twenty-three and already the leading money-winning rider in the nation in 1951, '53, and '54. Both owner Ellsworth and trainer Tenney were practicing Mormons who tithed the customary 10 percent to the church, and jockey Johnny Burton, who had ridden Swaps in his first five races, was also a devout Mormon. It was not until Burton left the stable to undertake a religious mission that Shoemaker took the saddle as Swaps's new jockey.

But despite the colt's substantially improved jockey situation, Californians were viewing Swaps no more optimistically as 1955 dawned. Making his first start as a 3-year-old at Santa Anita, Swaps was the 4-to-1 third choice in the San Vicente Stakes, which he won in the mud by three-and-a-half lengths. Adding injury to insult, the colt was then found to have incurred a hoof infection, which cost him a few days' conditioning after trainer Tenney drained the infection and created a cushioning pad to ride between the hoof and the shoe. Swaps next contested the Santa Anita Derby, still only the 7-to-2 second choice to the entry of Jean's Joe and Blue Ruler. He drew post position twelve in a fourteen-horse field and raced wide but nevertheless prevailed by a half-length.

And then, having perhaps finally convinced skeptical Californians that he belonged among Derby-quality 3-year-olds, Swaps was on his way to Kentucky to test his skills against those of Nashua, the elite Belair Stud's talented scion of Nasrullah, who had drawn headlines as a 2-year-old by winning six of eight starts, including such traditional East Coast champion-makers as the Hopeful and the Futurity, and $192,865 in purses. As the Run for the Roses approached, Swaps, with his southern California–based resume, was considered more an oddity than a legitimate Derby contender. Perhaps he could run his best race on Derby Day—and finish second.

For Nashua, runner-up to Summer Tan for 1954's 2-year-old championship, was enhancing his credentials as the deserving Derby favorite. He won Hialeah's Flamingo Stakes and the Florida Derby at Gulfstream, and New York's Wood Memorial, then contested at Jamaica. Coming through the first two unscathed, and prevailing over Summer Tan by a head nod in the Wood, Nashua arrived at Churchill Downs the obvious Derby Day choice.

Swaps, departing the Golden State in near anonymity, was entered in a six-furlong pre-Derby prep race at Churchill Downs and galloped home by eight-and-a-half lengths as the 3-to-10 favorite, with 2-to-1 Trim Destiny, a former claiming horse that had won the Arkansas Derby, the distant runner-up in an undistinguished field. With one week remaining following this modest workout of a victory, Swaps would remain on the sidelines until the First Saturday in May.

The eighty-first Run for the Roses began as many had predicted, with Shoemaker hustling Swaps, the 2-to-1 second choice in the wagering, into the early lead, with the gritty Trim Destiny second early, but soon to fade to last, and 6-to-5 Nashua and 9-to-2 third choice Summer Tan in close pursuit.

The Belair colt launched a determined challenge as the field turned into the stretch, moving alongside Swaps for a few strides, but

Shoemaker had nursed the California colt skillfully through the early furlongs, and Swaps repelled his rival's charge and pulled away, winning by a length-and-a-half, with Summer Tan another six-and-a-half lengths back. For the first time since Morvich in 1922, a California-bred was the Kentucky Derby winner.

Tenney, a truly dedicated horseman, reportedly had slept in the stall with Swaps the evening before the Derby, but he celebrated the colt's sensational victory with a rare night of luxury: Instead of bedding down with the Derby winner for the night, the trainer slept in his car, parked a few yards from the stable door.

To some, Swaps's surprising Derby triumph seemed worthy of poetry, and at least one example of Swaps-inspired verse made it to the *Louisville Courier-Journal* sports page. While it may not be Shakespeare, Wordsworth, or Frost, we applaud it as a worthy effort . . . and present, in all its glory, James O. Nall's "So, Swaps Wins the Derby":

SO, SWAPS WINS THE DERBY

By James O. Nall of Marion, Ky.

Here's to the horse that won it!
And here's to the race he won!
What other horse could have done it,
In the faultless way it was done?
His record will go on the roster—
His name, and the time and the date,
He'll rank with the great ones who've run here.
No matter how well they rate!

I don't know much about horses—
Yes, what I don't know fills a tome;
But Swaps—what a name!—struck my fancy,
And Shoemaker rode him home.

Here's to the crowd that saw it!
And here's to the race they saw!
What other racetrack could draw it
And run it without fuss or flaw?

The running will go on the record—
The date and the time and the place;
It equaled all others they've had here,
No matter what horse won the race!

It ain't the money I'm winning—
No, I won't vacation in Rome;
But Swaps looked the best for my money,
And Shoemaker rode him home.

Here's to the men who've done it!
And here's to the way it was done!
What other men could have run it,
In the perfect way it was run?
The record will stand for the ages—
The men, and the horse, and the day;
They'll rank with all others who've been here,
No matter the time or the May!

I took a look at the horses—
Yes, whirled 'em around in my dome;
But Swaps took my eye as a gamble,
And Shoemaker rode him home.

Back at Hollywood Park, Swaps both dominated his California-based rivals and began his assault on the record book. Following a twelve-length laugher in the Will Rogers Stakes, he overpowered a field of older rivals that included 1954 Derby winner Determine in the mile-and-a-sixteenth Californian Stakes, in the process clipping two-fifths of a second off the existing world record for the distance.

Following a six-length triumph in the ten-furlong Westerner Stakes, run in a sparkling but non-record-setting 2:00⅗, Swaps journeyed 2,000 miles to Chicago, where he won Washington Park's mile-and-three-sixteenths American Derby easily over Traffic Judge, handling turf for the first time and establishing a new American record of 1:54⅗.

Nashua by this time had won not only the Preakness and Belmont but the Dwyer and the Arlington Classic, and the racing world was clamoring for a return match with Swaps. This was arranged for Washington Park on August 31, 1955, at a mile-and-a-quarter. In what the sporting press dubbed "The Race of the Century," the purse would be $100,000—winner take all.

It had rained the night before, and Washington Park's drying-out track was labeled "good" at race time. What was known to Nashua's jockey, Eddie Arcaro, however, was that while the area nearest the inner rail was still fairly deep, the portion of the track away from the extreme inside had dried out nicely, but outside of that area was softer. The crafty Arcaro determined to place Nashua in the fastest area and keep Swaps in the deeper going. As the *Daily Racing Form*'s chart call described it, Arcaro implemented this strategy perfectly:

> *NASHUA hustled out of the gate, went to the front at once and set the pace under restraint for about five furlongs, then drew out slightly and, withstanding a mild challenge from SWAPS around the stretch turn, went rather wide on the bend seemingly in search of the best going, then drew out while not being put to severe pressure after entering the last quarter.*

Nashua's winning margin was six-and-a-half lengths, and possibly it was the exertion of that historic contest that caused him, three and a half weeks later, to lose as the odds-on favorite in Belmont Park's Sysonby Stakes. But the Belair colt came back to win the two-mile Jockey Club Gold Cup in the muck by five lengths and was an easy choice as not only the season's top 3-year-old but as Horse of the Year. Swaps, amid rumblings that an undisclosed injury may have affected him during the encounter with Nashua, would not race again in 1955. He, and Ellsworth and Tenney, endured a long, desolate train ride back to California.

Swaps began his 4-year-old campaign with a victory in a February 17 prep race, then was shipped to Florida's Gulfstream Park, where under a 130-pound impost he eclipsed the world record for one mile and seventy yards in winning the Broward Handicap with a 1:39⅗ clocking.

Returning to California, Swaps next started in Hollywood Park's one-and-a-sixteenth-mile Californian Stakes, the infamous "Shoe Blows One" race. Swaps's next engagement was in Hollywood Park's Argonaut

Handicap, where it was evident Shoemaker had learned to ride his mount from start to finish, running the mile in 1:33⅕, two lengths faster than Citation's existing mile record, in fractions—:22⅖ for the quarter-mile, 1:08⅘ for three-quarters, 1:20⅘ for seven furlongs—guaranteed to overwhelm the opposition.

Nor were the challengers going to approach more closely in Swaps's next start, Hollywood Park's mile-and-a-sixteenth Inglewood Handicap. Bobby Brocato tried front-running tactics this time, slowing the early pace to :23⅕ and :46, but neither he nor any of the other starters were up to a mile-and-a-sixteenth in a world record 1:39, and Swaps pulled away to an unchallenged two-and-three-quarter-length win. This triumph was followed by the traditional Hollywood Park Independence Day offering, the nine-furlong American Handicap, which featured Swaps, perhaps having an off day, merely equaling Noor's 1:46⅘ world record under 130 pounds.

There was no reason at this point for the Swaps entourage to forsake Hollywood Park's friendly environs, and ten days later Swaps was back, once again carrying 130 pounds, in the mile-and-a-quarter Hollywood Gold Cup. This time it was Rejected's 1:59⅗ track record that fell, by a full second, with Swaps merely galloping at the end. Had Swaps been challenged down the stretch, it is possible that he would have eclipsed Noor's 1:58⅕ world record for the distance.

Perhaps Swaps's greatest effort was to come next. Concluding his sensational run at Hollywood Park, the Ellsworth colt gave Honey's Alibi twenty-two pounds and a four-and-a-quarter-length shellacking in the season-ending Sunset Handicap, racing the mile-and-five-eighths in 2:38⅕, shattering the hallowed record that had once been set by Man o' War in his one-hundred-length Lawrence Realization runaway.

Swaps's record for the distance remains on the books as this sentence is being penned, some sixty-eight years later, and is one of the handful of racing records that seems unlikely ever to be bettered.

And now it was back to Chicago for an uncharacteristic seventh-place finish on turf in Washington Park's Arch Ward Memorial Handicap, followed by a victory at one mile on dirt in the Washington Park Handicap, establishing yet another track record with a 1:33⅖ clocking.

The public was again clamoring for another Swaps-Nashua rematch, but all possibility evaporated when Swaps, in Maryland preparing for the

Washington, D.C. International Handicap, fractured his right hind leg during a workout. There were hints that the colt's life was threatened, but Swaps responded readily to treatment. He entered stud duty at Darby Dan Farm and would ultimately live out his days at Spendthrift, in a stall not far from that of his Kentucky Derby victim, Nashua. Swaps died in 1972 at age twenty.

RECORD TIMES

Man o' War's and Swaps's track, American, and world records seen in tabular form are truly impressive:

Table 10-1: Records Set by Man o' War

Date	Track	Race	Distance	Time	Wt.	Record
19-May-20	Bel	Withers S.	1 mile	1:35⅘	115	NAR
12-June-20	Bel	Belmont S.	1⅜ mi.	2:14⅕	126	NWR
10-July-20	Aqu	Dwyer S.	1⅛ mi.	1:49⅕	126	NWR
21-Aug.-20	Sar	Travers S.	1¼ mi.	2:01⅘	129	ETR
4-Sept.-20	Bel	Lawrence Realiz.	1⅝ mi.	2:40⅘	126	NAR
11-Sept.-20	Bel	Jockey Club S.	1½ mi.	2:28⅘	118	NAR
18-Sept.-20	HDG	Potomac H.	1 1/16 mi.	1:44⅘	138	NTR
12-Oct.-20	Ken	Ken Pk Gold Cup	1¼ mi.	2:03	120	NTR

Table 10-2: Records Set by Swaps

Date	Track	Race	Distance	Time	Wt.	Record
12-June-55	Hol	Californian S.	1 1/16 mi.	1:40⅖	115	NWR
20-Aug.-55	Was	Amer. Derby	1 3/16 mi.	1:54⅗	126	ETR–T
14-Apr.-56	GP	Broward H.	1 mi. 70 yds	1:39⅗	130	NWR
9-June-56	Hol	Argonaut H.	1 mile	1:33⅕	128	NWR
23-June-56	Hol	Inglewood H.	1 1/16 mi.	1:39	130	NWR
4-July-56	Hol	American H.	1⅛ mi.	1:46⅘	130	EWR
14-July-56	Hol	Hol Gold Cup	1¼ mi.	1:58⅗	130	NTR
25-July-56	Hol	Sunset H.	1⅝ mi.	2:38⅕	130	NWR
3-Sept.-56	Was	Wash. Pk. H.	1 mile	1:33⅖	130	NTR

Comparing the two on the most basic level, Swaps set nine records of one sort or another; Man o' War set eight. Swaps was credited with five new world records (labeled "NWR" in the chart), another world record that he equaled on dirt (EWR), two new track records (NTR), and one track record that he equaled on turf (ETR-T). Man o' War was credited with two new world records (NWR), three new American records (NAR), two new track records (NTR), and with equaling another track record (ETR).

But it should also be noted that Man o' War's 2:01⅘ clocking in the Travers was considered merely a track record rather than a world standard only because it was being compared to Whisk Broom II's 2:00 clocking for the 1913 Suburban Handicap, at Belmont Park on June 28, 1913.

A separate finish line, some forty yards past the regular line, was used for the 1913 Suburban, and horsemen on the scene that day insisted that official clocker W. H. Barretto had snapped his stopwatch when Whisk Broom passed the original line, rather than waiting for the winner to reach the real finish. When Barretto insisted that his time was correct, it gained The Jockey Club's recognition as an official record, but there is lingering suspicion that Whisk Broom was incorrectly credited with the ten-furlong world standard.

It is therefore possible, even probable, that Sir Barton had run the fastest mile-and-a-quarter in history in winning the 1920 Saratoga Handicap in 2:01⅘, and that Man o' War equaled the world record when he earned the same clocking in winning the Travers three weeks later. In the absence of a time machine to return us to Belmont Park on Whisk Broom's controversy-ridden June day, we are inclined to credit Man o' War with equaling the world record, given the on-the-scene testimony of so many experienced horsemen regarding the Suburban.

Swaps's record times were uniformly faster than Man o' War's. His mile records were two seconds faster; his mile-and-a-quarter record was faster by more than three seconds. When Swaps shattered Man o' War's long-standing mile-and-five-eighths standard, he did so by running more than two seconds faster. But Swaps's faster times do not by themselves suggest that Swaps was Man o' War's superior. It is the nature of time records to improve; a slower time than the existing record is, by definition, not a record.

But unquestionably, the records that Swaps was overcoming were faster than the ones challenged by Man o' War. In no small measure, this relates to the number of horses that had raced to establish the records the two horses defeated. By the time Man o' War reached the races in 1919, approximately 69,274 Thoroughbred foals had been registered to race in America. Many of those foals never made it to the races; all but a handful were simply too slow to threaten even the records in existence at the time. The best of them, the ones whose times overcame the existing records of the day, were the ones whose records Man o' War outran.

For Swaps, foaled thirty-five years after Man o' War, the corresponding number of registered foals was roughly 250,618, or 3.6 times the number of runners that preceded Man o' War into the world. Which translates to this: Swaps overcame faster records in part because the runners who set those records were 3.6 times more likely to have included some who were faster than the runners who set the standards Man o' War had defeated.

Among the runners foaled between Man o' War in 1917 and Swaps in 1952 were some of the greats of the game: Zev and Princess Doreen; Blue Larkspur and Gallant Fox; Equipoise and Cavalcade; Myrtlewood and Omaha; Seabiscuit and War Admiral; Whirlaway and Alsab; Count Fleet and Twilight Tear; Gallorette and Assault; Citation and Noor; Bewitch and Two Lea; Bed o' Roses and Hill Prince; Tom Fool and Native Dancer. None of these outstanding Thoroughbreds, each with a plaque in the Hall of Fame, had yet drawn breath when Man o' War was shattering stopwatches; many had a role in setting the records smashed by Swaps.

Which, comparing Swaps to Man o' War, still does not necessarily make Swaps the better horse, or even the better record-setter.

There remain other factors to be considered—for example, whether Swaps might have raced over faster track surfaces than Man o' War. Hollywood Park, where Swaps felled most of his records, was a notoriously speed-favoring track, one that was maligned, particularly by the Eastern press, as being composed of India rubber, running downhill. That blazing-fast Hollywood Park track surface was surely an advantage that must be counted against Swaps.

But Man o' War also raced over track surfaces that had, at the time, been considered faster than normal, perhaps even deliberately made faster. An article in the Brooklyn *Times Union*, dated August 12, 1919 (ironically, the day before the Sanford Memorial), noted that "[n]early every winner yesterday [at Saratoga] ran his race in faster time than he had ever made before, and with no real stake horses starting, the time in two of the events missed the track record by only a fraction of a second." What could have caused such a phenomenon if not a hyper-fast track?

Dorothy Ours, in *Man o' War: A Legend Like Lightning*, noted that before the colt's record-shattering Lawrence Realization effort, the *Daily Racing Form* had stated that "the Belmont Park track is faster than ever before in its history." And Ours described how, according to one turf-writer, Kenilworth Park, site of Man o' War's career-ending confrontation with Sir Barton, had been worked into "perfect condition" for the race: "perfect for world-record speed, that is." Another knowledgeable observer described "the cement-like condition of the track."

Following his retirement, Swaps brought with him into the stud barn and ultimately into the afterlife an irrefutable reputation for blazing speed. The *American Racing Manual* described him as "endowed with a spectacular order of speed," and Edward L. Bowen, in *The Great Ones*, declared that in Swaps's case, "World Record" became virtually "a synonym for his name."

Swaps carried 130 pounds to victory six times in seven tries and set records on all six occasions; Man o' War carried 130 pounds or more to a record-breaking time only once (although it was, to be sure, a crushing 138-pound impost). And we must also consider that Swaps started twenty-five times, Man o' War only twenty-one. Give Man o' War those four more starts, and perhaps that one additional record would have been his.

It would seem almost a heresy to suggest that Swaps might be compared favorably to Man o' War. But one could certainly opine that Swaps held his own in the area of record-setting, and perhaps he more than held his own. It would take an extraordinarily talented racehorse to be declared unquestionably faster than this one.

Given all of the above, the decision between Man o' War and Swaps in the category Setting Records can only be a draw.

Kelso wins the 1961 Brooklyn Handicap. (Keeneland Library Morgan Collection)

CHAPTER 11

Awards

Man o' War vs. Kelso

How many times must a racehorse be voted the best before we agree, by acclamation, that he was, in fact, the best?

It is a question that fans of Kelso must surely have been asking themselves for years, a question that all of us, as racing fans, as racing historians, *should* have been asking ourselves since Mrs. Allaire duPont's magnificent gelding left the races in 1966 with thirty-nine victories in sixty-three starts and $1,977,896 in total earnings, a figure that would remain the pinnacle of equine earning power until Affirmed finally toppled him from the top spot in 1979, thirteen inflation-packed years later.

Voting for Horse of the Year and other divisional champions has been the province of various groups over the years, but despite this, the level of agreement among the voters regarding who should be the season-ending champions has been substantial. And between 1960 and 1964, there was no difference of opinion whatsoever as to who should reign as Horse of the Year. For five consecutive years, it was Kelso, Kelso, Kelso, Kelso, and Kelso.

From the beginnings of year-end championship voting, in 1936, until the present day, only Kelso has won five Horse of the Year titles. And when the editors of the *Blood-Horse*, in their work *The Great Ones*, pooled their considerable collective knowledge of the sport's history in an effort to determine champions from the days prior to that original 1936 poll, they could find no other horses, however dominant, however brilliant, deserving of more than two overall championships. Ten Broeck was found worthy of two, as was Hindoo, Miss Woodford, Salvator, Henry of Navarre, Commando, Hermis, Colin, Fitz Herbert, Sarazen, and Equipoise—great horses all, but they fell far short of Kelso's accomplishment.

If one goes back, then, as far as the *Blood-Horse*'s first unofficial award for the year 1870 and continues through 153 seasons of racing, concluding with the 2023 Eclipse Award presented to Horse of the Year Cody's Wish, it is Kelso and only Kelso who has won five Horse of the Year trophies. Forego won three, from 1974 through 1976, and the most for any other Thoroughbred racehorse is two. Kelso was better, longer, than any other horse in the history of the sport.

And it was not merely Horse of the Year trophies that Kelso dominated. Only Kelso has won double-digit championships of any kind. With 2023's year-end titlists in the books, the ten Thoroughbreds with the most divisional (i.e., other than Horse of the Year) championship trophies on their owners' overflowing mantels are Forego, John Henry, Kelso, and Round Table with five apiece; and Beholder, Buckpasser, Busher, Dr. Fager, Fort Marcy, and Wise Dan with four.

There are 21 who won three, 73 who won two, and 502, each an authentic champion and each richly deserving of our respect and admiration, have earned a single championship.

Five Horse of the Year titles, and ten year-end championships, are the unique legacy of Kelso. Can anyone reading this line, in this modern era of short equine careers and early retirements, imagine that there might be even one other horse that might possibly match, or even exceed, the gleaming hardware in the duPont family's trophy case attributable to this one extraordinary racehorse? Sixty years after Kelso won his fifth Horse of the Year title, nearly a half-century after Forego took home his third, the chances seem increasingly remote.

The Bohemia Stable's dark bay or brown gelding by Your Host out of the Count Fleet mare Maid of Flight (through his dam, Kelso was therefore a great-grandson of Man o' War) first faced the starter as a 2-year-old on September 4, 1959. He went into action as a gelding, having shown his first trainer, Dr. John Lee, that he would not race effectively with his original equipment. It is both racing's loss and racing's gain that while there would never be Kelso offspring, we did have the privilege of seeing Kelso at his best. And he was certainly something to see.

One of the more difficult tasks any handicapper must confront is determining which of a group of first-time starters in a 2-year-old maiden race is well intended and may be worthy of a wager, which ones will never be worthwhile, and which might be entered merely to gain the experience of racing. As readers of the various chapters of this volume will note, it is surprisingly easy to miss on the first start of what will one day be an equine superstar.

The handicappers at Atlantic City missed badly on the first start of Kelso, who won his maiden effort at 6-to-1 odds. Perhaps a few consoled themselves by noting that he covered the six furlongs in 1:13⅘, hardly an indication that this gelding might be anything out of the ordinary.

There was a good class of 2-year-olds at Atlantic City in 1959, and in his remaining juvenile starts Kelso ran afoul of two of them. Sent postward ten days later at 4-to-1 odds, he ran a close second to Dress Up, who the following year would be stakes-placed on the West Coast; returning nine days after that, the gelding was again second, this time by three-quarters of a length to Windy Sands, who would win stakes at four and five and earn nearly $200,000, not a pittance in those days.

There followed five and a half seasons of what can only be called exceptional brilliance. Allowed by new trainer Carl Hanford to mature until midyear of his 3-year-old season, and thereby missing the Triple Crown races, Kelso returned to the track in a six-furlong Monmouth Park allowance race, winning off by ten lengths and covering the distance in 1:10. He was in action again a few weeks later at Aqueduct, winning a one-mile allowance race by twelve lengths in a swift 1:34⅘. The New Jersey horseplayers hastily reconsidered: This gelding could, indeed, be something out of the ordinary.

After a dull effort in the Arlington Classic, Kelso rebounded to win Monmouth's Choice Handicap, traveling the mile-and-a-sixteenth in 1:41⅕. This was the beginning of an eleven-race winning streak that would both clinch Kelso's first Horse of the Year title and create a running start on a second title the following year.

It is tempting to simply follow Kelso, season by season, as he demolishes the best that each new generation of runners can unleash upon him: T.V. Lark and Beau Purple and Carry Back and Jaipur and Ridan and Crimson Satan and Never Bend and Mongo and Gun Bow and Roman Brother, among others, appearing, most of them multiple times, among Kelso's beaten foes. There are Hall of Famers among those names, and Roman Brother shared Horse of the Year honors with the filly Moccasin in 1965. But Roman Brother and Moccasin couldn't take home their shares of the trophy until Kelso was ready to relinquish it.

In the meantime, Kelso won five Jockey Club Gold Cups, this when the Gold Cup was a two-mile race with championship implications, three Whitneys and three Woodwards, two Suburbans and two Stymies and two Aqueduct Handicaps. He missed by a nose taking home a fourth Woodward trophy, missed a third Suburban by a head. He won thirteen times in twenty-four starts under 130 pounds or more, winning the 1961 Brooklyn under 136. By winning the Metropolitan, Suburban, and Brooklyn Handicaps, he became just the third horse—with Whisk Broom II in 1913 and Tom Fool in 1953—to sweep New York's historic Handicap Triple Crown.

Records? At age three, Kelso ran a 1:48⅖ in 1960's mile-and-an-eighth Discovery Handicap, clipping two-fifths of a second off the track record. He ran the Lawrence Realization in 2:40⅘, equaling Man o' War's time for the mile-and-five-eighths. His 3:19⅖ clocking for his first Jockey Club Gold Cup, this one run at Aqueduct, demolished the existing track and American record. As a 4-year-old, his 2:00⅗ in the Woodward equaled Aqueduct's mile-and-a-quarter track record; at five, the Jockey Club Gold Cup now moved to Belmont Park, Kelso won the race for the third time with a track record 3:19⅘ clocking.

In a single day, December 1, 1962, Kelso won the Governor's Plate at Garden State, became the fifth horse to exceed $1 million in total earnings, and set a new track record for the mile-and-a-half distance. Prepping at Saratoga for his fourth try at the Washington, D.C. International, Kelso tuned up with a 1:46⅗ mile-and-an-eighth, tying the American record for the distance on grass.

But before that D.C. International try, there would be a 3:19⅕ clocking for his final Jockey Club Gold Cup, which remains the fastest two miles on dirt any racehorse has ever run (or likely ever will). That historic two miles also placed Kelso in the unique position of having run the fastest, second-fastest, and third-fastest time for a major race, a feat he accomplished with his 3:19⅖ Jockey Club Gold Cup in 1960, 3:19⅘ in 1962, and 3:19⅕ in 1964.

I have searched in vain for another instance of a Thoroughbred winning a major stakes race five times. Exterminator won four consecutive Saratoga Cups between 1919 and 1922, but while one can give "Old Bones" his fair share of credit for this rare feat, four wins is not the same as five, and one of those Saratoga Cup victories was a walkover. Kelso faced live competition in all five of his Gold Cup victories.

There was one misstep along the way to immortality. A 1964 California foray was aborted early when he ran poorly in Hollywood Park's Los Angeles Handicap and Californian Stakes. Returned to more familiar environs, Kelso hefted 136 pounds and scored in an Aqueduct overnight handicap, won his fifth Jockey Club Gold Cup, and finally, after three agonizingly close misses in the Washington, D.C. International Stakes, powered away with a four-and-a-half-length victory. Russian jockey Nicolai Nasibov, aboard third finisher Aniline, was said to have described the race's climax in just two words, "Kelso . . . whoosh!"

At some point during this stretch of unexcelled excellence, even the hardened fans of New York racing adopted Kelso as more than merely a reliable win wager. A reporter noted one instance of this and recorded the emotional response of Mrs. duPont, Kelso's owner:

> [T]he field pulled up and Kelso jogged casually back to unsaddle. Perfect strangers thumped one another on the back. Rebel whoops and yells rent the welkin, and there was a continuous roar of applause that did not end until Kelso disappeared from view . . . the scene was like a Roman triumph . . . Mrs. duPont, damp eyed . . . remarked, "They really love him."

But by age eight, Kelso was no longer the colossus fans had come to appreciate over the previous five seasons, and he was sent to the track only six times, winning three. In September 1965, he was stricken with an eye infection that lingered far too long, jeopardizing and then destroying his chance at a sixth Horse of the Year trophy. At nine, he was tried in a six-furlong Hialeah allowance race in the hope of boosting his earnings total beyond the $2 million mark, but he managed only a dispirited fourth, and it was decided that $1.98 million would have to do.

It was a foregone conclusion that Kelso would be elected to racing's Hall of Fame in his first year of eligibility, and 1967 was his year of enshrinement. When trainer Carl Hanford was inducted at age ninety in 2006, he responded with humility, and accorded the champion all the credit he deserved. "It's a great honor," Hanford remarked, "but Kelso is the one who put me there."

AWARDS

Kelso is the greatest horse in the history of the American turf, if the sole criterion is awards won. His ten post-season awards top all Thoroughbreds, and even if we consider that official awards in racing did not begin until 1936, it seems certain that no other horse would have earned as many.

If we give full credence to the considered opinions of those who spend their years watching and writing about and evaluating the best racehorses in the country—and this author does emphatically grant them that credence—then Kelso's unremitting ability to project himself as the best of his kind, again and again (and again and again and again), demonstrates that he is not merely the most outstanding runner of his time. It creates a considerable argument that he may have been the best of all time. It is well within the realm of possibility.

Since Man o' War had no opportunity to earn year-end championship trophies, it may seem pointless to compare him to Kelso in this category. A 10-to-0 shutout for Kelso rings hollow if Man o' War was never even allowed to swing the bat.

But fortunately, the *Blood-Horse*'s important efforts to determine retrospective championships for those long-ago years provide a guideline. Their opinions regarding Horses of the Year, for example, allow us to improve the score to Kelso 10, Man o' War 1, for the latter's unquestioned rule over his magical 1920 season. The *Blood-Horse* editors also selected retrospective divisional champions for those years, and Man o' War was chosen the top 2-year-old of 1919 and the best 3-year-old of 1920. Who else could it have been? Now the score is Kelso 10, Man o' War 3.

And perhaps we can award Man o' War one more trophy. The *Blood-Horse*'s choice for best older horse of 1920 was Exterminator, who won ten times in seventeen starts and led the nation's older campaigners with earnings of $52,405. Exterminator would also earn at least a share of the handicap title for 1921 and 1922.

But Man o' War won all eleven of his starts at age three, gave older horses a shot in the weight-for-age Jockey Club Stakes (their owners declined the invitation), defeated 4-year-old Sir Barton with ease, and earned $166,340, nearly three times Exterminator's total. Man o' War earned more in that one race than all the purses Exterminator won for the entire year. Perhaps Man o' War was not, strictly speaking, a handicap horse, but he accomplished far more than any handicap horse active in 1920 and seems deserving of at least a share of the award, which would bring the score to Kelso 10, Man o' War 4.

It still isn't enough.

Both Kelso and Man o' War are longtime members of the Hall of Fame, and if there were an inner-sanctum Hall of Fame, with only the best of the best admitted, they would occupy that august plateau as well. Both will forever have their backers in racing's endless discussion of the most outstanding horses of all time.

But in the Awards category, even Man o' War falls short. It seems impossible that in this category any other racehorse in the long history of Thoroughbred racing can possibly be mentioned in the same breath with the mighty Kelso.

Spectacular Bid wins 1980 San Fernando Stakes. (Credit—Keeneland Library Mochon Collection)

CHAPTER 12

Money Earnings

Man o' War vs. Spectacular Bid

As noted in the Introduction, there is no shortage of ways a good racehorse can demonstrate its excellence: by dominating its opponents; by defeating horses of demonstrated talent; by winning as a juvenile and continuing to do so at ages three and four and, if asked to do so, thereafter; by winning gamely; by winning major races; by winning large amounts of money; by carrying high weights and defeating horses carrying less; by running record times; by winning year-end awards; by being selected to racing's Hall of Fame . . .

Spectacular Bid achieved every bit of this. And if one counts world records that are never broken as a particularly special feat, it can be said that Spectacular Bid achieved a nearly unique level of equine greatness.

On February 3, 1980, the recently turned 4-year-old broke from the Santa Anita starting gate in the Charles H. Strub Stakes. He had already won the first two legs of Santa Anita's unique Strub Series, races limited to the generation turning four years of age, scoring by five lengths in the seven-furlong Malibu Stakes and by a length-and-a-half at 1-to-20 odds in the mile-and-an-eighth San Fernando. The Strub Stakes was a mile-and-a-quarter, a distance that "The Bid," as Californians were now calling him, had handled with panache in the previous year's Kentucky Derby. Trainers had therefore sought easier challenges for many would-be Strub competitors: The Bid would face only three opponents in the race.

One minute, fifty-seven and four-fifths seconds after the starting gate sprang open, the big gray colt reached the finish three-and-a-quarter lengths clear of longtime foe Flying Paster. The Bid's clocking eclipsed by two-fifths of a second Noor's world record for the mile-and-a-quarter, commonly designated "America's classic distance." It had been on the books for nearly thirty years.

And as this chapter is being written, it is now precisely forty-four years and 168 days, or, if the reader prefers, 16,239 days and counting, since Spectacular Bid's record-demolishing run, and still nobody's horse has ever run a faster ten furlongs on dirt.

A $37,000 yearling purchase, Spectacular Bid began his career at Pimlico in June 1978 in a five-and-a-half-furlong maiden event, racing in the silks of the Hawksworth Farm. Trained by Grover "Buddy" Delp and ridden in his debut by eighteen-year-old apprentice jockey Ron Franklin, the son of Bold Bidder was dismissed by the Pimlico crowd as the race's fourth wagering choice, at odds of 6-to-1. His wire-to-wire win, accomplished in 1:04⅗, just two ticks off the track record for the distance, earned the winning stable a $3,000 check—the first handful of purse money for a colt that would eventually top the career earnings list. Those who had found something to like in Spectacular Bid's workouts earned a $12.60 win payoff for their perspicacity.

This captured the attention of Baltimore racegoers, so much so that in his next start the colt was anointed the 3-to-10 favorite. The 2-year-old performed like a runner with a future, swamping his four foes by eight lengths and shaving two additional stopwatch ticks off his debut's clocking. Seldom does a 2-year-old making his second lifetime start equal a track record, but it was becoming increasingly clear that standards for normal 2-year-olds might not apply to this one.

Having worn out his welcome with allowance-level 2-year-olds, Spectacular Bid was now elevated into the stakes ranks, perhaps a race or two too soon. As the 8-to-5 favorite in the second division of Monmouth Park's Tyro Stakes, Spectacular Bid was unable to overcome a sloppy track, a poor start, and a wide trip, sloshing home fourth behind the undefeated Groton High. That year's Tyro Stakes drew a decidedly better-than-average group of 2-year-olds: The first division was won by Coastal, who the following year would win the Belmont Stakes; the second division included Spectacular Bid, who would win the Derby and the Preakness.

Sent to Delaware Park eighteen days later and stretched to six furlongs in the Dover Stakes, The Bid again fell short, this time as the even money favorite, finishing two-and-a-half lengths behind Strike Your Colors, with Spy Charger five-and-a-half lengths farther back.

Two consecutive losses had temporarily given superstardom a less likely look for Spectacular Bid, an impression he utterly destroyed in his next start, the seven-furlong World Playground Stakes at Atlantic City. Sent off at generous 5-to-1 odds, Spectacular Bid broke with the early leaders and increased his margin from there, winning by fifteen spectacular lengths in 1:20⅘, a sensational time for a 2-year-old. This earned him a spot two weeks later in the Grade I Champagne Stakes.

The Champagne was viewed as a three-horse race, with Spectacular Bid, Calumet Farm's undefeated Tim the Tiger, and General Assembly, a son of Secretariat, the serious contenders in a field of six. With jockey Jorge Velasquez replacing Franklin in the saddle, Spectacular Bid quickly took over and pulled away, opening a lead that grew to four lengths at midstretch. Velazquez allowed The Bid to relax through the final furlong, and the pair completed the mile with a two-and-three-quarter-length lead, stopping the timer at a swift 1:34⅘.

"He's the champion," proclaimed trainer Delp. "If they want the crown, they're going to have to come to Laurel," where Spectacular Bid would be concluding his season in the rich Grade 1 Laurel Futurity. First, however, he would sidetrack to The Meadowlands for the $137,500 Young America Stakes, in those days another Grade 1 contest, and, with 122 pounds up and Velasquez in the saddle, would barely win in a three-horse driving finish, with Strike Your Colors hanging on stubbornly for second and Instrument Landing third.

The tight Young America finish might have reminded horseplayers that 2-year-old Spectacular Bid had been beatable at times, and the colt, who had been the 3-to-10 favorite at The Meadowlands, closed at

9-to-10 at Laurel, but the $142,280 Laurel Futurity provided almost no drama. Franklin—under orders from Delp to "ride him out. Keep on driving. I want these people to see how much horse he really is"—went to the whip at least ten times, pushing the colt to a lead that ultimately reached eight-and-a-half lengths, with a track record 1:41⅗ clocking, rendering General Assembly, Clever Trick, and Tim the Tiger little more than spectators. A season-ending six-length romp in the Heritage Stakes at Pennsylvania's Keystone Race Track cemented the 2-year-old championship, and with seven wins in nine starts and division-leading earnings of $384,484, Spectacular Bid went to the sidelines as the reigning favorite for the Kentucky Derby.

Having concluded 1978 on a five-race winning streak, Spectacular Bid resurfaced on February 7, 1979, in an early-season Derby prep, Gulfstream Park's $25,000-added Hutcheson Stakes. Sent off at 1-to-20 odds, the champion tracked Northern Prospect for a half-mile, then exploded into a lead that was three-and-a-quarter lengths at the wire, with Lot o' Gold, Northern Prospect, and Medaille D'Or well behind. It was an impressive seasonal debut, but this was merely a preview of the heroics that were looming on Spectacular Bid's horizon.

With romping victories in the Fountain of Youth (by eight-and-a-half lengths), the Florida Derby (by four-and-a-half), and the Flamingo (a twelve-length runaway), Spectacular Bid both padded his bankroll and proved conclusively that there was no 3-year-old in Florida that could challenge him, and then he surfaced in Keeneland's Blue Grass Stakes, where only three challengers could be found to take him on. At odds of 1-to-20 he galloped to a seven-length victory over the game but overmatched Lot o' Gold.

With the Kentucky Derby squarely in his crosshairs, Spectacular Bid's winning streak reached ten races. The Derby Day favorite at 3-to-5 odds, with California's Flying Paster second choice at 2-to-1, the Hawksworth Farm colt broke a bit awkwardly and dropped ten lengths behind the early pace, then surged into contention, then continued to surge into a comfortable lead. His winning margin was two-and-three-quarter lengths, with General Assembly second. Flying Paster straggled home fifth, ten lengths behind.

Seattle Slew won the Triple Crown in 1977, Affirmed in 1978. The twenty-five-year gap between Citation's 1948 series sweep and Secretariat's in 1973 convinced racing aficionados that Triple Crowns were a rarity, to be savored in those nearly miraculous years when a special 3-year-old surfaced and dominated their cropmates. Could Spectacular Bid destroy that notion by becoming the third horse in three years to take home the triangular gold trophy that the sport had commissioned specifically for those rare moments?

Nothing about the Preakness suggested otherwise. Stalking the early pace set by—who else?—Flying Paster and General Assembly, Spectacular Bid challenged the leaders with a half-mile to go, then accelerated into a lead that stretched to six lengths in the final furlong, then decreased to five-and-a-half lengths as the 1-to-10 favorite was allowed to coast home. With two-thirds of the Triple Crown in hand, a third consecutive sweep seemed little more than a formality.

But a bizarre incident was about to derail Spectacular Bid's chances. On Belmont Stakes morning, Delp noticed that his trainee had stepped on a safety pin hidden in the straw, embedding it in his hoof. It was removed, and when the colt appeared to be unperturbed, it was brushed aside as unimportant. Franklin had the 3-to-10 favorite running with the leaders early, then pushed him into a lead that grew to three lengths at the top of the lane, clocking the mile-and-a-quarter in 2:02⅖—the identical time of his Kentucky Derby victory.

But then, whether due to injury, distance, the pace, or simply the stress of three high-pressure races in five short weeks, Spectacular Bid wilted in the stretch, unable to hold off longshot Coastal and jockey Ruben Hernandez. Golden Act, third in the Derby and second in the Preakness, outfinished Spectacular Bid by a neck for second, and the Derby-Preakness winner was beaten. It was a disappointing conclusion to a Triple Crown chase that had begun with such promise and a strange, sad, and unsatisfying end to a twelve-race winning streak.

Spectacular Bid was given eleven weeks off and emerged from his vacation with a new rider in the irons. His former jockey, Ronnie Franklin, had been a teenager thrust into the media's harsh glare on racing's biggest and most public stage. Franklin would be replaced by the incomparable Bill Shoemaker, who would begin his tenure aboard Spectacular Bid with an easy task: an $18,000 allowance race at Delaware Park with just four unfortunate rivals and a slightly reduced burden of 122 pounds. It was the sort of race from which, had it occurred during the long-ago days of on-track bookies and auction pools, Spectacular Bid would probably have been excluded from the wagering, but the State of Delaware was legally mandated to reward even the most obvious of winning wagers at nothing less than a nickel on the dollar.

The Bid and The Shoe won by seventeen lengths over Armada Strike, with Not So Proud another seven lengths farther back in third; the mile-and-a-sixteenth was completed in 1:41⅗, setting a new track record for the distance. And in the post-race interview, the usually reticent Shoemaker volunteered to the press that "he's as good as any horse I've ever ridden, and I've ridden some of the greatest in the world," fulsome praise indeed from America's leading jockey.

Shipped next to Belmont Park for the mile-and-a-quarter Marlboro Cup, Spectacular Bid avenged his Belmont Stakes loss with a five-length victory over General Assembly, with Coastal third. Spectacular Bid covered the mile-and-an-eighth distance in a hasty 1:46⅗.

Next would come a true meeting of the titans in a classic race, the one-and-a-half-mile Jockey Club Gold Cup. This encounter pitted 3-to-5 favorite Affirmed, making the final start of his storied career under jockey Laffit Pincay Jr., against 7-to-5 second choice Spectacular Bid, with Shoemaker in the irons. Belmont Stakes winner Coastal and speedy Gallant Best were also entered, their owners hoping for a miracle that might bring them something better than show dough.

As so rarely seems to happen, this event was all that had been hoped and more. Affirmed, leading from the start under 126 pounds, briefly surrendered the lead to Gallant Best, then took over after the first half-mile, and spent the next eight grinding furlongs holding off challenge after challenge from Spectacular Bid and Coastal, never assuming full command from his rivals but never at any time relinquishing control. At the wire, it was Affirmed by three-quarters of a length over Spectacular Bid, with Coastal three lengths back.

With the victory, Affirmed clinched his second Horse of the Year title; Spectacular Bid, with ten wins in twelve starts and record seasonal earnings of $1,279,333, was forced to settle for the 3-year-old championship. But for a misplaced safety pin, could The Bid have taken home the Horse of the Year hardware? We will never know.

When Spectacular Bid returned it was at Santa Anita, where he began his campaign by shattering Imbros's twenty-four-year-old track record for seven furlongs, cruising the distance in 1:20 to win the Grade 2 Malibu Stakes by five lengths over old rival Flying Paster, who returned two weeks later in the nine-furlong San Fernando Stakes to run what was likely the finest race of his life, reaching the finish in a sparkling 1:48⅖. Spectacular Bid defeated him anyway, by a length-and-a-half, at 1-to-20 odds.

The climax of Santa Anita's Charles H. Strub Series for 4-year-olds was the Strub Stakes, named after the enterprising dentist who founded Santa Anita at the height of the Great Depression, and with Spectacular Bid's historic world record run, described earlier in this chapter, the 1980 running would become a classic.

The victory vaulted Spectacular Bid to fourth on the all-time earnings list, with $1,899,417; only Forego ($1,938,957), Kelso ($1,977,896), and Affirmed ($2,393,818) remained to be overcome. With the $350,000 guaranteed Santa Anita Handicap next on Spectacular Bid's calendar, and plenty of additional high-stakes races available thereafter, few doubted that the champion needed merely to remain healthy to leapfrog the remaining top earners.

Four weeks later, Flying Paster was back yet again, with six losses in six tries against Spectacular Bid, but ready nonetheless to take him on another time. Along for the Big 'Cap's minor awards would be Beau's Eagle, Silver Eagle, and Leonotis. A crowd of 49,285 turned up for the opportunity to see a one-of-a-kind horse in action, and they were not disappointed. On a day of driving rain, and in his first time on a sloppy track, Spectacular Bid demonstrated that mere track condition would not be an issue. None of The Bid's challengers would get close.

Spectacular Bid tracked Beau's Eagle's pace to the quarter pole, then ran past him and away from the rest, reaching the finish five lengths clear of Flying Paster in 2:00⅗. The remainder of the field resembled a parade: Beau's Eagle eight lengths behind Flying Paster, Silver Eagle fourteen behind Beau's Eagle, Leonotis twenty-two behind Silver Eagle.

With the victory and the $190,000 winner's check, Spectacular Bid's earnings totaled $2,089,417, just $304,401 short of Affirmed's record mark. With more than nine months remaining in 1980, The Bid seemed an inevitability as the eventual all-time leading earner.

Next, Spectacular Bid was vanned down the freeway to Hollywood Park, where he annexed the mile-and-a-sixteenth, $200,000-added Mervyn LeRoy Handicap by seven lengths under a career-high 132 pounds, with Flying Paster, back again for his eighth forlorn try, in the beaten field along with Beau's Eagle and the filly Life's Hope. The fractions for the LeRoy were brilliantly fast—:22⅗, :45⅖, 1:08⅘, and 1:33⅘—imperiling Swaps's record for the distance, but as Hawksworth Farm owner Harry Meyerhoff remarked after the race, "We're not interested in records, just the money-winning record."

And The Bid was closing in. The LeRoy's $120,400 winner's purse brought him to $2,209,817, just $184,001 short of Affirmed. This was a record that was destined to be broken—and soon.

Hollywood Park's mile-and-an-eighth Californian Stakes was next on Delp's agenda for Spectacular Bid, and there was nothing in California that was going to threaten the champion—even the previously omnipresent Flying Paster was staying in the barn. The Californian was run according to the increasingly familiar script: Spectacular Bid tracked the early lead, took over when Shoemaker was ready, and accelerated away. He was six lengths in front at midstretch, and Shoemaker settled for four-and-a-quarter at the wire, with the field strung out for thirty lengths behind. The time of 1:45⅘ established a new track record for the nine furlongs. And the Californian's $184,450 winner's purse put Spectacular Bid over the top, if barely, with $2,394,268, to Affirmed's $2,393,818—

a razor-thin margin of $450 that would only grow larger. It was, after all, still only June, with nearly seven months remaining in which Spectacular Bid could continue banking earnings.

Actually, two records had been set in Spectacular Bid's Californian, and quite possibly three. The Bid had certainly run faster than Hollywood Park's existing record for nine furlongs, and in so doing had also replaced Affirmed at the top of the leading earners list.

The possible third record is more speculative. A very fast horse named Rich Cream had established a new Hollywood Park mile-and-an-eighth record, 1:46⅕, about a half-hour before the Californian in a race called the Ack Ack Invitational Handicap, and it was in the very next race that Spectacular Bid supplanted him in the record book. Was this the shortest time any horse had held a track record before it was broken by another horse? It is entirely possible.

Spectacular Bid was scheduled to race once more at Hollywood Park, in the $400,000 Hollywood Gold Cup, but when trainer Delp considered the likely 134-pound weight assignment he chose an alternative course. The colt would instead attempt to conquer Chicago's best, shipping to Arlington Park for the Washington Park Handicap. For the second time in six weeks Spectacular Bid carried 130 pounds at one-and-an-eighth miles, and once again he set a new track record for the distance, 1:46⅕, obliterating his field by ten lengths at surprisingly generous 1-to-2 odds. Four weeks later, in Monmouth's Haskell Handicap, The Bid gave the following year's champion mare Glorious Song fifteen pounds, scoring a length-and-a-half victory.

Delp's next target for Spectacular Bid was a repeat victory in Belmont Park's Marlboro Cup, but the trainer took the colt out of the race when he learned that his charge had been assigned 136 pounds. "My first obligation is to my horse," Delp explained to the press, "and I did not feel it would be fair to him to run under the weights assigned." Instead, Delp opted for the weight-for-age Woodward Stakes, in which the colt would carry just 126 pounds.

This, however, created a different set of circumstances. Marlboro Cup winner Winter's Tale might have been his most serious competition in the Woodward, but a leg injury forced his withdrawal, and when the trainers of Belmont Stakes winner Temperence Hill and Seattle Slew's one-time conqueror Dr. Patches withdrew their horses rather than face Spectacular Bid under match race conditions, the race became a walkover, racing's greatest tribute to the talent of a racehorse. After receiving his instructions from Delp ("Hold on"), The Shoe piloted Spectacular Bid around the track in splendid isolation, reaching the finish in 2:02⅖, adding $73,300 to the colt's bankroll for the public exercise.

Walkovers are not exactly commonplace events. Owners and trainers tend to believe that second money in a two-horse race is a superior option to remaining in the barn, and the last previous walkover involving a prominent Thoroughbred had been Hall of Famer Coaltown's lone journey in Havre de Grace's Edward Burke Handicap on April 23, 1949, more than thirty years earlier. The last one before that had been Citation's Pimlico Special, on October 29, 1948.

Following Spectacular Bid's jaunt around Belmont Park, his bankroll stood at $2,781,608.

Next on Spectacular Bid's schedule was the Jockey Club Gold Cup, and he prepared for it with a powerful 1:10⅗ six-furlong workout. But a long-term injury flared up, and the decision was made that the colt had done enough and should not be risked. With nine wins in as many 1980 starts, Spectacular Bid was the consensus champion older horse and Horse of the Year. Syndicated for $22 million, he was retired to stud at Kentucky's Claiborne Farm, where his offspring, as might have been expected, failed to match their sire's extraordinary talent.

MONEY EARNINGS

We are all made forcibly aware on a daily basis that inflation impacts our lives. When prices rise and our earnings fail to keep pace, we find ourselves losing purchasing power. This has been an economic fact of life since before there even was an academic field of study called economics, and there has never been an election in America in which the economy was not a talking point for any and all presidential candidates.

But the inflation in purse money in Thoroughbred racing dwarfs the inflation that we all feel whenever we buy ten gallons of gas or a dozen eggs. Over the decades, inflation in purse money available renders virtually meaningless the total earnings of horses that raced prior to the sport's modern era. Man o' War himself can be used as an example of this.

In 1919, Man o' War earned $83,325; in 1920, his earnings were $166,140, for a lifetime total of $249,465. At the end of this two-season stretch, he was America's all-time leading money winner. For purposes of this discussion, Man o' War's record earnings are our baseline.

The rate for slightly over a century of inflation, from 1920 to 2023, is 15.81, reflecting that prices for a theoretical basket of goods has increased by a multiple of nearly sixteen during that period. Applying that rate to Man o' War's earnings would increase them to $3,944,042 very inflated dollars.

But Thoroughbred racing's purse inflation since 1920 vastly exceeds the level of inflation that applies to our daily trips to the grocery store. Total purse money for all American races, at all American tracks during Man o' War's two years as a racehorse, was $12,416,272; in the years 2022 and 2023, racetrack purses totaled $2,647,839,735. That's over $2.6 billion, with a *b*. Do the arithmetic and you'll find that purses have increased by 213.25 times between Man o' War's day and our own.

Applying this measure of inflation rather than the inflationary pressure we all face in our daily lives, Man o' War's purses grow to $53,198,411.

Perhaps the reader will be surprised to learn that in racing's 2024 season, the $20 million purse of a single race, the Saudi Gold Cup, exceeded the $18,555,680 paid out by all racetracks across the nation, for every one of the 16,094 races run as recently as 1943.

This immense increase in available purses, and in the ability of a racehorse to collect almost unimaginably large amounts of earnings for its owner colors every aspect of the sport's finances. In 2022 the year's leading earner, Country Grammer, earned $10,900,000 in a single year, racing but six times and winning but twice. Flightline, the second leading earner with $4,255,000, raced just three times in 2022, winning all three;

third on the list was Life Is Good, who raced six times, won four, and earned $3,482,500.

Does Man o' War's $249,465, over two seasons, still feel so meaningful?

Or consider this: It was 1951 before Citation became the first Thoroughbred to earn over a million dollars—$1,085,760, to be exact. Affirmed was the first runner beyond $2 million, earning $2,393,818, in 1980—roughly thirty years after Citation. He was surpassed the following year by Spectacular Bid, who won $2,781,607.

John Henry was the first runner over $3 million—and $4 million, and $5 million, and $6 million. When he was retired in 1984, he had more than doubled Spectacular Bid's career earnings, with $6,597,947.

By the conclusion of the 2023 racing season, John Henry's lifetime earnings had been surpassed by forty-two other racehorses.

Jump forward to 2022 and Country Grammer, and the leading earner's corresponding average earnings per race were $1,816,667. A total of forty horses earned at least a million dollars apiece in 2022 alone. Is each of those forty at least twenty times better than John Henry, or Spectacular Bid, or Affirmed, or Man o' War? Not a chance.

Leading the all-time money list in the modern era, then, is far more a measure of purse inflation than of equine quality. Arrogate, the all-time leading earner as this is being written, earned $17,422,600 in purses by winning just seven of his eleven races. Man o' War earned $9,275 for winning the Travers; Arrogate's owner received a check for a tidy $670,000, nearly triple Man o' War's lifetime earnings. Arrogate earned $3.3 million for the Breeders' Cup Classic, $6 million for the Dubai World Cup, and $7 million for the Pegasus World Cup, purses that were not available to Man o' War or Citation or even Secretariat.

As this is being written, none of racing's ten all-time leading earners raced in a calendar year beginning with a "1."

All of which can be summarized as follows, regarding Man o' War and Spectacular Bid: Both were phenomenal Thoroughbreds, both led the nation's top earners at the time of their retirements, both had numerous accomplishments beyond mere money earnings to amend their arguments for greatness. Man o' War reached the top of the American earnings list in his twenty-first and final start; Spectacular Bid supplanted Affirmed atop the list in his twenty-seventh.

The conclusion, in my view, is that topping the earnings list is a nearly unique accomplishment for the rare Thoroughbred that lasts long enough to poke its name above that of the previous leader. But the amount of earnings, in this time of purse hyperinflation, can no longer prove that one horse is better than another. Since Man o' War and Spectacular Bid both topped the all-time earnings list, the contest between the two in this category can only be adjudged a draw.

Exterminator with stable companion Peanuts the Shetland Pony. (Keeneland Library Morgan Collection—A36598)

CHAPTER 13

Carrying and Giving Weight

Man o' War vs. Exterminator

RACING HISTORIAN DAVID ALEXANDER, IN HIS BOOK *A SOUND OF HORSES*, paints a vivid picture of Exterminator's owner, Commodore Willis Sharpe Kilmer, as an intense, driven man with "the lowest boiling point of any man in the history of the turf's eccentrics."

> *He would boil over if you mentioned a patent nostrum called Swamp Root, which had been the basis of his fortune. He boiled over in a Chicago hotel room one day in 1931 when his Sun Beau, who was once the greatest money-winning horse in the world, was running in the $100,000 Caliente Handicap in Mexico. Sun Beau had to be rated back of the pace to run his best. When the radio announcer stated that Jockey Frankie Coltiletti had broken him on top, Kilmer destroyed the radio in his rage.*

But the issue that kept Commodore Kilmer at "a perpetual boiling point," suggested Alexander, was the refusal of Samuel Riddle, owner of Man o' War, to agree to a race with his remarkable gelding Exterminator.

Kilmer reportedly offered to take on Big Red at weight-for-age, which would have required the 5-year-old Exterminator to carry more weight than his 3-year-old rival. This was an offer rarely proposed to Mr. Riddle, whose already legendary colt routinely carried top weight in his races, while racing secretaries placed ever more feathery burdens on his rivals in the forlorn hope of creating something that might pass for a contest.

Alexander wrote that Kilmer was less than subtle in his dogged pursuit of Riddle. "He pursued Riddle from track to track and club to club," wrote Alexander, "shaking fifty thousand dollars in his face and demanding he put up the same stake for a race."

But Riddle had no interest in a race against Exterminator, under weight-for-age conditions or any other. "Riddle," wrote Alexander, "would merely smile and suggest that the two might meet in the normal course of their engagements," and would race his colt almost exclusively in races limited to other 3-year-olds.

And when Riddle eventually matched his colt against an older challenger, it was 4-year-old Sir Barton, and at a route, one-and-a-quarter miles, that would be to Man o' War and Sir Barton's liking, but slightly short for the distance-loving Exterminator. Despite Kilmer's blandishments and bluster, Exterminator and Man o' War would never meet on the track.

Some might suggest Kilmer should be relieved that Riddle never accepted this challenge; that this might be a case of "be careful what you wish for; you might get it." But while the popular perception of "Old Bones," as racing fans of the era dubbed the beloved Exterminator, is that of a stodgy old soul who won his marathon races by maintaining a constant pace until yet another field of rivals had been driven to the brink of exhaustion, in fact Exterminator was a versatile sort who could win a race with either speed or stamina.

He won eighteen times (not including the two occasions when he ran without a rival) in wire-to-wire or near-wire-to-wire fashion, broke his maiden at first asking, and won all four of his match races, in which his front-running speed was among the decisive elements. He once won a six-furlong race—with no less a competitor than future Hall of Famer Billy Kelly the runner-up—as a supposedly grizzled 7-year-old. Never mind his reputation—when Exterminator needed speed, it was there for him.

It may have been the 1920 Saratoga Cup, contested over a sloppy mile-and-three-quarters, that forever persuaded Riddle that a match with Exterminator might not be in Man o' War's best interest. Taking on the filly Cleopatra, one of the top runners of either gender in Man o' War's 1917 foal crop, Exterminator, carrying 126 pounds to the filly's 111, was first away from the tape and widened on his rival throughout, coasting to the finish under jockey Clarence Fairbrother with a six-length margin. This easy victory added $4,950 in purse money to Exterminator's steadily growing bankroll and demonstrated that the formidable gelding might be a difficult customer indeed, even in the one-on-one competition that Man o' War so routinely dominated.

But despite his prowess in match races, Exterminator is best remembered as a distance-savoring cup horse. He was able to win four of eight at distances of less than a mile, six of twelve at a mile or a mile and seventy yards, eleven of eighteen at a mile-and-a-sixteenth, and seventeen of thirty-nine in nine- and ten-furlong routes. He could manage only one win in ten tries at one-and-three-eighths miles or a mile-and-a-half, a statistical anomaly that must surely be a product of small sample size.

But give Exterminator a real distance, and he was virtual money in the bank. He won all four times he was tested at a mile-and-three-quarters, both times he tried two miles, and five of seven (with a second and a third) at two-and-a-quarter miles. It was an annual event to see him win the mile-and-three-quarters Saratoga Cup—he won four of them, once in a walkover—and to this he added three Pimlico Cups, two-and-a-quarter-mile marathons that he won under jockey Clarence Kummer in 1919, Lavelle "Buddy" Ensor in 1920, and Albert Johnson in 1921.

As Exterminator plied his trade with distinction over so many years, racing secretaries began adding weight to his burden, at first cautiously but soon with something approaching exuberance. The gelding carried 130 pounds or more a total of thirty-six times in his eight seasons on the track, winning twenty, with three seconds and six thirds, for a total of twenty-nine in-the-money performances. Some of his weight-conceding feats were little short of monumental. For example:

- In a Churchill Downs handicap on May 22, 1919, he carried 134 pounds to runner-up Flyaway's 97, defeating his rival by five lengths.

- In Woodbine's Toronto Autumn Cup on September 25, 1920, he carried 132 pounds to My Dear's 92, holding off that challenger by a head.
- In Belmont Park's Autumn Gold Cup on September 16, 1921, he carried 130 pounds to Bellostar's 104, winning by six easy lengths.
- In a Belmont Park handicap on June 5, 1922, he carried 133 pounds to Be Frank's 107, defeating his rival by a half-length.
- A few weeks later, in Aqueduct's Brooklyn Handicap, Exterminator carried 135 pounds to 129 for Grey Lag, edging the future Hall of Famer by a head. It would be Grey Lag's only loss of the 1922 season. The third finisher, Polly Ann, was another four lengths back under 103 pounds.
- In another edition of Woodbine's Toronto Autumn Cup, Exterminator carried 132 pounds to 102 for runner-up Guy, winning by a length-and-a-half.
- On April 21, 1923, at age eight, 1918 Kentucky Derby winner Exterminator, carrying 129 pounds, defeated 1919 winner Paul Jones, assigned 109, in the Philadelphia Handicap.

Exterminator was assigned 140 pounds in the 1922 Independence Handicap, but on a hot July 4th jockey Albert Johnson did not persevere after the gelding appeared to be in distress after one grueling mile. He won under 137 and 138, won twice under 135, twice more under 134, weights rarely seen in the modern era but assigned routinely to Exterminator until he reached his eighth birthday. Even as a superannuated 8-year-old, he was assigned 130 pounds in the ninety-fifth race of his career.

For over a century, Exterminator has been credited with the most symmetrical record in the long history of the Sport of Kings: exactly one hundred starts and exactly fifty wins, a precise 50 percent. He finished second seventeen times, third seventeen times, and out of the money sixteen times. It is a miracle of precision that over the course of his eight seasons on the track, during which time he was ridden by eighteen different jockeys and conditioned by eight trainers, in the United States, Canada, and Mexico, he achieved so nearly perfect a symmetry.

But there is an element to that allegedly perfect 50-for-100 record that fails to correctly state the facts of Exterminator's long career. It raises a question: Should Exterminator be credited with a fifty-first win, or should he be counted with fifty wins in just ninety-nine starts? As author Eva Jolene Boyd noted in her 2002 book *Exterminator: The Thoroughbred Legends*, the answer is to be found in a Chicago race that failed to draw so much as a single competitor for the phenomenal gelding.

On September 30, 1922, the newly reopened Hawthorne Race Course carded a special race intended to lure the enormously popular champion to Chicago. The race was to cover a mile-and-a-quarter, and Exterminator would be assigned a mere 126 pounds, which prompted the trainers of the race's other invitees to send their regrets. With no one to challenge their star attraction, the publicity department advertised the event as a race against the clock, presumably with Hawthorne's mile-and-a-quarter track record, 2:04⅗, as the target. Whether this was communicated to jockey Albert Johnson is unknown.

The presence of Exterminator drew nearly twenty thousand to Hawthorne, even on a day when the statutes still forbade wagering, but as a duel between the gelding and the clock, it was less than a rousing success. Breaking from the quarter-mile pole, Exterminator "came past the stand the first time with tail whisking as if in protest against the absence of competition." Without rivals to concern him, Johnson spent the early part of the race pulling hard on the reins to restrain Exterminator, who opened with a quarter-mile in :25, then consecutive one-paced quarters of :26⅘, :26⅘, and :26⅗, for a glacial 1:45⅕ mile. At this point, "as experienced racegoers were ready to voice disappointment," in the words of the *Chicago Tribune*, Johnson allowed the crowd a brief glimpse of Exterminator in a somewhat fuller stride, getting the final quarter in :24⅘ for a 2:10 final clocking. Johnson and Exterminator missed the track record by a rather considerable margin, five-and-two-fifths seconds.

Never mind a race against the clock; they could have timed this one with a sundial. It is surely the strangest race among the one hundred in which Exterminator participated, a walkover by anyone's definition— except that of the publicity department, whose definition of the event as a race against time must have prevailed, because ever since it has been counted as a loss.

As Boyd notes in her book, racing historian John Hervey was at Hawthorne that day and believed that the race should be considered an exhibition; he was "adamant about the race not counting." *Daily Racing Form* turfwriter John McEvoy concurred, stating, "I have no idea why a race against time would appear in Exterminator's career record as an unplaced finish. This should not be."

It is an unfortunate and erroneous blemish on the record of a phenomenal racehorse, one that is compounded because it is counted not merely as a loss but as an unplaced finish. Perhaps, one day, someone will review Exterminator's record and properly exclude this mile-and-a-quarter workout from the sport's official records.

Exterminator seemingly could win under any conditions. He raced at twenty different racetracks and won at sixteen. He raced thirty times over tracks labeled heavy, sloppy, or muddy, and came home first in nineteen of these, including the Kentucky Derby, which he won in his first start as a 3-year-old, as a 29-to-1 longshot substituting for Kilmer's preferred Derby colt, Sun Beau, and directly off a 296-day layoff. Seven of his victories in the slop were under weights of 130 to 138 pounds.

Exterminator was so docile that he became a favorite of starters, who in those days before the availability of starting gates would place him next to the most troublesome runner in the field. The sedate Old Bones would lean against the malcontent Thoroughbred, keeping the animal in line until the starter pulled the string.

By the time he was done, Exterminator had surpassed by precisely $3,531 the $249,465 earned by Man o' War, the rival he never was allowed to challenge on the track. By the time Exterminator surpassed his long-retired rival, however, 1923 Kentucky Derby–Belmont Stakes winner Zev had outearned them both, forever denying Exterminator a place at the top of the leading earners list.

In the ultimate game of life, however, Man o' War and Exterminator arrived at something of a dead heat, both succumbing at the advanced age of thirty.

CARRYING AND GIVING WEIGHT

We have discussed in some detail the various qualities a good horse will utilize in attempting to win a race. The most important tool in the racing secretary's arsenal as they engage in the never-ending effort to bring fields of horses together at the finish—or at least make the finish sufficiently palatable that a goodly percentage of those who wagered on the outcome accept that their interests were appropriately represented—is weight. More weight in the saddle of a heavily favored runner should, or so goes the theory, allow other horses their chance at an upset victory.

And yet, the precise impact of weight on the Thoroughbred is but one factor in a constellation of causes determining the outcome of a race. It is a topic that even the greatest of handicapping writers seemingly prefer not to tackle. There are simply too many other considerations that are more amenable to logic and rational thought.

Nonetheless, it defies reason to suggest that the weights carried by horses in a race are irrelevant. We may never be able to determine the precise impact of an additional one pound on a Thoroughbred; this will depend on the animal's size and strength, the level of its training, the condition of the racetrack, and (from this point the reader can append their own et ceteras). But weight is important in the racing game, and horses that can win with extremely high imposts, and defeat opponents carrying substantially less weight, have always been recognized with great appreciation by those who follow the sport.

Which brings us to two of the best weight-carriers ever seen on the American turf: Man o' War and Exterminator. Both will have their backers as the giant in this esoteric area of the sport, and both have earned the accolades. How would we rank them against one another? It is a difficult task.

Exterminator raced one hundred times, Man o' War twenty-one, so at the beginning of this discussion are problems of scale. Exterminator carried 130 pounds or more thirty-six times, nearly twice as many starts under high weight as Man o' War had starts. He won twenty races under 130 or more pounds; Man o' War won twenty races in total. On the surface, this may seem a mismatch; Exterminator accomplished so much more under high weights than his younger rival.

But it would be unfair to hand the victory to Exterminator by acclamation, for Man o' War was a prodigious weight-hauler who gave weight to his opponents whenever a racing secretary could find in the rules the opportunity to heap the avoirdupois on his broad back.

Man o' War carried 130 pounds in six of his ten starts as a 2-year-old, winning five. Never in my meanderings through the records of the sport have I found another racehorse asked to carry 130 pounds six times before its third birthday—or one who won under so much weight so often, and usually with such ease.

Weight carrying played an important part in the Man o' War legend, not merely because he carried so much, so early, but because, from his third start through the end of his 2-year-old season, the big red colt was also giving weight to every rival, in every race.

And in Man o' War's one loss, in Saratoga's Sanford Memorial Stakes, weight and weight differential were of crucial importance. It was the virtually unanimous opinion that had he not carried fifteen additional pounds, Man o' War would have overcome all the adversity he faced in the race and caught Upset before the finish.

Exterminator, who raced only four times as a 2-year-old, was assigned packages of 109 pounds in his debut, then 105, 105, and 112. And then, at exactly the point in Man o' War's career in which he began his six consecutive races under 130 pounds, Exterminator was purchased by Commodore Kilmer from his original owner, J. C. Milam, and sent to the sidelines to grow and develop. And, as matters evolved, to prepare for the 44th running of the Kentucky Derby.

Man o' War carried at least 130 pounds only three times as a 3-year-old. He of course won all three: by eight lengths over Yellow Hand in the Stuyvesant, carrying 135 and giving the runner-up thirty-two pounds; by six over Donnacona in the Miller under 131, giving the second finisher twelve; and by a length-and-a-half in the Potomac, carrying 138 and conceding thirty pounds to runner-up Wildair. He carried 129 in the Travers, administering a two-and-a-half-length beating to Upset, who carried 123.

Exterminator never carried more than 129 pounds in a race at age three. It would not be until his 4-year-old season, 1919, that he would begin his amazing weight-carrying exploits. Four times that year, Exterminator would heft 130 pounds or more in a race, winning two. Had he raced as a 4-year-old, Man o' War might well have been carrying the grandstand on his back, so much respect did he draw from track handicappers.

Given all the above, the verdict in this category must swing to Man o' War, who was carrying 130 pounds routinely at a far earlier stage of his career than was ever considered for 2-year-old Exterminator—or even the 3-year-old version. Exterminator is justly revered for his weight-carrying exploits and is deservedly a Hall of Famer for winning so often under such oppressive handicaps. But while we would award the gelding an A for his numerous victories under high weight, it is Man o' War who garners the A+.

Sunday Silence (racing on the inside) edges Easy Goer in the Breeders' Cup Classic.
(Keeneland Library Raferty Turfotos Collection)

CHAPTER 14

Crop Size

Man o' War vs. Sunday Silence and Easy Goer

A FOAL CROP IS THE ENTIRE YEAR'S PRODUCTION OF THOROUGHBRED foals. Two years after the foal crop comes into being, its most precocious members will be winning 2-year-old races, and the year after that the elite members will be competing for the Triple Crown. The more horses there are in a foal crop, the better the likelihood that the crop will produce a truly outstanding horse, and two truly outstanding horses, and three. And so on.

This is not genius-level mathematics requiring advanced calculus or the power of a supercomputer. If you own 1,680 random cats and your neighbor owns random felines totaling 51,296, then, all other things being equal, your neighbor is going to win the vast majority of the cat shows. It is the simplest of logic.

Now let's apply this reasoning to racehorses.

Which foal crop is more likely to have produced a truly outstanding Thoroughbred: The 1917 crop, second smallest of the twentieth century, which saw approximately 1,680 Thoroughbred foals born and registered with The Jockey Club to race in the United States, or the 1986 crop, the century's largest, with 51,296 Thoroughbred foal registrations swarming through The Jockey Club's computers? The commodity is different—cats vs. horses—but the numbers are interchangeable. All other things being equal, it is approximately thirty times more likely that you will get an outstanding runner from the larger crop than the smaller one.

Like so many matters of logic, sometimes there will be anomalies, years and horses that defy the numbers. Man o' War is an extreme anomaly; a member of 1917's tiny foal crop who had a nearly perfect racing career, he was enshrined in racing's Hall of Fame and is still believed by many to be the best racehorse ever.

But in most years, the logic stands. Table 14-1 lists the ten smallest foal crops of the twentieth century and the horses produced in those years that reached the Hall of Fame. (Note: Foal crops for the early years are approximations).

That's eleven Hall of Famers in ten lean years for stud farms everywhere (we'll discuss the reasons the foal crops were so small in a later chapter). The four smallest crops combined produced only a single Hall of Famer, and even if the one was Man o' War, that's still the closest thing possible to being shut out altogether from racing's most imposing shrine.

Table 14-1: Hall of Famers from Ten Smallest Foal Crops of the Twentieth Century

Year	Foals	HoF'ers	Name(s)
1919	1,665	0	
1917	1,680	1	Man o' War
1914	1,702	0	
1913	1,722	0	
1920	1,833	1	Zev
1912	1,900	1	Regret
1910	1,950	1	Pan Zareta
1918	1,950	1	Grey Lag
1921	2,035	4	Black Gold, Fairmount, Princess Doreen, Sarazen
1911	2,040	2	Old Rosebud, Roamer

Table 14-2: Hall of Famers from
Ten Largest Foal Crops of the Twentieth Century

Year	Foals	HoF'ers	Name(s)
1986	51,296	4	Easy Goer, Open Mind, Safely Kept, Sunday Silence
1987	50,917	3	Go For Wand, Housebuster, Paseana
1985	50,433	1	Winning Colors
1984	49,247	4	Alysheba, Bayakoa, Miesque, Personal Ensign
1988	49,220	4	Best Pal, Dance Smartly, Flawlessly, Lonesome Glory
1989	48,235	2	A.P. Indy, Lure
1983	47,237	1	Manila
1990	44,143	2	Cigar, Sky Beauty
1982	42,894	2	Lady's Secret, Mom's Command
1991	41,804	3	Heavenly Prize, Holy Bull, Inside Information

Applying the same test to the century's ten largest foal crops, we see that the logic remains: twenty-six Hall of Famers from the ten largest crops versus eleven from the ten smallest ones. The anomalies in Table 14-2 are the foal crops of 1985 and 1983—two birth years in which only two of 97,670 foals earned invitations to the Hall of Fame.

Unlike the ten smallest crops, all of which were foaled over a century ago, perhaps there will be more from these years, which still reside in Hall of Fame voters' recent memory. Among the 1983 foals with at least a slight chance of joining Manila in the Hall of Fame are the following champions: Family Style, Ferdinand, Groovy, Snow Chief, Steinlen, Tasso, and Tiffany Lass. Among the champion 1985 foals who could still earn Hall of Fame status are Blushing John, Epitome, Forty Niner, Risen Star, Sunshine Forever, and steeplechaser Highland Bud. Time will tell.

Two of the runners from that all-time largest American foal crop, Sunday Silence and Easy Goer, engaged in a battle for supremacy that lasted two seasons. They would meet four times on the track, in four of America's most important races: the Kentucky Derby, the Preakness and Belmont Stakes, and the Breeders' Cup Classic. In all four races they would finish first and second. They would be perceived as so closely matched that following their careers, the *Blood-Horse*'s compilation of the top one hundred US racehorses of the twentieth century would rank one at #31, the other at #34.

Sunday Silence and Easy Goer arrived at their initial confrontation in thoroughly different ways. Sunday Silence, by Halo out of an Understanding mare, went through the auction ring twice as a yearling without being bid on and finally was sold as a 2-year-old to Arthur B. Hancock for the somewhat bargain basement cost of $50,000. Trainer Charlie Whittingham, who would condition the colt, briefly owned a share but sold it to Ernest Gaillard. Whittingham, however, would be retained to train the colt.

Sunday Silence made a late start as a 2-year-old, beginning his racing career on October 30, 1988, and competed only three times as a juvenile, losing a six-and-a-half-furlong Santa Anita sprint by a head, winning by ten lengths in a six-furlong maiden event at Hollywood Park, and losing a six-and-a-half-furlong Hollywood Park allowance race by a head to Houston, who had been purchased for $2.9 million as a yearling. If anyone at that point believed that Sunday Silence might be a Triple Crown threat and a possible champion, they were not suggesting it publicly. Houston was perceived to be the major West Coast Derby horse.

There was nothing low-key about the preparation of Easy Goer for what was predicted to be a brilliant career. The son of Alydar and the champion mare Relaxing (herself a daughter of the immortal Buckpasser) was trained by Claude "Shug" McGaughey and would be ridden throughout his career by Pat Day. Easy Goer had caught McGaughey's eye almost from the first time the big colt went to the track. "He gave the impression he could gallop those horses to death," McGaughey recalled.

Like that of eventual rival Sunday Silence, Easy Goer's first race was a close but losing effort—but one that raised eyebrows among the media.

As "The Inside Track," a racing column in the *New York Daily News*, duly noted, "Making his debut in yesterday's third race, Easy Goer (by Alydar) broke slowly and was beaten by a nose. He was clearly best."

And for the remainder of his 2-year-old season, Easy Goer was, in fact, the best—or at least, the best in the East. He broke his maiden eighteen days later by an emphatic two-and-a-half lengths over a promising colt named Is It True. He then won an allowance race by five-and-a-half, and won the Cowdin Stakes by three, with Is It True, who had won his most recent start by fifteen-and-a-half lengths, disqualified from third. He won the one-mile Champagne, as the 1-to-10 favorite, by four, with Is It True second. By November, with the $1 million Breeders' Cup Juvenile the final race on his 2-year-old agenda, Easy Goer was regarded as a sure thing.

But over a muddy Churchill Downs oval, Easy Goer was bumped at the start and fell behind early, then lost his concentration down the stretch, hurdling the starting gate tracks as Is It True survived an early speed duel and held on to win what the *Lexington Herald-Leader* headlined the "Upset of the Day." Easy Goer would earn the juvenile championship anyway, but the self-evident superiority that had enveloped his image throughout his four-race winning streak was now open to question.

Both Sunday Silence and Easy Goer vacationed through the winter, and the pair returned almost simultaneously with the dawning of spring to stake their claims on a spot in the Kentucky Derby. March 2 saw Sunday Silence, in the California rain, win a six-and-a-half-furlong allowance race by four-and-a-half lengths, cruising wire-to-wire while defeating a field of made-to-order opponents. Two days later, Easy Goer stormed from eleven lengths behind to win Gulfstream Park's seven-furlong Swale Stakes by eight-and-three-quarter lengths. This was Easy Goer's third stakes win; Sunday Silence had yet to even compete in stakes company. No one was yet mentioning the two in the same sentence.

The San Felipe Stakes—originally the San Felipe Handicap, for older runners—has been run at Santa Anita since the track's opening in 1935; the Gotham Stakes has been a fixture on the New York racing schedule since Native Dancer and Laffango won divisions of the race in 1953. The 1989 renewals would provide stepping stones to the 1986 crop's two best runners, although it would require most of 1989 to confirm their status. Sunday Silence's San Felipe coming-out party was a length-and-three-quarters victory over Flying Continental, with heavily favored Music Merci a distant third.

Easy Goer's Gotham Stakes was more impressive. Not always the smoothest of starters, the public's 1-to-20 choice broke second, then relaxed in a striking position until the turn for home, when he seemed to begin moving twice as fast as the rest of the field. He pulled away to win by thirteen lengths, in the process shattering Aqueduct's fifteen-year-old track record by nearly a second with a 1:32⅖ clocking. Thirty-five years later, Easy Goer remains the track's co–record holder for the distance.

The Derby prep season continued, and now it would be Sunday Silence who made the headlines. On April 8, with jockey Patrick Valenzuela in the saddle, he entered the starting gate for the $500,000 Santa Anita Derby. One minute, forty-seven and three-fifths seconds later, Sunday Silence was a lonely figure breezing past the stands, eleven lengths clear of Flying Continental, with the rest of the starters scattered at various points down the stretch. It was no longer open to question which colt was the Golden State's reigning Derby contender.

Easy Goer's final Kentucky Derby prep was less compelling. As the Wood Memorial's 1-to-10 favorite, he broke with the field, took the lead early in the stretch run, and pulled away to a three-length victory in 1:50⅗. It was a workmanlike effort over a much slower track than the speedy Santa Anita oval, one that earned him the favorite's role in the Run for the Roses, now just two weeks away. McGaughey was doubtless satisfied.

And now began the series of races that would forever tie Sunday Silence and Easy Goer together in the public's perception. On Kentucky Derby Day, May 6, 1989, Easy Goer entered Churchill Downs starting gate stall #13 as the 4-to-5 favorite, coupled with entrymate Awe Inspiring. Sunday Silence, the 3-to-1 second choice, entered starting gate stall #10. The track was muddy; Secretariat's record clocking, 1:59⅖, would not be threatened on this Derby Day.

Neither colt had the cleanest of journeys. Easy Goer was bumped at the start and dropped into sixth position; Sunday Silence was jostled by another colt the first time down the long Churchill Downs stretch before settling into fourth. Approaching the final turn, Sunday Silence moved past the pacesetting Houston and into the lead while Easy Goer moved up menacingly on the outside. Down the stretch, Sunday Silence swerved repeatedly, keeping all competition at bay, while Easy Goer seemed to lose momentum in the final furlong. At the wire, it was Sunday Silence two-and-a-half lengths in front, with Easy Goer second.

The Preakness followed two weeks later, and no one who witnessed the Triple Crown's second jewel in person or via the airwaves will ever forget it. Once again Houston jumped to the early lead, once again Easy Goer lost a half-step with a poor start, and once again Sunday Silence found a comfortable stride early and moved into stalking position. Down the backstretch, Sunday Silence confronted Houston, only to be challenged almost immediately by Easy Goer, and as the Phipps colt made a powerful move on the outside, Sunday Silence took up sharply while in close quarters. A second or two to regather momentum, and Sunday Silence was after the leaders, then past them.

But now Easy Goer found his best stride.

The head-and-head stretch run found Sunday Silence on the outside, Easy Goer on the rail. Neither runner faltered, neither jockey—Patrick Valenzuela on Sunday Silence, Pat Day on Easy Goer—hesitated, and it was a battle all the way down the Pimlico stretch. At the finish, it was Sunday Silence by a nose, Easy Goer second, and third place Rock Point five lengths farther back. With a Triple Crown now on the line, Sunday Silence and Easy Goer were next sent to Belmont Park, where they—and the racing world—would await the Belmont Stakes.

With the return to the Empire State, the advantage shifted to Easy Goer. Sunday Silence had never raced in New York; Easy Goer had broken his maiden there, had won the Cowdin and the Champagne, the Gotham and the Wood, had won six of seven overall in the Big Apple, and but for a slow break in his first start would have won all seven. New York was Easy Goer's town, and the crowd that attended the Belmont was Easy Goer's crowd. He and jockey Pat Day went out and used that advantage.

It was Easy Goer's race almost from the break. Sunday Silence stalked the early pace of Le Voyageur and took the lead at the top of the stretch, but a few steps later Easy Goer caught his erstwhile conqueror and ran right on by. At the wire, Easy Goer was eight lengths clear of his rival and had run twelve furlongs in 2:26. In the thirty-four mile-and-a-half Belmont Stakes renewals since, no colt or filly has run the distance faster. And the score, kept scrupulously in the press, was now two victories for Sunday Silence, one for Easy Goer—and with Easy Goer's overwhelming Belmont Stakes score, Horse of the Year honors would be determined by the one race the two superb 3-year-olds would surely contest: the $3 million Breeders' Cup Classic, to be contested at ten furlongs on November 4, 1989, at Gulfstream Park in Florida.

But it would be 147 long days between the Belmont Stakes and Breeders' Cup Saturday, and the racing world would wait patiently for the opportunity to crown its champion. Sunday Silence and Easy Goer took radically different routes to the confrontation.

Sunday Silence would begin his trek to the Classic with a return to California and a startling loss at Hollywood Park in the $400,000 Swaps Stakes. Leading from the start and gradually opening a lead that grew to four lengths in midstretch, the Derby-Preakness winner abruptly lost his action and began bearing out. This allowed Prized, who would claim the $2 million Turf on Breeders' Cup Day, to blow past the 1-to-5 favorite to win by three-quarters of a length.

Given two months to thoroughly forget that decidedly odd race, Sunday Silence was next sent to Louisiana Downs for the $1 million Super Derby. This went according to plan, as Sunday Silence stalked Big Earl and then Le Voyageur through the race's early stages, then accelerated away, winning by six lengths. With a healthy boost to his earnings and a relatively easy prep for the Classic, now just forty days away, Sunday Silence seemed poised to run a big race at Gulfstream.

Easy Goer's route to Breeders' Cup Saturday involved a series of classic New York events, races that seemed to prepare him to run his best race in Florida. He began with a four-and-a-half-length victory in the Whitney, a race that had eluded even Secretariat, covering the mile-and-an-eighth distance in a sparkling 1:47⅗ and defeating older horses for the first time. How likely was the 3-to-10 favorite to win the Whitney?

Sportswriter Peter Giannetti in the *Glen Falls Post-Star* headlined his article, "Race Was Decided When Sun Came Up."

Next came Saratoga's classic Travers Stakes, a cruising three-length win, followed by a two-length score in the muddy mile-and-a-quarter Woodward, giving weight to older opponents, and then a four-length victory over distance-loving Cryptoclearance in the mile-and-a-half Jockey Club Gold Cup.

Finally, Breeders' Cup Day arrived, and the battle between two exquisitely talented 3-year-olds was joined.

Easy Goer and jockey Pat Day were the heavy favorites at 1-to-2 odds, with Sunday Silence, ridden by Chris McCarron while the colt's regular jockey, Patrick Valenzuela, was sidelined, the second choice at 2-to-1. The rest of the field, all of whom had earned their way into the contest through a long, arduous season, were largely ignored at the betting windows. As it had been whenever Sunday Silence and Easy Goer met on the track, the handicappers saw the Classic as strictly a two-horse race. And they would be largely correct this time but not entirely so. The unexpectedly strong performance of a 4-year-old dismissed at 21-to-1 would bring him an Eclipse Award.

As expected, Slew City Slew erupted out of the starting gate and went directly to the lead, setting suicidally rapid fractions of :22⅖, :46⅕, and 1:10⅖ while opening a lead that was three lengths after the first half-mile, still two lengths with a half-mile to go. Blushing John then opened a length-and-a-half lead as Slew City Slew inevitably retreated, and Sunday Silence and Easy Goer moved side by side to challenge. But now, for a few strides approaching the stretch, Easy Goer could not keep up. He seemed to run in place as Sunday Silence rallied.

Down the stretch, it was Sunday Silence and the game Blushing John, battling to the wire, with Easy Goer launching a powerful but belated bid on the outside. By the finish, Easy Goer had made up all of the margin but a decisive neck, with Blushing John a game third. Present Value, the fourth finisher, was nearly ten lengths farther back.

With Sunday Silence's victory came a 3-races-to-1 margin over Easy Goer and Horse of the Year honors. Blushing John's strong third-place finish, coupled with earlier victories in the Razorback Handicap, the Pimlico Special, the Hollywood Gold Cup, and the Washington Park Handicap, earned him an Eclipse Award as champion older horse. But Easy Goer's narrow defeat ensured that despite costing Sunday Silence the Triple Crown with a crushing eight-length defeat in the Belmont Stakes, he would earn no championship hardware as a 3-year-old.

Both Charles Whittingham and Shug McGaughey announced that their trainees would return for another year of competition in 1990, perhaps with thoughts of continued dominance on the one side, revenge on the other.

But racehorses are delicate creatures, and planning months in advance for triumphant campaigns is a pastime fraught with peril. Easy Goer returned to the races in May 1990 with an easy victory in a Belmont Park sprint; finished third in the Metropolitan Mile to the season's eventual Horse of the Year, Criminal Type; won the Suburban Handicap by nearly four lengths; then suffered a chipped bone in his right front ankle, and abruptly his racing career was over. "They told us even if you give him time and he's sound, he won't be a hundred percent," explained McGaughey. "He'll be ninety percent sound, but . . ." And big, powerful Easy Goer, for two years the toast of New York, was gone from the game.

A torn ligament below his left front ankle spelled the end for Sunday Silence. He returned in June at Hollywood Park, won the Californian Stakes while giving weight to two rivals, then lost the Hollywood Gold Cup to Criminal Type. He was in training for the Arlington Challenge Cup—initially planned as a $1 million race, but reduced to $600,000 when both Easy Goer and Sunday Silence were withdrawn—when he suffered his career-ending injury.

Both horses were retired to stud, and once again it was Sunday Silence who outfinished his rival. Easy Goer, retired to Claiborne Farm in Paris, Kentucky, sired three Grade 1 winners and nine stakes winners from 136 foals. He died at age eight in 1994 and was buried in Claiborne's impressive equine cemetery alongside the likes of Secretariat, Bold Ruler, and Buckpasser.

Exported to Japan, Sunday Silence became one of that nation's foundation sires in a breeding system whose seemingly limitless potential is beginning to produce quality Kentucky Derby challengers annually. Generations of Japanese Thoroughbreds, many with the blood of the 1989 Horse of the Year coursing through their veins, will go to the races, and the quality of the Japanese breeding program is already being seen annually, both in Japan and in the wider racing world. Sunday Silence died on August 19, 2002, at the age of sixteen, but his powerful and ongoing influence is already assured.

THE IMPACT OF CROP SIZE

Crop size is not, in itself, a quality; it is a factor that influences the number of good horses that *should* appear in a given year, without being a determiner of greatness. It is included in this book to demonstrate that while Man o' War was unquestionably one of history's most outstanding Thoroughbreds, there have been a great many crops that mathematically could be expected to have produced far more great foals, perhaps even better ones.

And so, if there is to be a winner in this category, it must be Man o' War, a member of the second-smallest Thoroughbred crop of the twentieth century who nonetheless proved to be a superhorse of overpowering talent. We would have expected that based on sheer numbers a Sunday Silence or an Easy Goer—or possibly both (or possibly many)—would have emerged from the huge 1986 crop; Man o' War's excellence was an anomaly of the first measure.

We will give Man o' War the victory here, with the recognition that for a horse as singular as Man o' War to emerge from a foal crop as small as that of his 1917 crop represents a happenstance so extraordinary as to be something close to impossible. If Man o' War qualifies as an outstanding horse, it is because of his success on the track; if he qualifies as verging on the miraculous, it is because he came from a foal crop so small it should never have been expected to produce a runner so phenomenally special.

Flightline romps in the Metropolitan Mile. (Bob Coglianese)

CHAPTER 15

Undefeated Records

Man o' War vs. Flightline

Sports fans hold a special fascination with teams and individuals that can boast of being undefeated. The 1972 Miami Dolphins are immortal in the National Football League's annals because they were a perfect 14-and-0 in the regular season, then won two playoff games and the Super Bowl. While the NFL's once-defeated squads are ultimately dismissed as yet another team that tried to achieve a perfect record but failed, it is the undefeated Dolphins who will forever be remembered as exemplars of perfection.

College football teams struggle to attain the same standard. A team that steamrolls through its regular season schedule undefeated, only to fall short in the championship game, will find its students dissatisfied, its contribution requests unanswered, its off-season highlighted by alumni grumbling. The word "undefeated," in the world of college football, implies more than mere perfection. An undefeated season confers a measure of immortality.

This is less true in Thoroughbred racing. While undefeated seasons may mean divisional championships or even Horse of the Year honors, there have been enough of them in the sport's lengthy history that racing authorities and enthusiasts may brush them off as lacking implications of greatness. We recognize Tom Fool's 10-for-10 1950 season as something extraordinary, and Personal Ensign's thirteen wins in thirteen career starts as history-making, but an undefeated season, or even an undefeated career, will not, in and of itself, confer greatness upon a Thoroughbred.

This is reflected in Table 15-1, listing American Thoroughbreds with unbeaten records of six or more races. Only three of the ten "perfect" runners were able to parlay undefeated careers into Hall of Fame

Table 15-1: Notable Undefeated American Racehorses

Horse	Foaled	Wins	Losses	Hall of Fame?
Peppers Pride	2003	19	0	No
Colin	1905	16	0	Yes
Personal Ensign	1984	13	0	Yes
Tremont	1884	13	0	No
Asteroid	1861	12	0	No
Handsomchamp	2002	10	0	No
American Eclipse	1814	8	0	Yes
Bullets Fever	2013	8	0	No
Rare Brick	1983	8	0	No
Sensations	1877	8	0	No
Cluster of Stars	2009	7	0	No
El Rio Rey	1887	7	0	No
Monarch	1834	7	0	No
Rodolph	1831	7	0	No
Bustin Stones	2004	6	0	No
Flightline	2018	6	0	*
Justify	2015	6	0	*

*NOT ELIGIBLE FOR ENSHRINEMENT AT THE TIME OF WRITING.

enshrinement. It is not merely the fact of an unbeaten record but the quality of the runner's career that confers greatness.

The Hronis Stable's Flightline had an undefeated career, one that is certain to earn him, after the minimum waiting period, a Hall of Fame plaque. The son of Tapit burst onto the American racing scene as an unraced 3-year-old on April 24, 2021, in a Santa Anita maiden race. He quickly outran his overmatched opponents, then began lengthening his lead, stretching his margin to four-and-a-half lengths on the turn for home, then to ten-and-a-half at midstretch. Under jockey Flavian Prat, the colt poured it on through the final furlong, reaching the finish thirteen-and-a-quarter lengths in front, in 1:08.75, an extraordinary performance for a first-time starter. But more—considerably more—was awaiting the racing world.

It was 124 days before Flightline's next appearance, at Del Mar in a six-furlong allowance optional claiming race for 3-year-olds and upward. These were better runners than the son of Tapit had dispatched at Santa Anita, but while Flightline and Prat allowed one of the other starters to lead briefly down the backstretch, the colt's 1-to-5 odds spoke to the near inevitability of the outcome. With a quarter-mile to go, he was a length-and-a-half in front; with a furlong remaining he had stretched the lead to eight yawning lengths. At the finish, the margin was twelve-and-three-quarters, this time in 1:08.05.

No one was rushing Flightline's timeline. Another 111 days passed, and on December 26, 2021, the opening day of Santa Anita's long winter/autumn season, Flightline's name again appeared in the program, this time as the 2-to-5 favorite in the Grade 1, $301,000 Malibu Stakes for 3-year-olds.

The Malibu drew some nice horses. As this book is being written, five of the six are stakes winners; third-place Stilleto Boy and Dr. Schivel, who trailed the winner by nearly twenty lengths, have banked more than a million dollars; and runner-up Baby Yoda has passed the half-million mark.

And Flightline treated them identically to the way he had disposed of all previous challengers. He started a half-step slowly, moved to the lead on his own, then gradually drew away from the competition to a lead that ultimately stretched to eleven-and-a-half lengths, ticking off rapid-fire fractions of :22.01, :44.48, and 1:08.72 on the way to a swift 1:21.37 seven furlongs.

With this, Flightline went on winter hiatus, one that lasted nearly to the beginning of summer. Trainer John Sadler, who had masterminded the colt's brief but spectacular season, will never be accused of over-racing the livestock in his barn.

This time, the gap was 167 days and approximately 3,000 miles, as Flightline, trainer Sadler, and jockey Prat next appeared at Belmont Park for the one-mile, $935,000 Metropolitan Handicap. Also in the field would be equine millionaires Happy Saver and Aloha West, and Speaker's Corner and Informative, with earnings of three-quarters of a million and a half-million, respectively. None of this mattered much to Flightline, who grudgingly allowed Speaker's Corner to set the pace through the first half-mile, then exerted himself and instantly left the others six lengths behind. The time, 1:33.59, was something of a stroll in the park by Flightline's standards. But if some actually found this race slightly disappointing—five other runners in recent years have posted sub-1:33 clockings in the Metropolitan—Flightline was about to demonstrate that his name belongs among those of history's very best Thoroughbreds.

The wait, however, would be a shorter one this time. John Sadler is a patient man, but Flightline was ready, and there is no point wasting time when a horse of this brilliance is at his peak. And so it was but eighty-four days after his Metropolitan Mile victory that Flightline, back in California, would electrify the racing world with a performance worthy of the rarest of Thoroughbreds.

Excluding years when Del Mar hosts Breeders' Cup, the Pacific Classic has been the seaside track's headline event since its inaugural running in 1991, when California-bred fan favorite Best Pal, then a 3-year-old, defeated Belmont Stakes winner Unbridled to give the million-dollar race instant credibility. The seaside track's featured event gained even greater stature in 1996, when the late-kicking Dare and Go, with assistance from front-running stablemate Siphon, abruptly and unexpectedly terminated two-time Horse of the Year Cigar's winning streak at sixteen.

The 2022 edition would include, in addition to 3-to-10 favorite Flightline, Country Grammer, who would close his career with earnings just below $15 million and a Dubai World Cup victory; $731,000 earner Royal Ship, a regular in top-level southern California stakes events since his arrival from Brazil in 2019; Express Train, who won the 2022 Santa Anita Handicap and would close his career with earnings of $1.4 million; the speedy Extra Hope, a stakes winner but entered mostly to ensure a realistic early pace; and millionaire Stilleto Boy, who had crossed paths with Flightline once before, and whose stable, given the experience, might realistically be in pursuit of the $200,000 runner-up share.

The others might as well have remained in their barns.

Flightline survived a bumping incident leaving the starting gate, then moved up to volley with Extra Hope for a half-mile. Shaking that competitor off while racing wide, Flightline began opening a gap on the field that began at "impressive," then increased to "amazing," and concluded somewhere in that seldom-explored region between "ridiculous" and "impossible." The *Los Angeles Times'* John Cherwa described the winning margin as "goosebumps-producing." It was an apt description.

But racing fans prefer numbers, so let's add here that the margin was ten lengths after a mile, thirteen after another furlong, and nineteen-and-three-quarters at the finish. The final time was 1:59.28, which would have eclipsed the stakes record, Candy Ride's 1:59.11 set in 2003, had Prat and Flightline not "coasted in the late [*sic*] to win impressively," in the words of *Equibase's* race chart.

Sixty-three days following this tour de force, Flightline would be in competition again. The aim this time would be the $6 million Breeders' Cup Classic at Keeneland, and the competition, of course, would be daunting. Flightline's seven challengers would conclude their careers with combined earnings of $22.3 million.

Travers winner Epicenter was injured early in the race and would never compete again; the remainder of the field was left to battle for the minor awards, as Flightline tracked the pace of $4.5 million earner Life Is Good, passed that horse with a quarter-mile remaining, and, with 45,973 watching from trackside and millions more gasping at their TV screens, pulled away to an eight-and-a-quarter-length victory, reaching the wire in a sensible 2:00.05.

Flightline would conclude both his 4-year-old season and his career as an undefeated, unchallenged racehorse and an unequaled stud prospect, and racing fans awaited the inevitable. The following day it was made official: After a brief but historically brilliant six-race career, Flightline would be retired to the breeding shed.

There were, of course, headlines yet to come. No one else was going to be named champion male dirt horse or Horse of the Year, and these became official with the Eclipse Awards ceremony in late January 2023. His Hall of Fame induction ceremony remains a few years off, but the vote for his enshrinement will undoubtedly be unanimous.

It was just a day after his retirement that one of forty breeding shares in Flightline, equivalent to 2.5 percent of his available breeding rights, were sold at a Keeneland auction for $4.6 million, suggesting that Flightline, as he began his breeding career, might have an equivalent value in the range of $184 million. Obviously, such matters had progressed well beyond the pace of inflation from those long-ago days when Secretariat was syndicated for just over $6 million.

And now we await the next important headlines: the first runner, the first winner, the first stakes winner, and, the Racing Gods willing, the first champion by a colt who raced only six times, at widely separated intervals, but when he did run brought back memories of Secretariat, Citation, Man o' War, and the very best of Thoroughbreds for the racing fans of the world.

UNDEFEATED RECORDS

Obviously, as has been noted already in this chapter, there have been multiple undefeated Thoroughbreds in the long history of the Sport of Kings. I have specifically used the word "multiple" here, rather than "numerous," to emphasize that while an undefeated record is not a unique occurrence, it is also far from commonplace. Any undefeated season borders on the extraordinary; it was the unique quality of Flightline's six victories that rendered them so special.

The question here is whether an undefeated record separates its owner from runners with a single loss—or even multiple losses—sufficiently to be considered a quality worthy of discussion in determining whether one Thoroughbred should be looked upon as greater than others. The National Museum of Racing and Hall of Fame, and the voters who elect the runners to enshrinement within its hallowed walls, are perhaps the most knowledgeable sources of a possible answer to this question.

And it appears that their answer is an emphatic "No."

As we saw in Table 15-1, only American Eclipse, Colin, and Personal Ensign among the ten American runners with undefeated careers totaling eight or more races have been seen as worthy of Hall of Fame induction. The seven others all remain eligible for the Hall, but for reasons that are likely different for each, they continue to be on the outside looking in.

Table 15-2, which lists American-based horses with at least eight victories plus a single loss, includes fifteen names, of whom six (40 percent)—Native Dancer, Man o' War, Zenyatta, Sysonby, Ruffian, and Majestic Prince—have been deemed worthy of the Hall of Fame's notice.

Apparently, that single loss did not sway the Hall of Fame's voters away from runners whose other qualities were considered worthy of a vote.

Table 15-2: Notable Once-Beaten American Racehorses

Horse	Foaled	Wins	Losses	Hall of Fame?
Lottery	1803	21	1	No
Native Dancer	1950	21	1	Yes
Man o' War	1917	20	1	Yes
Zenyatta	2004	19	1	Yes
Sysonby	1902	14	1	Yes
La Vraie Reine	1848	10	1	No
Leonatus	1880	10	1	No
Ruffian	1972	10	1	Yes
Awesome Feather	2008	10	1	No
Majestic Prince	1966	9	1	Yes
Phone Trick	1982	9	1	No
Stopshoppingdebbie	2010	9	1	No
Devil's Bag	1981	8	1	No
King Glorious	1986	8	1	No
Smarty Jones	2001	8	1	No

And I agree. The difference between a perfect record and one with a single loss is too trifling to confer greatness upon the runner that happens to have won every time, to deny it to the runner that fails by a single loss to achieve perfection. Is Flightline a better, more brilliant, more compelling runner than Man o' War, simply because the former won all six of his races, while the latter won "only" twenty of twenty-one? The answer, it seems obvious, is no. Man o' War's perfectly excusable loss should not elevate Flightline ahead of him.

In fact, I am inclined to give Man o' War the edge over Flightline in this battle of superstar Thoroughbreds of two distinct eras. Man o' War won more races, and as we have seen, he more than demonstrated his superiority over Upset by defeating him repeatedly. When comparisons between Man o' War and Flightline are proffered by the experts, the two will need to be evaluated on criteria other than that one unfortunate afternoon in August 1919. For purposes of comparing two unique race-horses, Man o' War's lone loss, and Flightline's unsullied record, are in and of themselves largely irrelevant.

Ruffian captures the Coaching Club American Oaks. (Bob Coglianese)

CHAPTER 16

What Might Have Been

Man o' War vs. Ruffian

THERE CAN BE NO SADDER RELIC OF THE SPORT OF KINGS THAN A photo or video of the grand filly Ruffian winning yet another of her victorious races. Racing for the Locust Hill Farm of Stuart and Barbara Janney, Ruffian won all ten of her completed races, most of them by substantial margins, most of them at the infinitesimal odds that are the result of a Thoroughbred's absolute, demonstrated superiority over the opposition, most of them in times that sportswriters and fans of the sport marveled were "more like you'd expect from a colt!"

She looked coltish, a big-bodied, strongly muscled filly, described by many writers as "coal black" in color, although of course one of the rarest things in the Thoroughbred is a pure black coat. She was too big, too perfect, to be anything but fast, and she went about her victories with a workmanlike approach that was part ability and part enormous, undeniable desire to forge ahead and never look back. At no point of call, in any of the ten races that defined her as one of the all-time champions, was Ruffian ever behind another filly.

Her unquenchable desire to be ahead, to be first in line, dictated that jockeys Jacinto Vasquez and Vince Bracciale Jr. would invariably launch her directly into the lead; she was going there regardless of her riders' intentions, so why fight the inevitable? And once in front, her raw ability and that burning desire to stay ahead ensured that no filly would ever pass her, through greater speed or superior stamina. Not a chance, not this filly, forget it.

In Ruffian's first start, a five-and-a-half-furlong maiden race on May 23, 1974, her name was unknown to all but the most savvy of New York horseplayers. Some doubtless made their wagers based on the newspaper column "Gelardi's Belmont Ratings" in the *New York Daily News*, which touted Ruffian as slightly the best wagering prospect in the day's third race, projecting lukewarm 3-to-1 odds. Gelardi nearly nailed it; as Ruffian and her nine opponents entered the starting gate, Belmont's tote board listed her at 4-to-1 odds that were actually 4.2-to-1, which must have seemed reasonable at the time but today reverberates through our subsequent experience as utterly ridiculous.

Ruffian was quick to correct her doubters, rocketing into a lead that was three lengths before some clockers thought to click their stopwatches and grew larger with every stride. She reached the finish fifteen lengths ahead, jockey Jacinto Vasquez sitting serenely as the clock stopped at 1:03, which happened to equal Belmont's track record for the distance. Never again would Ruffian go postward as anything other than the odds-on favorite.

Not bad for a first start, the fans must have thought, tossing off whatever losing tickets they hadn't already discarded when Ruffian was eight lengths clear at midstretch. Perhaps some wondered whether they had just seen a ringer in action—a good 3-year-old colt snuck into a 2-year-old maiden filly race in order to purloin a victory. But would the great Frank Whiteley, who had trained the likes of Preakness winner Tom Rolfe, the great Preakness–Belmont Stakes winner Damascus, Forego . . . would a trainer of his eminence risk entering an illegal runner in a maiden race to pursue a winner's purse of $5,400? No, it was impossible. And the racing world waited to see what Ruffian's next start might bring.

They would not have long to wait.

It was one day less than three weeks later that Ruffian's name appeared again in the entries for the following day. She would be racing in the five-and-a-half-furlong Fashion Stakes, a $27,580 event with a history going back as far as 1897. It had been a five-furlong race for nearly all of that time but had been increased by a half-furlong in 1972, when Queen's Mark won with a 1:05⅕ clocking. Last year, In Hot Pursuit had won in a sparkling 1:03⅕, with the eventual 2-year-old filly champion, Talking Picture, finishing third.

This time, the newspaper prognosticators were unanimous in assuring their readers that Ruffian would likely win, although the good filly Copernica also drew some respect. "Gelardi's Belmont Ratings" listed Ruffian first at even money; the unbeaten Copernica next at 8-to-5. The *Buffalo Evening News* and the *Syracuse Post-Standard*, among others, named Ruffian the most likely winner of the day for Belmont Park, particularly in light of the sensational three-furlong workout—she blazed the distance in thirty-three swift seconds—the filly had posted a few days before the Fashion.

Mostly, the prognosticators got this one right. Once again, Ruffian was perhaps a half-step slow leaving the gate; once again she blew immediately past the other fillies and grabbed a lead that quickly became insurmountable; once again jockey Jacinto Vasquez kept her to her task throughout the brief contest without asking her to do much more than she was doing on her own, despite which she again stopped the timer at 1:03, equaling the track record for the second time in her two starts. Copernica did indeed take second, some six-and-a-half lengths back.

Now discussion shifted to Aqueduct's $25,000-added Astoria Stakes, scheduled for four weeks later. By this time, horseplayers were ignoring the competition and placing their wagers almost exclusively on Ruffian, who would reign as the Astoria's 1-to-10 favorite. The big filly left nothing even slightly in doubt as she cruised to victory by nine ever-widening lengths over Laughing Bridge, who was another twelve lengths ahead of Our Dancing Girl, who was another three-and-a-quarter lengths clear of Jan Verzal. Jockey Vince Bracciale was in the irons this time, but it made little difference; Ruffian missed the track record by a fifth of a second, but otherwise the outcome was the same—an easy, impressive, fast, and decisive Ruffian victory.

The filly's next race, however, would be different, at least in one way. Taken on in Monmouth Park's six-furlong Sorority Stakes by Hot n Nasty, another prodigiously fast filly with an undefeated record, Ruffian found herself running second for the first hundred yards before she could apply her own blinding speed to the problem and wrest the lead away from the interloper. With Vasquez again aboard Ruffian, the fillies raced head-and-head for the first five furlongs before Ruffian, at 3-to-10 odds, gradually got the better of her stubborn rival, pulling away from Hot n Nasty in the final 220 yards to win by two-and-a-quarter lengths. Ruffian reached the finish in 1:09, by three stopwatch ticks the fastest Sorority Stakes in history. But even better yet was soon to come.

Four weeks later, Saratoga would card the six-furlong Spinaway Stakes. Contested at six furlongs since 1922, the Spinaway had never been completed in less than 1:09—until Ruffian, the 1-to-5 favorite, reached the finish in a preposterous 1:08⅗. Laughing Bridge, who had finished nine lengths back in the Astoria, was second again, this time twelve-and-three-quarter lengths behind.

It was announced that Ruffian had sustained a hairline fracture to her right hind leg and would be retired for the season, and the owners and trainers of other juvenile fillies breathed a brief sigh of relief. She would, however, be back in 1975, her goal for the coming season New York's Filly Triple Crown: the one-mile Acorn, the mile-and-a-furlong Mother Goose, and the mile-and-a-half Coaching Club American Oaks. Only three fillies—Dark Mirage, Shuvee, and Chris Evert—each a future Hall of Famer, had swept the series.

Before the Acorn, however, Ruffian would need to demonstrate that she had recovered fully from her injury. She began this process in a six-furlong $20,000 allowance race at Aqueduct on April 15. Ridden by Jacinto Vasquez, closely observed by trainer Frank Whiteley, the filly went to the post with bandages on both hind legs. An overpowering victory would not be necessary for Ruffian's human retinue; merely a win would be sufficient.

And so Ruffian, sent away as the 1-to-10 favorite, was allowed to lead by only a cautious half-length over Sir Ivor's Sorrow at the race's halfway point, which she reached in :45⅘, before pulling away through the stretch run to win by four-and-three-quarter lengths in 1:09⅖ for the distance, nearly a full second slower than the time she'd posted in winning the Spinaway as a 2-year-old.

When Ruffian was returned to her stall after this safe but unspectacular effort, the veterinarians determined that the filly had emerged from her first post-injury start unscathed. It was time, now that all was well, to find out just what this one-of-a-kind filly could accomplish as a sophomore.

The seven-furlong, $25,000 Comely Stakes would be Ruffian's final start before the Filly Triple Crown series, and this time the wraps would be off. Ruffian would face a small but excellent field of four: Aunt Jin, a Grade 1 winner at age two; Point in Time, who would win three stakes races as a 3-year-old, Proud Delta, who would receive an Eclipse Award as the nation's best Handicap Mare the following year, and Mirthful Flirt, a stakes winner at two and again at three. As in so many of Ruffian's races, the competition among even these fine 3-year-old fillies would be strictly for runner-up dough.

The Comely had been run as a seven-furlong race for 3-year-old fillies since 1960, and over its first fifteen years nobody had run the distance faster than Stacy d'Ette's 1:21⅗ in 1972, when she defeated champion Numbered Account in a shocking $21 upset. Ruffian took two-fifths off that stakes record, leading—how else?—wire-to-wire to win in 1:21⅕, with Aunt Jin seven-and-three-quarter lengths back and the rest trailing behind. With the Acorn Stakes just eleven days away, it was clear that Ruffian was ready for the challenge.

The first leg of 1975's New York Filly Triple Crown was less a classic horse race than a necessary step along the path to Ruffian's inevitable coronation. This was made abundantly clear when the 1-to-10 favorite led from flagfall to finish, leaving six good rivals farther behind at every call and flashing under the wire with an eight-and-a-quarter-length victory. The Acorn had been run since 1931, and no filly had ever run the race's one mile faster than future Hall of Famer Susan's Girl's 1:34⅗ in 1972 (with Stacy d'Ette third); Ruffian passed the photo finish camera a fifth of a second faster.

The $83,700 Mother Goose Stakes, run three weeks later, was, if anything, easier. Again facing six rivals, the daughter of Reviewer and Shenanigans nearly beat the starting gate, opening a length-and-three-quarters lead after the opening quarter-mile, then began pulling away rapidly, stretching the lead to eight lengths at midstretch and thirteen-and-a-half at the finish. The Mother Goose was a relatively new addition to the New York stakes schedule, debuting in 1957 as a mile-and-a-sixteenth event that was stretched another half-furlong, to a mile-and-an-eighth two years later. Since 1959, the fastest time for the distance had been 1:48⅖, set by Wanda in 1972 and equaled by Windy's Daughter the following year. Ruffian got the distance in 1:47⅘.

Clearly, this was the same Ruffian who had dominated her entire crop as a 2-year-old, but with another year's growth and maturity. She would surely be the odds-on favorite for the Filly Triple Crown's third jewel, the Coaching Club American Oaks.

But there were questions. Could a daughter of Reviewer, he a son of the great but allegedly distance-challenged stallion Bold Ruler, carry her front-running speed for twelve grueling furlongs? And if she did, could she challenge Secretariat's 2:24 Belmont Stakes clocking of four years earlier? The questions would be answered in just three weeks, on Oaks Saturday, June 21, 1975.

One of the answers was emphatically yes. Ruffian could, she demonstrated, go twelve furlongs in front, and although she was challenged on the final turn by 6-to-1 Equal Chance and 35-to-1 longshot Let Me Linger, she had more than enough stamina to pull away from her rivals and open three lengths at midstretch. Vasquez was content to let her relax the rest of the way, and the lead shrank to two-and-a-half, but the jockey never even considered going to the whip. "I never hit her, never hit her all this year," he reported after the race.

But the other answer was a firm no. Neither Ruffian nor anything else on hooves was going to challenge Secretariat's Belmont Stakes clocking. It was an exaggeration to suggest, as did the following day's *New York Daily News* headline, that "Ruffian Loafs (Ties Mark) to Triple Crown," but it was not a typical supersonic Ruffian performance. Vasquez conserved her energies and she won. That seemed more than enough. Ruffian had, at least, run the mile-and-a-half distance two ticks faster than Avatar, a colt, had clocked in winning the Belmont Stakes two weeks earlier.

There was a third question that no one thought to ask in the aftermath of Ruffian's Filly Triple Crown sweep, a question that only an extreme pessimist or possibly a clairvoyant might have thought to raise: Will this be the last time we enjoy the glory that is this amazing creature?

The answer turned out to be a tearful yes.

I do not enjoy rewatching the ill-fated Ruffian-vs.-Foolish Pleasure match race of July 6, 1975. Some events are simply too painful to be relived.

And so, in preparation for this chapter, I rewatched all of Ruffian's other races, observing, awestruck, as the big filly left field after field in the dust and the clock ticked off impossible fractions. I did not, however, rewatch the race in which the filly challenged the year's Kentucky Derby winner for a $350,000 winner-take-all prize, and I never will. I will not force myself to observe anew as the two leave the starting gate together and race around the clubhouse turn, two speeding blurs racing eye-to-eye until one of the runners takes an obvious misstep, slowing abruptly, and the other speeds on, the colt oblivious, jockey Braulio Baeza, aboard Foolish Pleasure, grimly knowing.

It was trainer Ron McAnally who would, fifteen years later, pronounce the ultimate epitaph for every Thoroughbred that loses its life giving more on the track than its bone and muscle and sinew will allow. In the aftermath of the horrific breakdown of another champion filly, Go for Wand, McAnally stared into the television cameras and said haltingly, fighting tears, "They give their lives for our pleasure."

If the reader is unaware of the grisly events that followed the fatal first quarter-mile of the Foolish Pleasure–Ruffian match race, there are enough sources available to fill in the missing pieces. Surgeons attempted to repair the damage to Ruffian's catastrophically injured leg, and as the filly rested, sedated, it seemed that they might succeed. But we shortly learned that Ruffian, awakening from the anesthesia, began thrashing uncontrollably in her stall, possibly believing she was still in the race, until the cast supporting her leg was in ruins and the rods and pins repairing the damage had loosened. The weary veterinary team asked owner Stuart Janney whether further life-saving efforts should be undertaken, but his response, that of a lover of the sport and of a great horse, was that she should be spared any more pain. Mercifully euthanized, Ruffian was buried a few days later in the Belmont Park infield.

The all-but-undefeated filly was inducted into the National Museum of Racing and Hall of Fame in 1976, the year following her tragic death. In 1976, the New York Racing Association debuted the Grade 1 Ruffian Stakes, honoring the filly with what began as a race conducted at one-and-a-quarter miles for 4-year-olds and up, fillies, and mares. Over the years, the race was gradually decreased to a mile-and-an-eighth, then a mile-and-a-sixteenth, to its current flat mile distance. In 2013 it was reduced to Grade 2 status. Memories, even of greatness, fade.

Ruffian, of course, is far from the only example of a Thoroughbred that was unable to realize its potential due to injury, early death, or other bitter circumstance. It is, sadly, all too easy to recall runners whose potential for greatness was not permitted to blossom by the fickle determinations of equine fate.

One thinks of Tim Tam, whose ten wins in fourteen starts included stretch-running victories in the 1958 Kentucky Derby and Preakness, but who fractured a sesamoid bone in his right foreleg during the Belmont Stakes and could hold only second place, while finishing on three legs. What feats might this game and talented Thoroughbred have achieved, had he not suffered this devastating injury at the peak of his career?

One thinks of Buckpasser, who won twenty-five of thirty-one starts, was named Horse of the Year for 1966, and earned a spot in racing's Hall of Fame but whose tender hooves cost him the opportunity to compete for the Triple Crown and sidelined him for swaths of time throughout his career. Once described as "the most perfectly proportioned Thoroughbred I've ever seen" by no less an expert than equine artist Richard Stone Reeves, who painted every top racehorse for generations, Buckpasser overcame his painful hooves often enough to become a champion, but how much greater might he have been, had he not been hampered by that one imperfection?

One thinks of Landaluce, the California-based filly who won all five of her starts as a startlingly gifted 2-year-old, averaging a victory margin of 9.3 lengths, then contracted deadly Colitis X and died in her stall while awaiting her next rousing victory. How much greatness might

Landaluce have shown us, with merely a normal equine lifespan? Sadly, we will never know.

And one thinks of—and wonders endlessly about—the dozens, or hundreds, or possibly thousands of other Thoroughbreds, with the blood of champions coursing through their veins and physical dimensions promising the brilliance of their forebears, who succumbed to illness or injury or fatal circumstance before they could demonstrate their ability on the racetrack. With names we will never hear, or, in some cases, having not survived long enough even to be given a name, they will forever linger on the edge of our awareness, tragic ghosts of opportunity that were denied their birthright by bitter fate.

"What might have been," indeed.

WHAT MIGHT HAVE BEEN

In most of the chapters of this book it has been my task to compare the immortal Man o' War with runners who exemplified a quality that professional horsemen and fans of the sport hold dear.

But in this chapter, discussing runners that might, given different circumstances, have been worthy challengers to the heritage of Man o' War, there is no comparison to be made. Man o' War had a full, if shortened career, was retired sound, and lived to age thirty, at which point he had done all that might have been asked of a vital young 2-year-old, a powerhouse 3-year-old, and a vigorous stallion. Ruffian died tragically on the track while still awaiting the races that might have demonstrated conclusively that she was a match for her predecessor.

Man o' War displayed his excellence for as long as he was allowed to compete; Ruffian displayed hers until one fatal misstep ended her career and her life. Few of us today saw both Man o' War and Ruffian race; the beginning of Ruffian's career occurred nearly fifty-four years after Man o' War's retirement. And so, as racegoers, as devotees of the game, the most it is possible to say is that it was our rare good fortune to have experienced the greatness of one and learned of that of the other.

As fans, it is our fervent hope that we will again encounter their like, and that we can thrill once more to the unique brilliance that they brought to the sport, and to our lives.

PART II

GREATNESS—
A PLACE IN HISTORY

"Few individuals significantly alter the course of history."

—STANLEY WOLPERT, *JINNAH OF PAKISTAN*

IT IS HERE THAT WE CONFRONT A DIFFERENCE IN DEFINITIONS THAT will become crucial in the final sections of this volume. Throughout these pages, I have attempted to use the term "excellence" to describe the athletic accomplishments our most successful Thoroughbreds have achieved on the racetrack. "Outstanding" is the term I have attempted to use to describe the Thoroughbreds themselves. Every fast furlong, every stakes victory or year-end trophy or Hall of Fame vote is a marker for the outstanding Thoroughbred, a confirmation of their excellence. "Extraordinary" is another word I have used to describe horses and performances that I found to be exceptional.

"Greatness" is a word I have tried to give a separate meaning. Rather than mere racetrack accomplishments resulting from physical traits—speed, power, stamina—greatness is intended to describe Thoroughbred accomplishments that have significantly impacted the sport of racing itself. Horses whose achievements have transcended mere racetrack victories deserve to be considered truly great.

The thesaurus tells us that "excellence" and "greatness" are intended to have different meanings. "Excellence" is defined as fineness, brilliance, superiority, distinction, merit.

And these are certainly desirable qualities, whether in a state-of-the-art sports car, or a work of art, or a successful entrepreneur, or a fine Thoroughbred racehorse. But they are not quite greatness, which the thesaurus defines as importance, prominence, significance, weightiness.

They're different words. And when we're assessing the accomplishments of racehorses, the difference is important.

Consider Swaps, for example. He was an excellent racehorse, something he demonstrated conclusively and repeatedly by coming home first in nineteen of twenty-five races, winning major stakes, emerging victorious over a very good group of 3-year-olds in the 1955 Kentucky Derby, setting numerous track and world records, earning a Horse of the Year trophy, and being honored with a plaque in racing's Hall of Fame. He did virtually everything we expect of a top Thoroughbred.

But do fans of Swaps have reason to suggest that he earned a higher level of acclaim? Other than displaying enormous talent on the racetrack and indicating to the skeptical Eastern press that a top California colt could compete with the best Thoroughbreds in the East, did Swaps make contributions to the sport that place him above the merely excellent? Did he enhance the future of the sport? Did his importance as a racehorse surpass that of other Hall of Famers who also set records in abundance and won major races? Did Swaps, in short, achieve greatness?

I don't see it.

People flocked to racetracks to see races that included Swaps, but not in numbers creating a visible blip on the economy of the times, or even the economy of the tracks that featured him. Many of those who saw him win the Santa Anita Derby, the Kentucky Derby, the American Derby, and the Hollywood Gold Cup would have been there anyway, to see a famous and historic race, to drink a mint julep, to wager their dollars, to enjoy the company of friends, or to revel in an afternoon in the sun.

And the same is almost certainly true for the Thoroughbreds used in this book as exemplars of some particular Thoroughbred virtue. Exterminator and Ruffian and Affirmed and the others were spectacularly outstanding examples of the Thoroughbred breed at its most talented. We have honored them during their careers with race trophies and year-end titles, named important races after them, voted them racing's most coveted honors. They have thrilled us with their brilliance and enriched our memories with their enormous hearts and their beauty. They have earned our acclaim.

But as we are defining it in these pages, they have not earned the mantle of greatness. We reserve that term for a very few, for those Thoroughbreds whose importance extends beyond the mere physical task of winning races. A Thoroughbred described as "great" should be more important than merely "one of the ones," as the old racing phrase goes.

There is a long-standing debate in the sphere of presidential history over whether "the man makes the times or the times make the man." Would Lincoln have seemed as great, had the questions of slavery and maintaining the union been solved by an earlier president? Would our relatively obscure peacetime presidents have earned more respect, had they been required to guide the nation through difficult eras of military conflict?

Does it seem odd to bring so exalted a standard to the realm of racehorses? If so, let's continue our discussion with Swaps as the example.

Swaps raced during the mid-1950s, a period when racing had largely recovered, first from the Great Depression and then from World War II and the war in Korea. The number of races each year was on the upswing and had been since 1946, when the Second World War was behind us and the increased tax rates required to wage a full-scale war had been reduced to less draconian levels. Dwight D. Eisenhower was in the White House, a symbol of peace and prosperity during what was a tension-filled but less difficult "cold war."

At American racetracks, purses were keeping pace, increasing in most years, occasionally consolidating, then again leaping upward. Total purses would reach $100 million in 1962, $200 million in 1971, $300 million in 1976. The number of races being contested was growing by the year, topping 20,000 in 1946, 30,000 in 1953, 40,000 in 1961, 50,000 in 1969. The number peaked at 82,705 in 1989.

The breeding industry, with the rest of the sport, was booming, and Thoroughbred foals were being bred in record numbers. It was in 1956, Swaps's final year on the track, that the number of registered American foals exceeded 10,000 for the first time. Although the annual count of registered foals peaked in 1986 with 51,296 and has been decreasing ever since, the number has never again approached a count as low as 10,000. Probably it never will.

If Swaps had an influence on any of this, it was surely no greater than other Derby winners who set records and earned copious newspaper coverage. Was Swaps more responsible for racing's growth during his period than Citation was during the late 1940s and early '50s? Than Native Dancer, who first drew television viewers to the sport, in the 1950s? Than Carry Back in the 1960s? It is difficult to make this case.

In short, Swaps arrived at a time when racing was in stable health. There was not much that needed to be done, or could be done, by an individual horse to speed the upswing or ensure that the sport did not fall back into the doldrums. Times were good.

Man o' War's career began under vastly different circumstances, at a time when racing was on a downturn and beset by issues that literally threatened its existence. As we will explore in more detail, these issues were:

- The so-called "Progressive Era" of American politics, lasting roughly from 1890 through the early years of the "Roaring '20s," which included a strong and committed anti-gambling faction that for a time gained the upper hand over forces favoring racing.

- World War I, which began in Europe in 1914, was joined by a reluctant United States in 1917, and had a substantial impact on American Thoroughbred racing before the Allied forces gained victory in 1919.

- The scandal that beset sports in Man o' War's day. Baseball, in particular, was viewed as a dirty sport in which cheating, including throwing games or bribing other players to do so, was commonplace. The 1919 Black Sox scandal, in which eight members of the American League Champion Chicago White Sox participated in a clumsy but ultimately effective conspiracy with gamblers to deliberately lose that season's World Series to the National League Champion Cincinnati Reds, was strongly rumored in 1919, considered a likelihood in 1920, and became headline news in 1921. Thoroughbred racing, in which wagering is a central aspect of the sport, has always been a particular target for those who believe that fixing races is the constant aim of the seediest form of sporting miscreants, and the sport was inevitably stained by the issues besetting the National Pastime.

Man o' War's role in overcoming such weighty issues may have been nothing less than the salvation of his sport.

Sheepshead Bay Speedway in 1916, no longer a horse racing venue. (Wikimedia Commons)

CHAPTER 17

The "Progressive Era"

THE PROGRESSIVE ERA, WHICH BEGAN AROUND 1890 AND IS CONSID-
ered to have lasted until roughly the end of the First World War, albeit
with influence for years after, was not primarily involved with racing,
or with sports at all. It was rooted in the rapid-fire industrialization of
America during this period, accelerating urbanization of populations
as jobs moved increasingly to cities, and the results of those dynamics,
especially as reflected in the poor living conditions for so many hand-to-
mouth, working-class families.

There are many other aspects to the Progressive Era as well: concerns
about the "boss" governing system in American cities; the initially slow
but ultimately successful movement toward women's suffrage; and the
effort to bust trusts, eliminate monopolies, and promote fair competition
for the good of the nation and its people. All of this, and still more, com-
prised the Progressive Movement, an era widely reported in newspapers,
discussed in books, and debated by politicians seeking office, up to and
including the highest office in the land.

But those elements of the Progressive Era are well beyond the
scope of this book, which is, after all, about Man o' War and his place in
the history of the Sport of Kings. What we will be considering in this
chapter is the element of Progressive politics that focused on gambling
and on the efforts—largely successful, at least for a while—to eliminate
the perceived evils that operated daily at the nation's racetracks, which
included bookmaking, wagering pools, parimutuel wagering, and the

other structures and processes that powered the ultimate aim of such pursuits: winning money.

In this small but significant subgenre of the overall Progressive platform, there was nothing more important to the Empire State's coalition of conservative politicians and religious leaders than doing away with gambling. Gambling was the plunderer of families, the path to bankruptcy, to madness, to suicide, to perdition for those caught up in its spell. Racetrack gambling was certainly a target, but for New York City (and doubtless all large cities), another perceived evil was the poolroom, which existed not merely as a site for friendly billiards matches but as a backdrop for betting on games of chance and, of course, on the horses, in the form of backroom bookie joints.

We will focus here on New York City, which at the time was presenting the nation's most important and most opulent racing, and that arguably had the most public relations–conscious politicians. Thoroughbred racing, exemplified by both wealthy owners and two-dollar racegoers, would shortly face the challenge of a series of anti-gambling governors and legislatures who would eventually succeed in closing every racetrack in the great city. The ban would be relatively brief, but the economic impact on racing would be felt long after racetrack gambling was restored to legal status.

New York's first state constitution, adopted in 1777, was the most basic of documents for the governance of a state. It was a combination Declaration of Independence and constitution, focusing largely on "the tyrannical and oppressive usurpations of the King and Parliament of Great Britain on the people of the American colonies" as the rationale for forming an independent governmental entity. It established basic structures of government, but for the most part declined to dictate which laws to pass or which to prioritize for enforcement.

It was with the second New York Constitution, passed in 1821, that the topic of gambling is first mentioned at so important a level. Article VII, §11 reads: "No lottery shall hereafter be authorized in this state; and the legislature shall pass laws to prevent the sale of all lottery tickets within this state, except in lotteries already provided for by law."

This didn't particularly impact racing in the Empire State. Bookies operated on the racecourses; spectator-to-spectator wagers were treated as private business transactions rather than criminal enterprises. If there was an effort to discourage gambling, it was probably felt most acutely in the poolrooms, which were a flourishing presence in New York City and would remain so for decades to come.

The third New York Constitution, established in 1846, addressed the issue in Section 1, Article 1, §10, which read, "[N]or shall any lottery hereafter be authorized, or any sale of lottery tickets allowed within this state."

The wording is not much different, but the attitude is becoming more anti-gambling, and there began to be concern about increased police presence at the tracks and the occasional highly publicized raid. This was not creating insuperable problems for racetrack bookies, bettors, or track owners; the concern was that it *could*, should the police choose to interpret the law to prohibit racetrack gambling. Raids on poolrooms continued, with lurid newspaper reports of gamblers' skin-of-the-teeth escapes and police destruction of gambling paraphernalia. The party in power trumpeted the success of productive police actions; the opposition's post-raid critiques were publicized at every opportunity.

In 1887, with the Ives Pool Bill, the racing industry began seeking a legislative path around the possibility of a statutory ban on racetrack gambling. And the anti-gambling authorities—police, jurists, politicians, and members of the clergy—began pushing back.

The Ives Bill was intended to permit racing in New York for thirty days each year, with "pool selling" (selling of wagering chances on the races) permitted. As a condition of operating, the racing associations were to pay a percentage of their gate receipts as a fee or tax, which would then be allocated to agricultural associations to be used for the purpose of improving the breeds of cattle, sheep, and horses. The aim of this money transfer did not reflect any interest on the part of racing's supporters in the improvement of non-equine breeds; the intent was to garner legislative support from the agricultural associations.

The Ives Bill created a firestorm of opposition. Passage of the bill in the legislature was a four-month-long ordeal of spirited and often acrimonious debate, with legislators, clerics, and racing organizations battling over gambling's legality and morality. Finally called for a vote, the Ives Pool Bill passed its final legislative hurdle on May 12, 1887, and became law on May 25, when Governor David B. Hill, declining to affix his signature to a bill condoning gambling, allowed it to pass unsigned into law.

An uneasy truce ensued between the racetracks and the anti-gambling forces, culminating with the Empire State's 1894 Constitution, New York's fourth. It is here that the anti-gambling influence of what would soon be full-blown Progressive Era politics can be seen, and it is here that racing's supporters faced their sternest challenge.

Article 1, Section 1, §9 of the 1894 Constitution took dead aim at racetrack wagering with wording far more explicit than in previous documents: "[N]or shall any lottery or the sale of lottery tickets, pool-selling, book making, or any other kind of gambling hereafter be authorized or allowed within this State; and the Legislature shall pass appropriate laws to prevent offenses against any of the provisions of this section."

The key words here are "pool-selling, book making, *or any other kind of gambling*" [italics the author's], which strikes not only at two of the most popular racetrack wagering schemes of the day but also at any other that might be invented to replace them.

With the fourth constitution, on-site racetrack gambling was, to all intents and purposes, no longer a legal possibility in the state of New York, and police raids on racetracks increased dramatically. In one such instance, a raid at Brooklyn's six-year-old Brighton Beach racetrack caught the eye of a reporter for the *Penn Yan (New York) Chronicle-Express* on June 3, 1885. His pessimistic appraisal was roughly a quarter-century ahead of its time, but otherwise it was all too accurate:

> *Pool selling at Brighton Beach was rudely interrupted on Memorial Day by the arrest of the chief law breakers. This will probably lead to the abandonment of that race course.*

Although our focus here is on New York, the reader should not have the impression that the Progressive Movement, and its anti-gambling aspect, was anything less than a national phenomenon. As New York was moving haltingly toward a ban on all gambling, other states, slightly ahead of the curve, had already enacted measures and were actively enforcing them. Other areas were enacting similar statutes, their police forces adopting similar attitudes.

And thus, on January 28, 1900, Mayor George H. Clark of Sacramento directed the city's chief of police to shut down all gambling houses in the city. "All gambling that is against the law must be discontinued. You and I are called upon to enforce the laws as we find them, and if any law of this State is being violated in our community our plain duties require us to punish the offender and to prevent repetitions of such violations." On March 29, 1907, Governor Thomas Mitchell Campbell of Texas signed a bill declaring all forms of gambling a felony. On June 29, 1907, the Tennessee Supreme Court overruled the state's criminal court by declaring the Volunteer State's anti-race gambling law to be constitutional, ending horse racing in the state.

When Exterminator ran his "race against time" at Hawthorne Park, discussed in chapter 13, it was the highlight of the first day of racing following an eighteen-year ban in Illinois. Under the law, no wagering was permitted on any of the day's seven races, and police were on the grounds to ensure that any violations were cited. The feature article in the *Chicago Tribune* was headlined "20,000 Cheer Race Revival at Hawthorne / No 'Open' Betting as Police Watch."

There is no quicker way to destroy a gambling-based sport such as racing than to sever its lifeblood by outlawing wagering. For years, then decades, the racetracks and their backers sought legislation that would keep the sport viable by allowing some form of betting. Each new bill, each new law, sent the anti-gambling forces back to the law books, the courtrooms and the legislatures seeking new ways to prohibit wagering. Each law was slightly different from earlier ones, but each represented another hurdle to be overcome by the pro-racing forces.

There was, for example, the 1895 Percy-Grey Bill, which would have permitted racing to continue but prohibited bookmaking, pool-selling, and pari-mutuel machines at racetracks and at non-racing venues, while also banning the use of telegraphic wires to transmit race results to poolrooms and other interested locations. There was the 1904 Dowling-Wainwright Anti-Gambling Bill, which not only would have banned gambling but also would have compelled gamblers to testify against themselves under threat of contempt of court citations. There was the 1905 Cassidy-Lansing Bill, intended to make gambling anywhere in New York a felony. There were the 1906 Moreland and Coggeshall Bills, which would have continued racing and increased the stake of agricultural associations from the Ives Bill's initial $50,000.

The election of anti-gambling governor Charles Evans Hughes, who assumed office on January 1, 1907, was the nearest thing yet to a death blow for racing in the Empire State. Hughes's inaugural address did not specifically mention gambling, but it did allude to "complacent inactivity" and the "toleration of wrongs made possible by defective or inadequate legislation or by administrative partiality or inefficiency," and added that "many of the evils of which we complain have their source in the law itself, in privileges carelessly granted, in opportunities for private aggrandizement at the expense of the people . . . in failure to safeguard our public interests." It would not be a long reach to apply all of these comments to horse racing still having a foothold in the state.

Nor would it be difficult, given those strong words from a newly elected governor known to be anti-gambling, to believe that the ongoing fight to eliminate racing was about to escalate dramatically.

Clearly, the anti-gambling clergy had a new and powerful ally. Governor Hughes's father was a retired minister who was seated on stage for the new governor's inaugural address, and there were few among religious leaders or the press who failed to understand the implications. The clergy ramped up its efforts to defeat the racing forces once and for all with mass meetings designed to enlist ever greater support and sermons teeming with anti-gambling rhetoric.

In July 1907, Governor Hughes announced that he was "preparing for action" against racetracks and the ever-present poolrooms, informing the district attorney of Albany County that he was "not satisfied with the manner in which the laws against gambling, vice, and the sale of liquor on Sundays and after hours were being enforced." The forces seeking to maintain racing braced for yet another blow. It was not long in coming.

In his January 1, 1908, message, Governor Hughes urged the legislature to "carry out the clear direction of the people against racetrack gambling as embodied in the Constitution, to repeal the Percy-Gray Act . . . and to impose a penalty of imprisonment upon bookmakers." With this encouragement, the assembly quickly passed two new anti-racetrack gambling bills. One, which would amend the Percy-Gray Law out of existence by disallowing all forms of racetrack gambling, passed the assembly by a 126-to-9 vote; the other, imposing a year's imprisonment for those found to be professional gamblers, bookmakers, or pool sellers, passed 126-to-7.

With this, the writing was on the wall for some racetrack owners. On March 26, 1909, Brooklyn's Brighton Beach racetrack closed its doors forever to the equine sport. It would reopen as a motordrome, the sound of hooves replaced by the roar of automobile engines, but by the 1920s real estate investors had purchased the land. The former racetrack facilities were demolished, and the land rededicated to residential housing.

On June 15, 1910, Governor Hughes's signing of three bills collectively known as the Agnew-Perkins Laws ended Thoroughbred racing in New York. One of the bills made it a misdemeanor punishable by imprisonment for up to a year for anyone to make book on a horse race, "with or without writing," which made criminals even of private individuals making oral bets among themselves. Another of the bills specifically applied the anti-gambling sections of the Penal Code to racetracks.

It was the third of the bills, however, that spelled doom for racing in New York. The Percy-Gray racing law had exempted from personal liability the trustees and directors of racing associations. The new law ended this exemption, holding track owners criminally liable for gambling at their tracks. Unwilling to assume personal liability for every potential instance of gambling, they had little choice but to close down their tracks.

While tracks in various states were shut down for a variety of different periods, the New York tracks were shuttered for two years, from 1911 to 1913. Gone were the great events that had previously highlighted the racing calendar: the Belmont Stakes, the Travers, the Brooklyn Handicap, the Suburban, the Metropolitan, the Futurity. Even when the sport was finally restored, New York racing would recover from the ban with painful baby steps.

The first day of renewed racing was Friday, May 30, 1913, at Belmont Park. An overflow crowd estimated at 25,000 attended, and newspapers published photos of Whitneys, Vanderbilts, and other leaders of high society sunning themselves on the track's balconies and enjoying the ambience and the fine foods. The featured event on the six-race card was the twentieth running of the Metropolitan Handicap, won by the future Hall of Fame combination of Whisk Broom II, jockey Joe Notter, and trainer James Rowe.

But the racing industry was on the razor's edge following two years without revenues. While the cost of horse ownership was what it had always been, the ability to earn purse money was reduced substantially. It would require years to build back to the level of a half-decade earlier.

This is reflected in the substantially reduced purses of the historically important races. When the horse Joe Madden won the Belmont Stakes in 1909, he earned a winner's purse of $24,550; when Prince Eugene won the race in 1913's reduced circumstances, the winning purse was $2,825. When Novelty won the 1910 Futurity, he earned $25,300; Pennant's winning purse three years later was $15,060. Novelty's bankroll increased by $19,140 when he won the 1910 Hopeful Stakes at Saratoga; Bringhurst's 1913 Hopeful victory earned just $4,100. Fitz Herbert's winning share of the 1909 Lawrence Realization Stakes was $14,900; Rock View's winner's share in 1913 was $2,475.

In some ways, the sport would never recover: Brooklyn had been the flourishing home to three major racetracks: Gravesend, where the Brooklyn Handicap and Tremont Stakes were launched and the Preakness resided for fifteen years when Maryland racing was on the verge of bankruptcy; Brighton Beach, where on July 17, 1900, James R. Keene's 6-year-old stallion Voter had set a new world record for the mile with a clocking of 1:38; and Sheepshead Bay, where the Suburban Handicap and the Futurity had begun and the first twenty-two Lawrence Realizations had been contested.

None would ever reopen as a horse racing venue, and Brooklyn would never again play an important role in the sport. Nationally, dozens, perhaps hundreds of tracks that had thrived in the days before the Progressive Era were lost to the sport in the nationwide flurry of legislation.

It would require years—and one incredible racehorse—to bring New York racing back to its full-blown glory. But from that gorgeous May afternoon of magnificent rebirth, the Sport of Kings in America could once again look forward to a hopeful future.

World War I American troops passing through a small French town. (Wikimedia Commons American First World War Official Exchange Collection Q85388)

CHAPTER 18

The War to End Wars

We honour the memory
Of the peoples who suffered through war.
We remember their citizens who were persecuted
And who lost their lives.
We remember those killed in action in the World Wars.
We remember the innocent who lost their lives as
A result of war in their homeland, in captivity
And through expulsion.

We remember the millions of Jews who were murdered.
We remember the Sinti and Roma who were murdered.
We remember all those who were killed because of their
Origin, homosexuality, sickness or infirmity.
We remember all who were murdered
Whose right to life was denied.

We remember the people who had to die
Because of their religious or political convictions.
We remember all those who were victims of tyranny
And met their death, though innocent.

We remember the women and men
Who sacrificed their lives in resistance to despotic rule.
We honour all who preferred to die rather
Than act against their conscience.

We honour the memory of the women and men
Who were persecuted and murdered
Because they resisted totalitarian dictatorship.
—Inscription at Neue Wache, Central Memorial of the Federal
Republic of Germany to the Victims of War and Tyranny,
Berlin, Germany

WORLD WAR I REPRESENTED THE FIRST TIME IN AMERICAN HISTORY
that the nation would send its sons—and a handful of pioneering daughters—into a foreign war for the purpose of defending other nations' soil. America's entry into the war came after years of often acrimonious public debate about whether the nation should join the battle in the time of our allies' greatest need or remain on the sidelines. When America did choose to involve itself, the nation's addition to the Allied war machine would prove decisive.

Historians generally agree that World War I's origin can be found in the assassination of Archduke Franz Ferdinand of the Austro-Hungarian Empire by a Serbian nationalist named Gavrilo Princip, at 11:15 a.m. on June 28, 1914. The European nations had, for years, forged complex alliances calling for countries to reinforce one another in times of conflict, and now matters spiraled. In a slow unfolding toward inevitability, those European alliances were called into play, and hostilities between nations escalated.

The conflict lasted for four bloody years, pitting the Central Powers—Germany, Austria-Hungary, Bulgaria, and the Ottoman Empire—against the Allied Powers: Great Britain, France, Russia, Italy, Romania, Canada, Japan, Belgium, and, eventually, the United States. Russia's involvement, however, would be cut short. The overthrow of Czar Nicholas II in the Bolshevik Revolution of 1917 would end czarist rule and would also bring an abrupt end to Russia's participation in World War I.

Of the major Allied powers, Russia had committed a land force totaling 1,400,000; France 1,290,000; Serbia 190,000; and Belgium 186,000. Great Britain could send only a 120,000-man army into the fray. The ground forces of the Central Powers were primarily composed of Germany's 1,900,000 soldiers and 450,000 from Austria-Hungary.

As the war began, the British could boast of a substantial advantage in sea power: twenty Dreadnought battleships to fourteen for the Germans; nine battle cruisers to the Germans' four; thirty-nine pre-Dreadnought battleships to the Germans' twenty-two; thirty-four armored cruisers to the Germans' nine; sixty-four other cruisers to the Germans' forty-one; 301 destroyers to the Germans' 144; and sixty-five submarines to the Germans' twenty-eight. Without massive production of additional naval vessels—and training of the men required to operate them—Germany's sea force would rely to a great extent upon the aggressive use of submarines, and British superiority on the waters would remain a powerful factor in the Allies' favor. President Wilson's address to Congress asking for a declaration of war against Germany took place on April 6, 1917; the United States would declare war against Germany's ally, the Austro-Hungarian Empire, eight months later.

The United States had begun the war as little more than a spectator nation. A policy of neutrality was favored by President Wilson, reflecting to a great degree the belief of the typical American that the nation should avoid participation in what was perceived as a European war. The United States engaged in commerce with countries on both sides, largely without regard to their politics or military coalitions.

By 1915, Germany had declared the waters surrounding the British Isles part of the war zone, and German submarines began sinking commercial and passenger vessels. Maintaining neutrality became an increasingly difficult proposition for the United States, as the German Empire escalated its submarine warfare, including attacks involving ships carrying noncombatant American passengers. Neutrality would receive a jolt whenever a US ship was hit.

No one writing about World War I can avoid discussing the sinking of the British passenger ship RMS *Lusitania*, torpedoed by German submarine U-20 eleven miles off the coast of Ireland on May 7, 1915. Of the 1,960 people aboard the ship, which was also carrying war materiel for the British Army, 1,193 died, including 128 Americans. Americans responded with the outrage and indignation that might have been predicted, but the nation's reluctance to engage in a war on foreign soil held strong. It would be another two years before the Americans declared war.

Another event serving to incite America's entry into the hostilities was the Zimmermann Telegram, a communication from German foreign minister Arthur Zimmermann inviting Mexico to ally with the German Empire. The Mexican government was promised not only money but the return of the territories of Texas, New Mexico, and Arizona, lost by Mexico seventy years earlier in the Mexican-American War.

But British intelligence intercepted the telegram, and when President Wilson gave it to the press for publication it fired Americans' righteous anger, leading to a much greater willingness to join the fight against Germany and its allies.

Even when the outraged American public was sufficiently affronted to make a war effort feasible, preparations of historic levels would be necessary. At the time of the declaration of (in Wilson's words) "a war to end all wars" and a war to "make the world safe for democracy," the United States had a standing army of just 127,000, including officers and soldiers, fewer available troops than thirteen of the nations already fighting.

German soldiers outnumbered their American counterparts by a margin of nearly twenty to one, and it is likely that this very numerical superiority emboldened the Central Powers, and Germany in particular, to discount the likelihood that America could influence the war's outcome. Germany began employing its submarines to sink ships of all sorts in the effort to prevent troops and war materiel from reaching their intended destinations, and in the hope that the war could be ended, with a treaty advantageous to the Central Powers, before America, perceived as a dangerous but lumbering giant, could both declare and prepare for war.

Obviously, if the United States planned to have a real impact, it would need considerably more fighting men, and after passage of the Selective Service Act of 1917, considerably more would be provided. By the end of the war, 10,000 American soldiers were arriving in France each day, and some 4 million men had served in the US Army, of whom approximately 2 million—1.4 million would see active combat—were assigned to the American Expeditionary Force (AEF). Another 800,000 served in other branches, including naval and Marine forces. The AEF tipped the balance of power as the war neared its climax, retaking more than 200 miles of French lands that had been seized by foreign armies.

Even as these millions of American troops were being trained and prepared to fight, other concerns needed to be addressed. Aside from lacking a viable army, the United States faced the necessity of ramping up the production of supplies, equipment, and rations that would be required in huge quantities for a fighting force of the intended magnitude. Even the transport ships that would be needed to bring troops to Europe were scarce, and building warships is not an overnight process. The military commandeered cruise ships, hastily repaired captured German vessels, and borrowed ships of other Allied nations to transport soldiers to the war zone.

Nor was the peacetime American economy sufficient to support a war effort of this magnitude, and as the all-out push was implemented to raise and supply an army of sufficient size, the governmental structure swung into action to find the funding required for essential materiel, munitions, and food. Aiding in this effort would be the Sixteenth Amendment to the US Constitution, passed by Congress in 1909 and ratified on February 3, 1913, which allowed Congress to levy an income tax.

But the raising of such enormous amounts of additional funds would require both mandated and voluntary revenue sources. The cost of the war would eventually be $33 billion, some forty-two times the level of 1916 Treasury receipts.

The first step would be to raise the income tax level substantially. The tax rate for individuals who had been paying 2 percent income taxes in 1917 was increased to 12 percent in 1918. Additional surcharges ranged from 1 percent for incomes above $5,000 to 65 percent for incomes above $1,000,000. Businesses paid additional taxes, including excess profit taxes of 20 to 80 percent above pre-war levels. Excise taxes were added for purchases of luxury items such as automobiles, motorboats, and jewelry.

Additionally, Americans were urged to purchase war bonds, which were marketed through campaigns that touched everyone who read a newspaper, purchased a magazine, or saw any of the millions of posters that blanketed public spaces during the years of America's involvement. At public meetings and celebrations, over the wireless, and in the moving picture theaters that were becoming increasingly popular, well-known celebrities explained the importance of purchasing war bonds. The Boy

Scouts of America undertook campaigns to help sell bonds. More than half of all American families subscribed, raising more than $21 billion to support the war effort.

The American workforce found ways around the loss of workers engaged in military service. Trade unions such as the American Federation of Labor had actively encouraged their younger members to enlist in the war effort, which created a need for others to join assembly lines and work in production centers. As men were recruited, trained, and sent into the fray, large numbers of American women began performing jobs that were traditionally reserved for men, the first time in history this had occurred on so broad a scale. Additional millions of women joined the Red Cross as volunteers, working to assist servicemen and their families.

The impression many have of World War I is a tableau of grinding trench warfare, with battle lines moving forward or back in frustratingly small increments as one side or the other gained the momentary upper hand. The sheer manpower required to replace dead or injured troops and continue fighting such a war was enormous. By war's end, it was estimated that Germany and France had sent as much as 80 percent of their male populations between the ages of fifteen and forty-nine into combat. The arrival and increasing participation of American troops was welcomed heartily by the exhausted Allies—who had, after all, been fighting the war since 1914—and contributed to lessening the morale of Central Powers troops and leadership.

While Allied leaders might have preferred that American troops be combined with the existing armies already fighting the war, President Wilson deemed it essential that the American Expeditionary Forces remain an independent and separate fighting force on a par with other Allied armies. Wilson's goal was long-term and intensely political, based on his belief that only an independent American effort would be seen by the combatants as entitling the president to significantly influence peace negotiations at the conclusion of hostilities.

At the time, World War I was by far the deadliest conflict in history, both for those on the front lines and for the civilian populations of participating nations. It is estimated that the death toll from all aspects of the war—from death in battle to starvation, disease, genocide, and the horrors of being held as prisoners of war—may have totaled as many as 16.5 million, including 9.7 million soldiers and sailors who died in battle, and more than 6.8 million civilians. The carnage exacted from the fighting was so extensive, the battle zone so enormous, that historians continue to debate the actual numbers killed.

The war's historically enormous death toll can be attributed in part to the improved technology that made the fighting forces ever more capable of inflicting death on a large scale. World War I was the first war in which aircraft played an important role, the first to feature extensive trench warfare, sophisticated use of submarines, tank battles, aircraft carriers and aerial warfare, machine guns, flamethrowers, and poison gas and gas masks.

And thus, the almost incomprehensible carnage. On the Allied side, nearly 900,000 British lives were lost, France lost nearly 1.4 million, Russia over 1.8 million, Italy 651,000, Serbia 275,000, and the United States approximately 116,000. Of the Central Powers, the German Empire suffered more than 2 million deaths, Austria-Hungary 1.1 million, the Ottoman Empire 2,150,000, and Bulgaria 87,500. One American soldier was reportedly killed in the final minute before the armistice was declared and the war officially ended.

It is estimated that the United States sustained more than 320,000 casualties during World War I, with over 53,000 killed in action and an estimated 63,000 noncombat deaths. Approximately 204,000 were wounded. With troops engaged in trench warfare inevitably being in close proximity for extended periods, a deadly form of influenza, which surfaced as a raging pandemic in the early months of 1918, exacted a disproportionate toll. One source believes that 45,000 American troops died of the flu. Troops returning to the home front brought the virus with them, exacerbating the disease as a global horror.

In the most severe pandemic of modern times until COVID-19, the "Spanish Flu"—so named not because it originated in Spain but because it was first publicized there—infected approximately one-third of the world's population, an estimated 500 million people, and caused 50 million deaths worldwide. In the United States, one-quarter of the population became ill, with the death toll estimated to be 675,000. New

York City alone experienced three distinct waves of infection, sustaining approximately 30,000 flu-related deaths in its population of 5.6 million.

On September 1, 1919, approximately two years after the arrival of the first American troops in France, with victory won and many of its fighting men already returned to their homes, the American Expeditionary Forces were officially deactivated.

Sadly, "the war to end wars" proved to be anything but. The League of Nations, Wilson's hope to create a forum to adjudicate and de-escalate disputes among states, was a dismal failure, not even gaining enough support in Congress to permit the United States to join and participate. Barely more than a decade following the conclusion of World War I, Adolf Hitler had arisen in Germany, and as new alliances formed and new and even deadlier weaponry rolled off factory assembly lines, a second world war, even more devastating than the first, meant death for more millions of fighters and peacemakers, politicians and civilians. Not only political goals were pursued by the combatants, but bitter religious and cultural hatreds led to genocidal efforts, some of which came far too close to succeeding.

The Second World War lasted from 1939 until 1945, and the nations of the world did not wait long to plunge into yet another war, and another, and ever more. Whether the human race can ever find its way to peaceful solutions cannot be predicted, but as the conclusion of the first quarter of the twenty-first century approaches, nations continue to embrace war as a legitimate solution to their conflicts.

And what, you might ask, does all of this have to do with Man o' War?

President Wilson's address to Congress asking for a declaration of war against Germany occurred just eight days after Man o' War was foaled, on March 29, 1917, at August Belmont Jr.'s Nursery Stud. Mr. Belmont, then age sixty-five, had chosen to serve overseas and was commissioned a major and assigned to the Quartermaster Corps. In his honor, Belmont's wife, Eleanor, who had the annual task of naming the burgeoning farm's foals, chose to honor her husband by giving one of the more promising colts the name Man o' War.

Just over two years later, on June 6, 1919, Man o' War would begin his career at Belmont Park. And just over sixteen months after that, on October 20, 1920, Man o' War would race for the final time, in his Kenilworth Park match race with Sir Barton. The armistice ending The Great War had become official on November 11, 1918. Man o' War's entire career therefore passed during the post-war era, with surviving soldiers, some grievously wounded, returning to their pre-war homes, less fortunate others remaining behind, victims of the ferocious fighting. The high taxes necessary to prosecute a war would be reduced now that peacetime had returned, but the money that had already been spent on war was gone, permanently unavailable for such discretionary uses as racetrack wagering.

Man o' War raced at a time of relative scarcity, particularly given the reduced number of races and racetracks that resulted from the so-called Progressive Era. As we will see, racing was experiencing the same scarcity that faced America at the time, and Man o' War would race under post-wartime conditions that affected every aspect of the sport.

He would be a significant player in the sport's recovery.

The 1919 Chicago White Sox. (Wikimedia Commons)

CHAPTER 19

The Black Sox Scandal

THE PHOTO THAT BEGINS THIS CHAPTER DISPLAYS BOTH THE FOURTEEN Chicago White Sox players who were not involved in throwing the 1919 World Series to the Cincinnati Reds, and the eight who crushed the hopes of the team and the city of Chicago by selling out to gamblers and stealing the post-season glory that had seemed not merely possible but almost a certainty from the season's opening game.

Swede Risberg (top row, 5th player), Fred McMillen (top row, 6th player), Shoeless Joe Jackson (top row, 9th player), Happy Felsch (middle row, 5th player), Chick Gandil (middle row, 6th player), Buck Weaver (middle row, 7th player), Ed Cicotte (bottom row, 3rd player), and Claude "Lefty" Williams (bottom row, 5th player) were the players who forever turned that exceptional White Sox team into the Black Sox, remembered today for the harm they did to the team, the city, and the sport. In the end, the eight were banned from baseball by the sport's commissioner, Kenesaw Mountain Landis. Occasionally, one might apply for reinstatement, but Judge Landis was not having players capable of inflicting such a devastating blow on the game. None of the eight ever returned to baseball.

Considered one of the best teams of the era, the White Sox had earned the championship of the talent-laden American League, overcoming the Cleveland Indians and New York Yankees in a pot-boiling pennant race to prevail in the regular season. Chicagoans reveled in their championship and in their champions, and they awaited the World Series with near certainty: The White Sox were the better of the two World Series teams by a wide margin, and surely would prevail in the post-season.

But the fans were to be disappointed, then embittered, when it was learned that their beloved White Sox had thrown the World Series, accepting gamblers' money to lose the Fall Classic to the upstart and decidedly less talented National League entrant, the Cincinnati Reds.

It was then, and remains over a century later, the most egregious scandal in the long history of Major League Baseball.

This was to be a historic World Series, the first to be played following the end of the devastating Great War, the first World Series that would be seen by American soldiers returning from the long and brutal conflict that had cost so many lives in Europe. And it seemed especially appropriate that the Chicago White Sox, comprising everything excellent about the National Pastime, and by reflection so much that was great about America, should be one of the teams in this one-for-the-ages World Series.

The 1919 White Sox featured solid hitting, led by the immortal "Shoeless Joe" Jackson, who batted .351 with a team-leading (tied with co-conspirator Happy Felsch) seven home runs in that dead ball–era season, and future Hall of Famer Eddie Collins, who played an athletic second base while batting .310 and driving in eighty runs. And the team could claim the league's best pitching, led by co-conspirators Eddie Cicotte, with twenty-nine wins and a 1.82 earned run average, and Lefty Williams, who won twenty-three games and posted an ERA of 2.64.

But then, the American League was a collection of star-studded franchises. The runner-up Cleveland Indians were led by future Hall of Famer Tris Speaker and Elmer Smith, whose nine home runs led the team. The infield was anchored by Bill Wambsganss, who the following year would glove a line drive, step on second base, and tag the runner coming from first to complete the only unassisted triple play in World Series history. Twenty-eight-year-old Ray Chapman, a solid .300 hitter and excellent shortstop, was another mainstay whose seemingly limitless future would be tragically cut short the following year when a fastball thrown by the Yankees' Carl Mays hit him in the head. He died the next day, the only player in Major League history to lose his life in an on-field incident.

The third-place Yankees, still a year away from obtaining the immortal Babe Ruth from the Red Sox, featured third baseman Frank "Home Run" Baker, whose ten round-trippers led the team, and twenty-game-winning pitcher Bob Shawkey. The fourth-place Detroit Tigers featured the fiery Ty Cobb, who batted .384 that year and intimidated infielders with his aggressive baserunning, and fellow Hall of Famer Harry Heilman, who batted .320 with eight home runs. Tigers outfielder Bobby Veach batted .355 and led the team with 97 RBIs.

The fifth-place St. Louis Browns would finish twenty and a half games back despite the batting feats of future Hall of Fame first baseman George Sisler, with his .352 batting average and ten homers. And the sixth-place Boston Red Sox somehow managed only a 66-71 record despite the exploits of George Herman (Babe) Ruth, who clobbered a record twenty-nine home runs and led the league with 114 RBIs, 103 runs scored, a .456 on-base percentage, and a .657 slugging percentage. When he wasn't clearing the fences with titanic home runs, Ruth also found time to pitch in seventeen games, winning nine and losing five, with a sterling 2.97 ERA.

Even the hapless Washington Senators, who won but fifty-six games, could boast of outfielder Sam Rice, who batted .321, and future Hall of Fame pitcher Walter Johnson, who had already won 277 Major League games and in 1919 would win twenty more, with a 1.49 ERA.

It was sportswriter Charley Dryden, dubbed by some "the Mark Twain of Baseball," who would one day describe Washington as "first in war, first in peace, and last in the American League," but thanks to Philadelphia Athletics owner/manager Connie Mack (nee Cornelius McGillicuddy), who a few years earlier had cut costs by selling off, trading, or releasing many of the Athletics' best players, the lowly A's managed to be even worse, winning just 36 of 140 games. Here was the wasteland of the star-studded American League: The 1919 A's were essentially a minor league team masquerading as a major league squad.

In the National League, the Cincinnati Reds had coasted to a nine-game victory over the runner-up New York Giants, winning ninety-six games and losing just forty-four. They were led by future Hall of Famer

"Big Edd" Roush, who batted .321 and drove in a team-leading seventy-one runs. Heinie Groh, their lead-off batter, batted .310, and their pitching staff included twenty-one-game winner Slim Sallee, as well as Hod Eller and Dutch Reuther, each of whom won nineteen games. But despite their abundant talent and a feeling among the people of Cincinnati that this "miracle team" was destined to bring a World Series victory to the Queen City, the Reds, as the post-season approached, were a decided underdog to the celebrated White Sox juggernaut.

But the White Sox were a team with grievances, most of which revolved around the players' loathing of their penny-pinching ownership, which followed each season with one-sided management-player negotiations intended to minimize salaries and thereby maximize the profits of owner Charles Comiskey. Despite their accomplishments, despite their high level of performance, the White Sox were reputedly among the league's lowest-paid teams.

Joe Jackson, whose career was certainly on a Hall of Fame trajectory but whose meager education did not allow him to prevail in a salary negotiation with the skilled attorneys employed by Comiskey, earned but $6,000 per season, less than half of what Columbia-educated Collins had been able to negotiate with the A's Mack before being sold to the White Sox. Mainstay third baseman Buck Weaver was paid $6,000; first baseman Chick Gandil and centerfielder Happy Felsch $4,000. Lefty Williams's salary was $3,000.

And Comiskey's refusal to part with money to support the team was seen in other ways: their $3 per day meal money (other teams typically received $4), or the fact that the White Sox often took the field in uniforms bearing the grass and dirt stains from the previous day. Daily laundering, after all, cost money.

If Comiskey wouldn't pay the players what they believed they deserved, and wouldn't provide the basic benefits taken for granted on less celebrated teams, perhaps they could earn what they felt they deserved in other ways.

It was the players, in fact, who reportedly solicited the gamblers' involvement in the scheme, rather than the other way around. As Eliot Asinov described it in his classic baseball book *Eight Men Out*, Chick

Gandil reached out to known gamblers, demanding $80,000 for himself and his seven teammates to throw the Series, and received assurances that this could be arranged. In fact, the players eventually received considerably less, but by the time the final accounting was in, the deed had been done, the Series lost.

It was said that Jackson, for example, despite being the team's unquestioned superstar, received only $5,000 for his role in losing the World Series; Cicotte admitted to receiving $10,000, having demanded his share up front, before he would throw so much as a single pitch. With Cicotte scheduled to pitch the first game of the Series for the Sox, his involvement was considered by both the gamblers and the players to be essential, as was the participation of second-game starter Lefty Williams, who also arranged to lose his initial World Series start.

Cicotte's agreement to deliberately lose the first game was to be signaled to the gamblers through a method that would be unmistakable: He would hit the first Cincinnati batter with a pitch. It was Reds shortstop Heinie Groh who had the painful misfortune to be on the receiving end of this message; the second pitch of the game plunked him in the ribs, and from that point both the players and the gamblers knew that the fix was in, although there were times that the White Sox, who were receiving their payments inconsistently and in amounts less than promised, decided that they would play to win.

But any player rebellion would be short-lived. When a gambler, concerned that his wagers on Cincinnati were at risk because the White Sox were belatedly winning games, sent a hitman to threaten Williams and his wife with physical harm, the hurler deliberately pitched poorly in Game 8, and Cincinnati emerged with a five-games-to-three World Series victory.

The Black Sox scandal, which exploded into public view in 1920 with accusations in the press and a sensational trial, was baseball's most publicized involvement with gamblers, but there had been fixed games in the sport for years and rumors of fixes that probably reflected but a small fraction of the illicit business being perpetrated in the shadowy back rooms of America's National Pastime. Indeed, as historian and scientist Stephen Jay Gould noted in his introduction to Asinov's book, "[T]he game had been in trouble for several years already. Attendance was in decline and rumors of fixing had caused trouble before."

First baseman Hal Chase had been, according to baseball historian Bill James in *The New Bill James Historical Baseball Abstract*, "accused by his manager, George Stallings, of trying to throw a game in 1910," "formally charged by Christy Mathewson, his manager in 1917, with throwing games that year," and "[c]harged by [player] Lee Magee with bribing him to lose games in 1918," before being "suspended by [the] Giants for allegedly throwing games during 1919." A total of twenty-two former and active players were banned from baseball between 1917 and 1927, most of them expelled from the sport for life.

The player suspensions and rumors of fixed games were reported in the press. People knew, and the threat to baseball—and to all sports, since all were susceptible to the gambler's influence—grew as the news of the Black Sox and their inexcusable actions approached ever closer to its explosive revelation during the 1920 season.

It hit, in fact, as Man o' War was completing his undefeated 3-year-old season, drawing glowingly positive notice to the Sport of Kings as the tarnish of scandal was increasingly affixing itself to Major League Baseball. As baseball was branded as a scandal-ridden and dirty sport, Man o' War was attracting fans to Thoroughbred racing with his string of victories, his superiority so evident that no hint of race-fixing would ever attach to him.

Racing, of course, is a sport in which the suspicion of fixing is forever present. It relies on a daily infusion of gambled money, not merely for success but for its very survival. There are features of racetracks that are absent in the venues of any other sport: the betting windows and cashiers' cages; the *Daily Racing Form*–obsessed fans studying the next race in a constant effort to discern the possible winner; and the discarded losing tickets, reflecting the difficulty in separating the merits of one flesh-and-blood, half-ton creature from another, sometimes overflowing from trashcans but just as likely to be scattered on the ground, where they remain in plain sight for all to see. Each of these is an unmistakable sign that here is a gambling game that withers and dies without a daily infusion of wagered cash.

Without it, there is no purse money, no racetracks, no racing newspapers, no television racing networks, no Kentucky Derby, no breeding industry.

No Thoroughbred racing.

The idea of the fixed race is part of the sport and likely has been since the earliest days of organized racing. Indeed, books have been written, most notably Milton C. Toby's *Unnatural Ability: The History of Performance-Enhancing Drugs in Thoroughbred Racing*, detailing how, when, and where improvements in drugging techniques have been achieved and allowed the fixers, all too often, to remain a step ahead of the authorities. Rumors and speculation about drugging are embedded deeply in racing and likely always will be.

In part, this tendency to assume the worst about the sport flows from the nature of racing itself and the followers of the sport who struggle, often in vain, to turn a profit at the betting windows. Handicapping is a difficult, complicated pursuit that is all the more so because governmental entities and the racetrack itself siphon off a significant percentage of each wager before returning a fraction of the betting money to those who win their bets. A handicapper might outthink the ponies, but few prevail in the long run against the takeout.

And the sport ultimately depends upon the abilities of animals—whose physical skills can be manipulated, whose ability to run to those skills even when human manipulations are not being attempted may vary from their on-paper winning chances, leaving handicappers to win on some days and lose—wagering on exactly the same Thoroughbreds in largely identical fields—on others, with no clues as to why a horse that won today might not repeat the performance two weeks later.

It was Man o' War whose pristine, nearly perfect persona drew fans to the sport and money to the tracks at a time when the rumors, and then the actuality of baseball's corruption, threatened to submerge all of sport. It was Man o' War, with his string of uncontestable victories, who became the positive public face of racing when the sport most needed one.

It was Man o' War, with his unmistakable excellence, his unquestioned ability to earn victory over all challengers, who may have saved a sport on the brink of disaster.

CHAPTER 20

A Sport in Peril . . .
and a Sport Resurrected

PART 1: A SPORT IN PERIL

If Figure 20-1 resembles a sinking ship, or at least a failing business, to the reader, you deserve congratulations for your business acumen. The graph displays an industry that, beginning in 1907 and continuing through 1917, was engaged in a business—in this case, Thoroughbred racing—that was producing results at a more or less consistent level. With the exception of the curious—and largely unexplained—drop-off

Figure 20-1 Number of Races by Year, 1907–1918

in 1908, the sport conducted approximately 6,000 to 7,000 races per year for more than a decade. It appeared a model of consistency and stability, until 1918, when the business graph turned suddenly and alarmingly downward.

In 1918, the number of races presented at racetracks throughout America fell by nearly 2,000, from 5,899 to 3,968. It was a 32.8 percent drop-off in a single year, a loss for American racetracks of approximately one-third of their business. This fall-off must surely have been perceived as an ominous trend, but one that was understandable for those who followed the world events of the time, the politics of the nation.

In that sudden fall-off of 1918, we see the stubborn continuation of the anti-gambling aspects of the Progressive Movement. No longer are the legal mechanisms of the New York State Legislature amenable to creating more statutes penalizing gamblers at properly constituted and licensed racetracks; this area is settled law, and racetracks, those still remaining after the Progressive Movement's anti-gambling fervor passed over like a brief but exceptionally violent thunderstorm, are free to operate, though in reduced circumstances.

There are fewer tracks, and fewer racing states, and perhaps there is a disinclination on the part of some even to attend the races in states where the sport survived the battle. Churches continue to preach from the pulpit on Sundays opposing gambling and even spending a day at the racetrack, and they will continue to do so, in greater or lesser numbers, for perhaps a decade to come. Religious crusades, political movements, and societal norms move slowly and change over generations, not merely years, and racing's recovery will be a slow one. Doubtless, some churchgoers will always perceive racing as an evil enterprise, a gambling-based game that should be avoided at all costs.

As the years tick by and racing continues treading water, at least in terms of the numbers of races being presented, an inevitability begins to be felt increasingly throughout the nation: The Great War is on the horizon, and while America resists entering this pan-European skirmish for as long as it might, it eventually becomes obvious that the nation will enter the war.

This becomes necessary, or at least grows gradually in popularity, for two reasons. First, it is not in the American mentality to fail to respond to an ally on the brink of defeat. And second, with German submarines increasingly sinking ships on the open sea, some of them American vessels, some of them foreign ships carrying American passengers, some of them supporting American allies, the revenge factor begins to grow more important.

America will join the war, and what we are seeing in 1918 is one result of that decision. In 1917, more American funds are diverted to war efforts and away from leisure activities. More men are being trained for war and shipped abroad to fight, diverted from leisure-time pursuits. The Great War is the primary factor in the sudden and profound fall-off in the numbers of races being offered.

One thing is certain: The 1907–1918 graph is anything but a model of growth. As racing learned when the minions of the Progressive Movement began shuttering racetracks, and as the sport relearned with even more bitterness as the nation began preparing for and then implementing its war efforts, the trend of Thoroughbred racing was one of stagnation. And this would be made even clearer as America entered the war: The sport's finances largely cratered, and its supposed health was demonstrated to be a myth.

Racing, in fact, was a sport in peril.

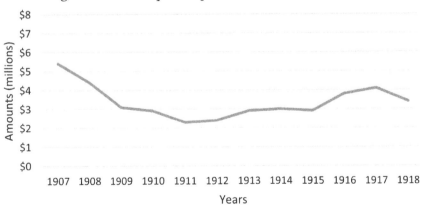

Figure 20-2 Gross Purses in American Thoroughbred Racing, 1907–1918

As Figure 20-2, reflecting gross purses in American racing over the same period, indicates, the sport's trend toward financial disaster was reflected not merely in the reduced number of races but, even more importantly, in the reduced amount of cash available for the purse money that supported racing stables, racetracks, and everyone else attempting to earn a living in the sport. Total national purses, relatively healthy at $5.4 million in 1907, had declined by nearly 60 percent, to $2.3 million by 1911 and $2.4 million in 1912.

Nor does the trend following these two extremely alarming years move energetically upward afterward: The numbers are $2.9 million in 1913, $3 million in 1914, down again to $2.9 million in 1915, and still, three years later, only $3.4 million in 1918, some 37 percent below the peak of nearly a decade earlier.

It must have been an anxious period for horsemen attempting to wring an honest profit from this difficult sport. There can be little question that, emerging from the anti-gambling mindset of the Progressive Era and grinding slowly toward war and the deprivations that inevitably accompany it, racing was becoming an underfunded, underattended afterthought. Fewer races were being run and less money wagered and distributed. The number of racing days had dropped 40 percent since 1907. The number of starters were down, from nearly 6,000 in 1907 to barely over 3,500 in 1918 and 1919, and each starter in each race was earning less money to support the racing operations of its owners. If you were an owner, a breeder, a racing association in 1918, you were surely looking for something—anything—that might turn the trendline upward before more tracks began closing for lack of funds, and the sport itself descended into unsustainability.

A sport in peril, indeed, with war on the way and the Black Sox scandal soon to add yet another element to the downward pressures on racing's ever-more-delicate economy.

Figure 20-3, the trendline for registered American foals for the period 1907 to 1918, completes a decidedly gloomy picture for the sport of Thoroughbred racing and the Thoroughbred industry as a whole. It

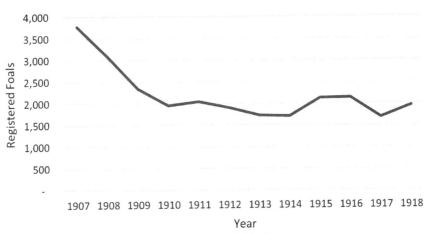

Figure 20-3 Registered American Foals, 1907–1918

reflects a truism about the Sport of Kings: If racing is not flourishing, if purses are down and the demand for more racehorses is reduced, there is no reason for the businessmen who have dedicated their lives to the production of Thoroughbred foals to produce more animals.

And as the second decade of the twentieth century progressed, that is exactly what happened.

As Figure 20-3 displays, production of Thoroughbred foals in Kentucky and California, Florida and Virginia, and throughout the nation slowed. The reductions were less dramatic, less instantaneous than those in races and purses, but they were no less vital to the survival of the sport. Foal crops, which had numbered 3,500 animals to nearly 4,000 annually from 1904 through 1907, declined to just 3,080 in 1908, then into the 2,000s the following year, and averaged just 1,881 for the decade-plus beginning in 1910 and continuing through 1920.

This period included the two smallest foal crops of the twentieth century, 1919's 1,665 foals and 1917's 1,680, which, as we have seen, against all odds happened to produce a Man o' War. And that, as we will see, is the event that, with the end of the war and the reduced reach of the Progressive Era, may well have saved Thoroughbred racing and ushered it into what would become, decades later, the Golden Age of the Sport of Kings.

As 1917 and 1918 were emerging as disastrous years for the sport, some surely must have been asking: Will racing still be in business when the war is done, the corruption of baseball handled and no longer constantly in the press, the fading remnants of "progressive" politics finally at its much-desired conclusion?

It was anything but an idle question.

PART 2: A SPORT RESURRECTED

In 1919, American Thoroughbred racing remained on the razor's edge. As Figure 20-4 indicates, the number of races continued to be depressed. The precise number, just 4,408 races for the entire nation, for the entire year, was more than 2,000 fewer than in the sport's peak year, 1910. Figures 20-5 and 20-6 on the next few pages demonstrate that available purse money and numbers of foals likewise remained at a low ebb.

But there were positives on the horizon. The war was over. The Progressive Era was winding down.

And Man o' War had arrived on the scene.

Figure 20-4 Annual Number of Races, 1919–1930

It is debatable which was the most important. Was it the return of gambling-aged men and the reinvestment in non-war activities and salaries that turned the tide for racing? Was it the ultimate victory of the pro-gambling forces over those who wanted to ban gambling nation-wide? Was it the willingness of a sports-obsessed nation to accept a level of corruption, even in the so-called National Pastime, and, by implication, in other sports, including racing?

Or was it the presence of the 2-year-old Man o' War, soon to reign as both the best runner in the sport and as the "Turf's Public Relations Man," in the words of one writer, that was racing's salvation? The precise configuration of factors bringing about the sport's resurgence can never be determined with certainty.

But Man o' War certainly played an important role in drawing fans' attention back to the sport. His obvious superiority demonstrated to doubters, even in the face of baseball's ongoing gambling woes, that Thoroughbred racing could be trusted, at least with this one powerful horse, to be aboveboard.

And racing began to revive. As Figure 20-5 shows, in 1920, with Man o' War's brilliant 3-year-old season, the money available to winning horses increased by 67 percent, from $4.6 million to $7.8 million,

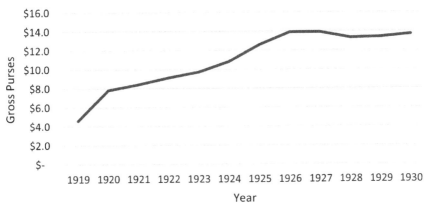

Figure 20-5 Gross Purses in American Thoroughbred Racing, 1919–1930

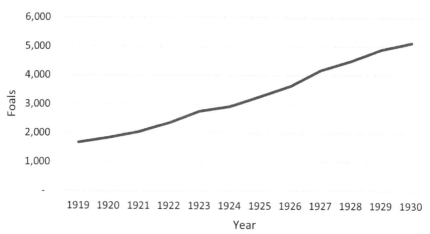

Figure 20-6 Registered American Foals, 1919-1935

in a single year. Relatively little of that increase was the result of race-goers passing through the turnstiles on the days Man o' War raced, although doubtless the increased attendance on those days did move the needle fractionally. Much more was the result of people reading and hearing about Man o' War's exploits and responding with curiosity, wishing to experience the excitement, at a distance, but still in the same pursuit.

Soon enough, the increases in races and dollars, and most importantly in reborn enthusiasm in racegoers, would be felt as well in the breeding industry, with more foals being produced each year. The trend, as reflected in Figure 20-6, is unfailingly upward over the course of this twelve-year period, and would continue on this trajectory, with only brief negative stretches during the Great Depression and the Second World War, which turned resolutely positive with the nation's economic recovery and victory in the war.

The nation, understandably, had other things on its mind than horse racing during those difficult and chaotic periods.

Through wars and pandemics and political upheavals and the growth of other sports and other entertainments competing fiercely for each discretionary dollar, racing would never again face the grim realities of the twentieth century's first eighteen years. With a crucial assist from one brilliantly unbeatable racehorse, racing would survive and, in the decades ahead, would flourish.

Man o' War, 1920. (Wikimedia Commons, New York Public Library Digital Collection)

CHAPTER 21

The Greatest Racehorse?

As we have observed throughout this volume, a great many outstanding racehorses have competed in America over the more than three centuries since the first pair of riders challenged one another to a race down the hopefully deserted main street of their small town. Determining the greatest of those Thoroughbreds is a task that can probably never be accomplished to the satisfaction of every opinionated fan of the sport. In this book, however, I committed to the attempt, and I believe I have decided, for myself in any case, who among the very best racehorses produced in America can be considered the greatest.

After considerable thought, enough statistical review to challenge my supply of headache medication many times over, and literally decades of discussion with anyone I could find with an opinion, I settled on three horses that I believe may be the most important or, in a word I now feel comfortable using, the greatest in the history of American Thoroughbred racing.

I did not arrive at my decision lightly.

In addition to Citation, Kelso, and Seattle Slew, featured in the preceding chapters, I considered American Eclipse (1814–1847), whose perfect record, eight wins in eight starts, was earned in three- and four-mile heats when England was racing's great power and America's voice not yet even a minuscule quaver in the discussion. American Eclipse burned through opponents until there was nothing left to rival him, then was retired to a magnificently successful stud career. He is important because he was among the first to set a high standard for American racing, and because his offspring helped populate the racetracks with finer specimens of Thoroughbreds than had ever been seen on our shores.

I considered Boston (1833–1850), "Old White Nose," who was once returned to his breeder by a disgruntled buyer who famously recommended that the dangerous, evil-tempered colt be "castrated or shot, preferably the latter." From there, Boston won forty races in forty-five lifetime starts and sired the great racehorse and phenomenal stallion Lexington.

I considered Ten Broeck (1872–1887), the superhorse of the 1870s, who won twenty-three times in twenty-nine starts, who made the historic three-horse Pimlico race described in the following section both possible and important by his mere presence, and who once held six separate American records, at distances from one to four miles.

I considered Parole (1873–1903), who won 59 of 138 races over the course of a twelve-year career, including the great 1877 race at Pimlico (defeating Tom Ochiltree and Ten Broeck, both future Hall of Famers); and, shipped overseas, defeated the mighty British colt Isonomy, becoming one of the first American horses to demonstrate to the haughty British that despite the Americans' alleged breeding shortcomings, they could more than hold their own on the world stage.

I considered Sysonby (1902–1906), who won fourteen times in fifteen starts and might have equaled Colin's perfect 15-for-15 record, had he not been drugged into defeat—or so it is alleged—in the 1904 Futurity.

I considered Colin (1905–1932), undefeated in fifteen races and quite possibly America's premier racehorse before the coming of Man o' War.

I considered Fair Play (1905–1929), an exceptional racer whose record would have been even more impressive, had he not been unquestionably the second-best runner in unquestionably first-best Colin's magnificent 1905 crop. From that start toward greatness, he added mightily to his ranking among the most important Thoroughbreds in the sport's long history by siring not just Man o' War—although this was certainly a huge contribution—but classic winners Display, Chance Shot, and Mad Play, and Hall of Fame steeplechaser Fairmount.

I considered Bold Ruler (1954–1971), who followed a successful racing career—twenty-three wins in thirty-three starts, including the

Futurity at age two, the Preakness as a 3-year-old, and the Suburban at age four—with a brilliant career at stud, which included eight years as America's leading sire. Bold Ruler sired eleven champions, including Hall of Famer Gamely and Triple Crown winner Secretariat. His impact on Thoroughbred racing will last as long as the sport does.

And I considered Zenyatta (2004–), all but unbeaten over a twenty-race career, whose popularity drew fans to the track and reminded us all that the girls can hold their own against the boys with a sensational stretch-running victory in the 2009 Breeders' Cup Classic and a near repeat in the 2010 edition.

And then, after considering each of these immortal Thoroughbreds in turn, pondering race records and stud careers, post-career awards and fan favoritism, I arrived at my choices for, in the slightly paraphrased words of Spectacular Bid's trainer, Grover (Buddy) Delp, "the greatest horses ever to look through a bridle."

Lexington, Man o' War, and Secretariat.

Lexington (1850–1875) because he was a superb racehorse, winner six times in seven starts and holder of the American record for four miles when that was a distance the racing world cared about passionately. Retired because his failing eyesight no longer allowed him to comfortably navigate turns and avoid other horses, Lexington then became the most successful stallion America has ever seen, the "Blind Hero of Woodburn," topping the sire list for fourteen consecutive years from 1861 through 1874, then heading it again in 1876 and 1878. His sixteen seasons at the top set a standard that no Thoroughbred, however prolific, had approached before or will again.

It is yet another demonstration of the lasting impact of Lexington that of the seventeen immortal Thoroughbreds highlighted in the chapters of this volume, sixteen—all but Citation, whose pedigree is the most European of the group—have Lexington's name in their lineage.

Man o' War (1917–1947) because he won all but one of his twenty-one races but even more because he won them with a power, a dominance, an uninhibited joy that quickened the heartbeats of grizzled horsemen who had wrongly believed they had seen the breed at its absolute best when Ten Broeck, then Sysonby, and then Colin passed before their eyes.

Man o' War reinvigorated a sport that had been at least a decade in the doldrums and brought fans back to the races in droves to experience even a glimpse of the wonder he created. He set stakes, track, American, and world records in profusion and, for most of his 3-year-old season, caused trainers to send their top runners to other venues in search of easier competition when Man o' War's name appeared among the entries.

Man o' War was a successful stallion who can be credited with bringing champions and Hall of Famers to the sport, and his offspring, both male and female, created champions of their own, though none as speedy and powerful as their immortal progenitor. There is no question—and it has been a long time since anyone suggested otherwise—that Man o' War belongs at or near the top of history's greatest Thoroughbreds.

Secretariat (1970–1989) because the second Big Red, like Man o' War, brought a generation of fans back to the races. He did so by winning a Triple Crown that many thought, after a twenty-five-year hiatus since Citation's sweep of the series in 1948, might never be seen again. Secretariat was a rarity, a Horse of the Year at age two who won the title again the following year and gave a generation of television viewers an opportunity to see what a truly great racehorse looks like. Secretariat, through race caller Chic Anderson, brought to the consciousness of viewers a phrase—"he is moving like a tremendous machine!"—that resonates today as a testament to his impossibly powerful, yet precise and rhythmic stride. He defeated the best of his own generation, then the best of the previous generations, winning on dirt and rampaging past the competition on turf. A generation of racing fans wept at news of his untimely death, at age nineteen, in 1989.

And, at long last, I determined that the greatest of these three, the greatest racehorse in the history of American racing, was unquestionably Man o' War.

The big red colt who was all but unbeaten during his brief two-year reign on the track was not merely the most outstanding racehorse of his day—and arguably of any other day—but a Thoroughbred of exceptional consequence in rescuing his sport from a period of malaise that could easily have seen it flounder and die due to profound economic and social concerns.

But Man o' War's influence does not stop there. It was not merely the racetracks and the horse owners and the many individuals necessary to present a racing program, but also the breeders who the great horse salvaged from the possibility of bankruptcy. For who, after all, needs stud farms, stallions, and broodmares if there is no sport remaining to give value to the horses they produce?

The sport's recovery, and the breeding industry's salvation, began with one horse, the immortal Man o' War, who drew fans back to the races and showed those who oversaw the sport that it could succeed in spite of its many obstacles.

Man o' War: the swiftest racehorse? Possibly. The strongest racehorse? Perhaps. The most outstanding racehorse? He is certainly one of a number of legitimate challengers for the title, but it is, and likely will always remain, a matter of opinion.

But the greatest racehorse? Yes. Unquestionably. It can only be Man o' War, who ran faster than the wind and by doing so helped rescue and save a sport.

Acknowledgments

"Silent gratitude isn't much use to anyone."

—Gertrude Stein

The Greatest Racehorse? is the fourth book I've been permitted to publish through the auspices of the Globe Pequot Publishing Group, Lyons Press, and Eclipse Press, and if there's one thing I've learned from the experience, it's that writing a book is a team process. The better the team, the smoother the process.

I've had a great team.

It all begins with my wife of twenty-five years, Dr. Fran Wintroub, who performs so many vital roles in my life that to list them all would push me far beyond my allotted word count. Suffice it to say that she is my *sine qua non*, the one person without whom everything else would be, at the very least, a whole lot less fun.

Greg Aunapu of Studio B Productions has again served as my agent, helping me deal with many of the technical issues that inevitably arise in publishing one of these things. Greg is patient and kind and knowledgeable and everything else you'd want your agent to be, and he has now carried me through four volumes. As always, Greg, thanks for all you do.

Three librarians deserve credit here. Vivian Montoya of the California Thoroughbred Breeders' Association Library has been a kindly force throughout my writing career, guiding me to books and old newspapers and magazines, and giving sage advice when such was needed. Roda Ferraro, library director of the Keeneland Library, has been the most supportive of resources whenever I've requested assistance with a question or project, and Kelly Coffman, the research services librarian at Keeneland

Library, has, among other functions, been my guide through Keeneland's extensive photo collection, not merely making many of the photos in this book available but also making the first run through the collection and selecting the best of the best. Kelly is to be thanked for many things, not the least of which is the photo of Man o' War on this book's cover.

It has been my great good fortune to work with Brittany Stoner at Globe Pequot, and a more accommodating, more knowledgeable editor would be difficult to imagine. I learned early in our relationship that Brittany's grandfather was a Man o' War man, who often spoke of the marvelous horse's legacy while passing down his love of racing. This book was written in part to celebrate Brittany's progenitor and his symbolic connection with this project.

And while associate marketing manager Jason Rossi has yet to apply his fine skills to the marketing of *The Greatest Racehorse?*, he was certainly a huge help with my last book, *The First Kentucky Derby*. I thanked him dozens of times via email and phone call for his considerable assistance with that last book, and he will doubtless earn more for the prodigies of effort he'll perform with this one. And thank you to everyone at Globe Pequot who has had a hand in this book without my ever learning your name.

Tracy Gantz-White is a longtime friend who has often engaged with me in discussions of Man o' War's place among the best horses of all time, and her arguments are always thought-provoking. More often than not, our debates wind up with an agreement that "we'll just have to agree to disagree." Tracy's husband, Jon White, is another knowledgeable and opinionated soul who has always insisted that Man o' War belongs atop the all-time list of American Thoroughbreds. We can now agree that Man o' War is the greatest racehorse, although we'll continue to debate whether Man o' War or some other racehorse may have been the best.

So many others! Frank Tocher, who does technical things with old and fuzzy photos that renders them suitable for inclusion in a book; Brien Bouyea of the National Museum of Racing and Hall of Fame, who is informative and encouraging, and has twice welcomed Fran and me to Saratoga Springs to sign books in the museum; the good people at Newspapers.com, without whom this book would have been stillborn for lack of information and data; *Daily Racing Form* and *Equibase*, whose charts informed the stories of so many of the great horses in this volume; the *Blood-Horse*, whose magazine is a nearly daily read, and whose two great publications, *The Great Ones* and *Thoroughbred Champions: Top 100 Racehorses of the 20th Century*, were valuable resources as I pursued this project.

And finally, thank you to everyone who has encouraged me along the way: the teachers and magazine editors—Les Woodcock at *Turf & Sport Digest* and Jim Corbett and Joe Girardi at *American Turf Monthly* particularly stand out—and family members whose pride in my work helped me carry on. One of these is my son, Sean Shrager, who is anything but a racing fan but who listens patiently when I have a book-related issue to discuss. Believe me, it helps.

Writing a book is a long and not always easy task, and having supportive friends and family members is one of the necessities for preventing the writer from losing his mind during the process. There are too many of these incredible people to acknowledge, people who allow me to talk about the sport that is my passion when perhaps their preference might be some other topic. They know who they are. Thanks to all of you for the support and assistance you have always given me.

Mark Shrager
August 25, 2024

Bibliography

BOOKS

Alexander, David, *A Sound of Horses*, New York: The Bobbs-Merrill Company, Inc., 1966.

American Racing Manual, 1947 Edition, Chicago and various other cities: Daily Racing Form, Inc., 1947.

American Racing Manual, 1952 Edition, Chicago and various other cities: Daily Racing Form, Inc., 1952.

American Racing Manual, 1969 Edition, Chicago and various other cities: Daily Racing Form, Inc., 1969.

American Racing Manual, 1970 Edition, Chicago and various other cities: Daily Racing Form, Inc., 1970.

American Racing Manual, 1972 Edition, Chicago and various other cities: Daily Racing Form, Inc., 1972.

American Racing Manual, 1973 Edition, Chicago and various other cities: Daily Racing Form, Inc., 1973.

American Racing Manual, 1974 Edition, Chicago and various other cities: Daily Racing Form, Inc., 1974.

American Racing Manual, 1975 Edition, Chicago and various other cities: Daily Racing Form, Inc., 1975.

American Racing Manual, 1977 Edition, Chicago and various other cities: Daily Racing Form, Inc., 1977.

American Racing Manual, 1994 Edition, Phoenix and various other cities: Daily Racing Form, Inc., 1994.

Asinov, Eliot. *Eight Men Out: The Black Sox and the 1919 World Series*, New York: Henry Holt and Company, 1963.

Auerbach, Ann Hagedorn, *Wild Ride*, New York: Henry Holt and Company, 1994.

Blood-Horse, The, *Thoroughbred Champions: Top 100 Racehorses of the 20th Century*, Lexington, Kentucky: The Blood-Horse, Inc., 1999.

Bowen, Edward L., *Man o' War: Racehorse of the Century*, Essex, Connecticut: Eclipse Press, 2022.

Boyd, Eva Jolene, *Exterminator: The Thoroughbred Legends*, Essex, Connecticut: Eclipse Press, 2002.

Carroll, Linda, and David Rosner, *Duel for the Crown: Affirmed, Alydar and Racing's Greatest Rivalry*, New York: Gallery Books, 2014.

Chew, Peter, *The Kentucky Derby: The First 100 Years*, Boston: Houghton Mifflin Company, 1974.

Churchill Downs, *124th Kentucky Derby, Saturday, May 2, 1998* (*Kentucky Derby Press Guide*), published 1998.

Cooper, Page, and Roger L. Treat, *Man o' War*, Yardley, Pennsylvania: Westholme Publishing, 2004.

Daily Racing Form, Champions: The Lives, Times, and Past Performances of America's Greatest Thoroughbreds, Third Edition, Champions from 1894-2010, New York: The Daily Racing Form, LLC, 2011.

Farley, Walter, *Man o' War*, New York: Random House, 1962.

Fleming, Mary, *A History of the Thoroughbred in California*, Arcadia, California: California Thoroughbred Breeders Association, 1983.

Heller, Bill, *Graveyard of Champions: Saratoga's Fallen Favorites*, Lexington, Kentucky: Eclipse Press, 2002.

Hollingsworth, Kent, *The Great Ones*, Lexington, Kentucky: The Blood-Horse, Inc., 1970.

Hollingsworth, Kent, *The Kentucky Thoroughbred*, Lexington, Kentucky: University of Kentucky, 2009.

Hornbaker, Tim, *Turning the Black Sox White: The Misunderstood Legacy of Charles A. Comiskey*, New York: Sports Publishing, 2014.

James, Bill, *The New Bill James Historical Baseball Abstract*, New York: The Free Press: A Division of Simon & Schuster, 2001.

Jockey Club, The, *2023 American Racing Manual*, New York: The Jockey Club, 2023.

Longrigg, Roger, *The History of Horse Racing*, New York: Stein and Day, 1972.

McGraw, Eliza, *Here Comes Exterminator!*, New York: St. Martin's Press, 2016.

New York Racing Association Yearbook & Media Guide, 2002.

Ours, Dorothy, *Man o' War: A Legend Like Lightning*, New York: St. Martin's Press, 2006.

Palmer, Joe, *This Was Racing*, New York: A.S. Barnes and Company, Inc., 1963.

Parmer, Charles B., *For Gold and Glory*, New York: Carrick and Evans, Inc., 1939.

Perdue, Mary, *Landaluce: The Story of Seattle Slew's First Champion*, Lexington, Kentucky: University Press of Kentucky, 2022.

Pimlico Press Book, 1967.

Quirin, William L., PhD, *Winning at the Races: Computer Discoveries in Thoroughbred Handicapping*, New York: William Morrow and Company, 1979.

Robertson, William H. P., *The History of Thoroughbred Racing in America*, New York: Bonanza, 1964.

Scanlan, Lawrence, *The Horse God Built: The Untold Story of Secretariat*, Toronto: HarperCollins Publishers Ltd., 2006.

Toby, Milton C., *Unnatural Ability: The History of Performance-Enhancing Drugs in Thoroughbred Racing*, Lexington, Kentucky: University Press of Kentucky, 2023.

Travathan, Charles E., *The American Thoroughbred*, New York: The McMillan Company, 1905.

Vosburgh, W. S., *Racing in America 1866-1921*, New York: The Jockey Club (privately printed), 1922.

Wickens, Kimberley A., *Lexington: The Extraordinary Life and Turbulent Times of America's Legendary Racehorse*, New York: Ballantine Books, 2023.

Willett, Peter, *The Thoroughbred*, New York: G.P. Putnam's Sons, 1970.

Winn, Matt, as told to Frank G. Menke, *Down the Stretch*, New York: Smith & Durrell, 1945.

MAGAZINES AND NEWSPAPERS

Articles by the following bylined reporters and columnists contributed to this volume:

Abbott, Bion (*Los Angeles Times*), Ashford, Ed (*Lexington Herald*), Austin, Dale (*Baltimore Sun*), Ayres, Ray (*Lexington Leader*), Barrett, Ray (*New York Daily News*), Barry, Howard (*Chicago Tribune*), Barry, Mike (*Louisville Courier-Journal*), Bates, Ray (*New York Daily News*), Bayliss, Skip (*Los Angeles Times*), Bolus, Jim (*Louisville Courier-Journal*), Boniface, William (*Baltimore Sun*), Bozich, Rick (*Louisville Courier-Journal*), Cady, Steve (*Lexington Leader, Sacramento Bee*), Chandler, John (*Lexington Herald*), Cherwa, John (*Los Angeles Times*), Christine, Bill (*Los Angeles Times*), Comeford, Ed (*Newsday [Suffolk, NY Edition]*), Condon, David (*Chicago Tribune*), Considine, Bob (*Pasadena [CA] Independent*), Copland, Al (*New York Daily News*), Corbett, James J. (*San Francisco Examiner*), Cronin, Ned (*Los Angeles Times*), Culpepper, Chuck (*Bradenton [FL] Herald*), Daley, George (*Miami [FL] News*), Danforth, Ed (*Louisville Courier-Journal*), Daniel (*New York Herald*), Delp, Doug (*Fort Lauderdale News*), Denberg, Jeffrey (*Miami [FL] News*), Devine, Tommy (*Dunkirk [NY] Evening Observer*), Eck, Frank (*Paducah [KY] Sun*), Evans, Luther (*Miami [FL] Herald*), Ferman, Gary (*Miami [FL] Herald*), Field, Bryan (*Saturday Evening Post*), Fife, George Buchanan (*Atlanta Journal*), Finley, Bill (*New York Daily News*), Forbes, Gordon (*Philadelphia Inquirer*), Fox, John W. (*Brooklyn Citizen*), Gaffer, Wes (*New York Daily News*), Gay Jr., Marvin N. (*Louisville Courier-Journal*), Geyer, Jack (*Los Angeles Times*), Giannetti, Peter (*Glen Falls [NY] Post-Star*), Grace, Art (*Miami [FL] News*), Graves, Gary B. (*Philadelphia Inquirer*), Hall, Bill (*Philadelphia Inquirer*), Harris, Russ (*New York Daily News*), Hayward, Barry M. (*San Francisco Examiner*), Hebert, Bob (*Los Angeles Times*), Hunt, Helm (*Louisville Courier-Journal*), Hovdey, Jay (*Los Angeles Times*), Husar, John (*Chicago Tribune*), Isaacs, Stan (*Newsday [Suffolk, NY Edition]*), Joyce, Dick (*Bridgewater [NJ] Courier-News*), Kellner, Jenny (*New York Daily News*), Kelly, Billy (*Buffalo Courier Express*), Kelly, Joseph B. (*Baltimore Sun*), Kemp, Abe (*San Francisco Examiner*), Kiley, Mike (*Chicago Tribune*), King, Henry V. (*New York Herald*), Klessel, Steve (*Philadelphia Daily News*), Krehbiel, George (*Louisville Courier-Journal*), LaBelle, Fran (*South Florida Sun Sentinel*), Lee, Joe (*Brooklyn Daily Eagle*), Leonard, Andrew G. (*Lexington Leader*), Linthicum, Jesse A. (*Baltimore Sun*), Lowry, Paul (*Los Angeles Times*), MacBeth, W. J. (*New York Tribune*), McCarthy, Paul (*Redwood City [CA] Tribune*), McCarthy, Richard (*Newsday [Suffolk, NY Edition]*), McCully, Jim (*New York Daily News*), McGraw, Eliza (*New York Times*), McIntyre, Bill (*Shreveport [LA] Times*), McIntyre, Christy (*Lexington Herald-Leader*), McLaughlin, Joe (*Miami [FL] Herald*), McLean, Gene (*Lexington Herald-Leader*), McNerney, Jerry (*Louisville Courier-Journal*), Metivier, Don A. (*Glen Falls [NY] Post-Star*), Moon, Wes (*Asbury Park [NJ] Press*), Moran, Paul (*Newsday [Suffolk, NY Edition]*), Morey, Charles (*Pasadena [CA] Post*), Mozley, Dana (*New York Daily News*), Munick, Ernie (*New York Daily News*), Myers, Bob (*San

Bernardino [CA] County Sun, Valley [North Hollywood, CA] Times, Santa Barbara [CA] News-Press, Santa Ana [CA] Register), Nack, Bill (Newsday [Suffolk, NY Edition]), Nall, James O. (Louisville Courier-Journal), Newland, Russ (Fresno Bee), Nichols, Joe (Lexington Leader), Nickleson, Al (Toronto Star), Ortell, Frank (Miami [FL] News), Phelps, Frank T. (Lexington Leader), Price, Harry N. (Washington Post), Privman, Jay (Oakland [CA] Tribune), Quinn, James T. (Troy [NY] Times Record), Rand, Jonathan (Miami [FL] Herald), Rasmussen, Fred (Baltimore Sun), Reed, Don (Baltimore Sun), Rees, Jenny (Louisville Courier-Journal), Rice, Grantland (Buffalo Evening News), Rivera, Thomas (Chicago Tribune), Ross, James M. (Louisville Courier-Journal), Sainsbury, Ed (Lexington Leader), Scherf, Chris (Syracuse Post-Standard), Schuyler Jr., Ed (Frankfort [KY] State Journal, Lexington Herald, Louisville Courier-Journal), Sevier, O'Neil (Butte [MT] Miner), Shearer, Lloyd (San Bernardino [CA] County Sun), Shevlin, Maurice (Chicago Tribune), Shrager, Mark (American Turf Monthly), Sisti, Tony (Newsday [Suffolk, NY Edition]), Sorkin, Dick (Newsday [Nassau, NY Edition]), Sparrow, Edward C. (Baltimore Evening Sun), Swift, George (Miami [FL] Herald), Tanenbaum, Joe (Louisville Courier-Journal), Tracy, Len (Lexington Leader), Treanor, Vincent (New York Evening World), Trimble, Joe (New York Daily News), Trost, Ralph (Brooklyn Daily Eagle), Vance, Kyle (Frankfort [KY] State Journal, Vreeland, W. C. (Brooklyn Daily Eagle), Wall, Maryjean (Lexington Herald-Leader), Ward, Gene (New York Daily News), Wesson, Al (Los Angeles Times), Whelan, Tom (White Plains [NY] Daily Argus, New Rochelle [NY] Standard-Star), Williams, Joe (Buffalo Evening News), Woodruff, Harvey (Chicago Tribune), Wooster, Len (Brooklyn Times, Brooklyn Times Union), Youll, Chet (Buffalo Evening News), Ziegel, Vic (New York Daily News), Ziff, Sid (Los Angeles Mirror News), Zimmerman, Paul (Los Angeles Times).

In addition to the above, unbylined articles from the following newspapers contributed to this volume:

Atlantic City [NJ] Press, Binghamton [NY] Press and Sun-Bulletin, Blood-Horse, Brantford [Ontario, Canada] Expositor, Brooklyn Daily Eagle, Brooklyn Standard Union, Brooklyn Times-Union, Buffalo Commercial, Buffalo Courier, Buffalo Courier-Express, Buffalo Enquirer, Buffalo Review, Buffalo Weekly Express, Canandaigua [NY] Daily Messenger, Cincinnati Enquirer, Daily Racing Form, Decatur [IL] Daily Review, Decatur [IL] Herald and Review, Elmira [NY] Star-Gazette, Harrisburg [PA] Evening News, Hollywood [CA] Citizen-News, Ithaca [NY] Journal, Lafayette [LA] Daily Advertiser, Modesto [CA] Bee, Montreal Daily Star, Montreal Gazette, New Rochelle [NY] Standard-Star, New York Sun, New York Times, New York Tribune, New York World, Oakland [CA] Tribune, Oklahoma Miner, Olean [NY] Times Herald, Ossining [NY] Citizen Register, Passaic [NJ] Herald-News, Penn Yan (NY) Chronicle-Express, Rochester [NY] Democrat and Chronicle, Salisbury [MD] Daily Times, Sun and the New York Herald, Tennessean, Toronto Star Weekly, Torrance [CA] Daily Breeze, Yonkers (NY) Herald Statesman.

WEBSITES

Aimone, Francesco, NCI, "The 1918 Influenza Epidemic in New York City: A Review of the Public Health Response," https://www.ncbi.nlm.nih.gov/pmc/articles /PMC2862336/

Bartholomew, Kaeli, "Louis Feustel and Man o' War: The Unbeatable Team," https://www .champsofthetrack.com/post/louis-feustel-and-man-o-war-the-unbeatable-team

Bayer, Barbara, Bloodhorse.com, "Derby Winner, Top Japanese Sire Sunday Silence Dies," https://www.bloodhorse.com/horse-racing/articles/186630/derby-winner -wop-japanese-sire-sunday-silence-dies

Bryant, Manly, Countryrebel.com, "Stories Behind Dead Jockeys That Haunt the Grounds of Churchill Downs," https://countryrebel.com/stories-behind-dead -jockeys-that-haunt-the-grounds-of-churchill-downs

Conway, Terry, America's Best Racing, "Horse Racing's First Superstar of the 20th Century: Undefeated Colin," https://www.americasbestracing.net/the-sport/2022 -horse-racings-first-superstar-the-20th-century-undefeated-colin

Drager, Marvin, Britannica, "Man o' War," https://www.britannica.com/topic/Man-o-War

Ehalt, Bob, Americasbestracing.net, "John Henry: An Undersized $1,100 Purchase Who Became the People's Champion," https://www.americasbestracing.net/the -sport/2023-john-henry-undersized-1100-purchase-who-became-the-peoples -champion

Goldberg, Ryan, DRF.com, "The Golden Era of Brooklyn Racing," https://www.drf.com /news/golden-era-of-brooklyn-racing

Hall, Tom, BloodHorse Daily, "Man o' War's 1920 Preakness Silences All Doubters," https://www.bloodhorse.com/horse-racing/articles/241200-man-o-wars-1920 -preakness-silences-all-doubters

Haskin, Steve, Bloodhorse.com, "Hangin' With Haskin: The Selling of the 1989 Triple Crown," http://cs.bloodhorse.com/blogs/horse-racing-steve-haskin/archive /2014//03/03/the-selling-of-the-1989-triple-crown.aspx

History.com editors, History, "World War I," https://www.history.com/topics/world-war -I/world-war-I-history

Horgan, John, World History Encyclopedia, "Germ Theory," https://www.worldhistory .org/Germ_Theory/

Johnson, J. Keeler, America's Best Racing, "August Belmont II: The Man Who Bred Man o' War," https://www.americasbestracing.net/the-sport/2020-august-belmont -ii-the-man-who-bred-man-o-war

Kelly, Jennifer, Twinspires Edge, "True Crime in Horse Racing: Lost at Sea," https:// www.twinspires.com/edge/racing/true-crime-in-horse-racing-lost-at-sea

Kiger, Patrick J., History, "How Many People Died in World War I?" https://www.his tory.com/news/how-many-people-died-in-world-war-I

Mitchell, Ron, Bloodhorse.com, "Triple Crown Winner Affirmed Euthanized," http://www.bloodhorse.com/horse-racing/articles/194804/triple-crown-winner -affirmed-euthanized

Monaco, Pete, The Spectrum, "The Incredible Journey of Legendary Thoroughbred Race-horse Man o' War," https://www.thespectrum.com/story/sports/mesquite/2018/10 /09/eighth-pole-life-and-legacy-famed-racehorse-man-o-war/1501815002/

Pedulla, Tom, America's Best Racing, "Sunday Silence: The Star No One Wanted," https://www.americasbestracing.net/the-sport/2024-sunday-silence-the-star -no-one-wanted

Peters, Anne, Thoroughbred Heritage, "Portraits: Fair Play," https://www.tbheritage.com/Portraits/FairPlay/html

Schwartz, Larry, ESPN Classic, "Man o' War Came Close to Perfection," https://www.espn.com/classic/biography/s/Man_o_War.html

Showalter, Dennis E. and Royde-Smith, John Graham, Encyclopedia Britannica, "World War I," https://www.britannica.com/event/World-War-I

Skinner Jr., Harold Allen, 1914-1918 Online International Encyclopedia of the First World War, "American Expeditionary Forces," https://encyclopedia.1914-1918-online.net/article/american_expeditionary_forces

Stanek, Anna, Horsey Hooves, "8 Interesting Facts About Man o' War (History, Stats & FAQs)," https://horseyhooves.com/man-o-war-racehorse/

Swancer, Brent, Journalnews.com.ph, "The Bizarre Sea Vanishing of the Jockey Albert Snider," https://journalnews.com.ph/the-bizarre-sea-vanishing-of-the-jockey-albert-snider

American Classic Pedigrees, "Affirmed (USA)," http://www.americanclassicpedigrees.com/affirmed.html

American Classic Pedigrees, "Easy Goer (USA)," http://www.americanclassicpedigrees.com/easy-goer.html

Avalon Law, Yale Law School, "Constitution of New York: April 20, 1777," https://avalon.law.yale.edu/18th_century/ny01.asp

Claiborne Farm, "1986-1994 Easy Goer," https://claibornefarm.com/history/hof/easy-goer/

Equimed, "Equine Diseases & Conditions: Osselets," https://equimed.com/diseases-and-conditions/reference/osselets

History NYCourts.gov, "Third Constitution of New York, 1846," https://history.nycourts.gov/wp-content/uploads/2019/01/Publications 1846-NY-Constitution-compressed.pdf

History NYCourts.gov, "Fourth Constitution of New York, 1894," https://history.nycourts.gov/wp-content/uploads/2019/01/Publications1894-NY-Constitution-compressed.pdf

JCSA.sa, "The World Awaits. Saudi Cup 2005," https://www.jcsa.sa.sa/en/saudi-cup

Keeneland Library, "1919 Belmont Futurity," https://keenelandlibrary.omeka.net/exhibits/show/manowar/1919/1919belmontfuturity

Keeneland Library, "1919 Sanford Memorial Stakes," https://keenelandlibrary.omeka.net/exhibits/show/manowar/1919/1919sanfordmemorialstakes

Keeneland Library, "1920: Three-Year-Old Season," https://keenelandlibrary.omeka.net/exhibits/show/manowar/1920

Keeneland Library, "1920 Lawrence Realization Stakes," https://keenelandlibrary.omeka.net/exhibits/show/manowar/1920/1920lawrencerealization

Keeneland Library, "1920 Travers Stakes," https://keenelandlibrary.omeka.net/exhibits/show/manowar/1920/1920traversstakes

Keeneland Library, "1936 Conformation, Man o' War," https://keenelandlibrary.omeka.net/exhibits/show/manowar/retrospective/1936conformationmanowar

Keeneland Library, "A Retrospective," https://keenelandlibrary.omeka.net/exhibits/show/manowar/introduction

Keeneland Library, "At Faraway," https://keenelandlibrary.omeka.net/exhibits/show/manowar/studcareer/faraway

Keeneland Library, "Head Shot, Man o' War," https://keenelandlibrary.omeka.net/exhibits/show/manowar/retrospective/headshotmanowar

Keeneland Library, "Introduction," https://keenelandlibrary.omeka.net/exhibits/show/manowar/introduction

Keeneland Library, "Man o' War, Andy Schuttinger Up," https://keenelandlibrary.omeka.net/exhibits/show/manowar/retrospective/manowarandyschuttingerup

Keeneland Library, "Man o' War, Clarence Cummer Up," https://keenelandlibrary.omeka.net/exhibits/show/manowar/retrospective/manowarclarancecummerup

Keeneland Library, "Man o' War, Johnny Loftus Up," https://keenelandlibrary.omeka.net/exhibits/show/manowar/1919/man-o----war--johnny-loftus-up

Keeneland Library, "Man o' War, Kummer Up, 1920 Dwyer Stakes," https://keenelandlibrary.omeka.net/exhibits/show/manowar/1920/1920dwyerstakes

Keeneland Library, "Man o' War, Kummer Up, 1920 Stuyvesant Handicap," https://keenelandlibrary.omeka.net/exhibits/show/manowar/1920/1920stuyvesanthandicap

Keeneland Library, "Man o' War, Sande Up, 1920 Miller Stakes," https://keenelandlibrary.omeka.net/exhibits/show/manowar/1920/1920millerstakes

Keeneland Library, "Man o' War, Schuttinger Up," https://keenelandlibrary.omeka.net/exhibits/show/manowar/1920/manowarschuttingerup

Keeneland Library, "Man o' War, Stripped," https://keenelandlibrary.omeka.net/exhibits/show/manowar/studcareer/manowarstripped

Keeneland Library, "Man o' War and John P. Grier," https://keenelandlibrary.omeka.net/exhibits/show/manowar/1920/manowarandjohnpgrier

Keeneland Library, "Man o' War Receiving Visitors," https://keenelandlibrary.omeka.net/exhibits/show/manowar/retrospective/manowarreceiving visitor

Keeneland Library, "Man o' War Regarding His Prototype," https://keenelandlibrary.omeka.net/exhibits/show/manowar/retrospective/manowarregardinghisprototype

Keeneland Library, "Man o' War with Exercise Rider," https://keenelandlibrary.omeka.net/exhibits/show/manowar/retrospective/manowarexerciserider

Keeneland Library, "Man o' War with John Buckner," https://keenelandlibrary.omeka.net/exhibits/show/manowar/studcareer/manowargroomjohnbuckner

Keeneland Library, "Man o' War with Will Harbut," https://keenelandlibrary.omeka.net/exhibits/show/manowar/retrospective/manowarwillharbut

Keeneland Library, "Man o' War Working Out," https://keenelandlibrary.omeka.net/exhibits/show/manowar/1919/manowarworkingout

Keeneland Library, "Man o' War's Transport Van," https://keenelandlibrary.omeka.net/exhibits/show/manower/studcareer/manowartransportvan

Keeneland Library, "More About Man o' War: Recollections & Reservations," https://thevaulthorseracing.wordpress.com/2019/02/07/more-about-man-o-war-recollections-reservations

Keeneland Library, "With Will Harbut," https://keenelandlibrary.omeka.net/exhibits/show/manowar/stud career/willharbut

Lusitania Resource, "Lusitania Home," https://www.rmslusitania.info/

National Museum of Racing and Hall of Fame, "Affirmed (FL)," https://www.racing museum.org/hall of fame/horse/affirmed-fl

National Museum of Racing and Hall of Fame, "Clarence Kummer: A Quiet Path to Greatness," https://racingmuseum.org/blogs/clarence-kummer-quiet-path-greatness

National Museum of Racing and Hall of Fame, "Colin," https://www.racingmuseum.org/sites/default/files/hall-of-fame/horse/past-performances/Colin.pdf

National Museum of Racing and Hall of Fame, "Earl Sande," https://www.racing museum.org/hall-of-fame/jockey/earl-sande

National Museum of Racing and Hall of Fame, "James G. Rowe Sr.," https://www.rac ingmuseum.org/hall-of-fame/trainer/james-g-rowe-sr

National Museum of Racing and Hall of Fame, "Sunday Silence (KY)," https://www.racingmuseum.org/hall-of-fame/horse/sunday-silence-ky

National Museum of Racing and Hall of Fame, "William J. Knapp," https://racing museum.org/hall-of-fame/jockey/william-j-knapp

On This Day, "Clarence Kummer," https://www.onthisday.com/people/clarence-kummer

Pedigree Online, "Thoroughbred Database," https://www.pedigreequery.com [followed by the name of the horse]: various horses

Prabook, "Andy Schuttinger," https://prabook.com/web/andy.schuttinger/2580077

Roadside America, "Man o' War's Grave," https://www.roadsideamerica.com/story/3613

Southern Calls, "Man o' War's Funeral," https://southerncalls.com/article/man-o-wars-funeral

Stars and Stripes, "The American Expeditionary Forces," https://www.loc.gov/col lections/stars-and-stripes/articles-and-essays/a-world-at-war/american-expedi tionary-forces/

U.S. Inflation Calculator, "The U.S. Inflation Calculator Measures the Dollar's Buying Power Over Time," https://www.usinflationcalculator.com

USRacing.com, "Affirmed," http://www.usracing.com/famous-horses/affirmed

Vault, "More About Man o' War: Recollections and Reservations," https://thevaulthorse racing.wordpress.com/2019/02/07/more-about-man-o-war-recollections -reservations/

Wikipedia, "List of Leading Thoroughbred Racehorses," https://en.wikipedia.org/wiki/list_of_leading_thoroughbred_racehorses

Wikisource.org, "New York Constitution of 1821," https://en.wikisource.org/wiki/New_York_Constitution_of_1821

Index

259